Terence Rattigan

Plays : One

French Without Tears, The Winslow Boy,
The Browning Version, Harlequinade

'Few dramatists of this century have written with more understanding of the human heart than Terence Rattigan'   *Michael Billington*

'One of the most reliable entertainers in the English theatre'
                                                    John Russell Taylor

This selection of Rattigan's best work from the thirties and forties includes his first, phenomenally successful comedy *French Without Tears*, about a group of 'bright young things' attempting to learn French on the Riviera amid myriad distractions. The second play, *The Winslow Boy*, based on an actual case, is the powerful, deliberately 'well-made' drama of a father's attempts to clear his cadet son's name against the assembled might of the naval Establishment. Completing the volume are the two one-act plays *Harlequinade*, a sustained joke against some well-worn theatrical conventions, and *The Browning Version*, a small masterpiece in its portrait of the disliked classics master, Crocker-Harris, on the point of retiring after eighteen years of unsuccessful teaching.

The introduction is by Anthony Curtis, literary editor of the London *Financial Times* and author of studies of Maugham and Rattigan.

Terence Rattigan was born in 1911. He won scholarships to Harrow and to Trinity College, Oxford. His first play, French Without Tears (1936), ran for over 1000 performances, as did the war-time farce While the Sun Shines (1943). Further successful comedies were Love in Idleness (1944), Who Is Sylvia? (1950) and The Sleeping Prince (1953). More serious plays at this time included Flare Path (1942), which ran for 670 performances, The Winslow Boy (1946), which ran for 476 performances, winning the Ellen Terry award and the New York Critics' award, The Browning Version (1948, in double-bill with Harlequinade), The Deep Blue Sea (1952: over 500 performances) and two linked plays, Separate Tables (1954: over 700 performances). He wrote biographical plays about Alexander the Great (Adventure Story, 1949), Lawrence of Arabia (Ross, 1960: over 700 performances) and Nelson (Bequest to the Nation, 1970). Other later plays include Man and Boy (1963), In Praise of Love (1973), Cause Célèbre (1977) and the television play Heart to Heart (1962). Most of his plays have been filmed and televised. Rattigan was knighted in 1971. He died in 1977.

Other writers in the Master Playwrights series

John Arden
Brendan Behan
Edward Bond (two volumes)
Noël Coward (five volumes)
Henrik Ibsen (four volumes)
Molière
Clifford Odets
Joe Orton
Harold Pinter (four volumes)
August Strindberg (two volumes)
J. M. Synge
Oscar Wilde

TERENCE RATTIGAN

Plays : One

French Without Tears
The Winslow Boy
The Browning Version
Harlequinade

With an Introduction by
Anthony Curtis

The Master Playwrights

METHUEN . LONDON

A METHUEN PAPERBACK

This collection first published in 1981 by Methuen London Ltd,
11 New Fetter Lane, London EC4P 4EE
by arrangement with Hamish Hamilton Ltd.
Reprinted 1984

French Without Tears and *The Winslow Boy* were included in Volume One of
The Collected Plays of Terence Rattigan. *The Browning Version* and *Harle-
quinade* were in Volume Two. Both volumes were published in 1953 by
Hamish Hamilton Ltd.

This collection copyright © Eyre Methuen Ltd 1981

Printed in Great Britain by Richard Clay (The Chaucer Press) Ltd,
Bungay, Suffolk

ISBN 0 413 49070 X

Contents

Introduction

The four plays in this volume are among those most successfully performed in the British theatre in the twentieth century.
With *French Without Tears* Terence Rattigan made his name
as a playwright in London in 1936. It ran for more than one
thousand performances. *The Winslow Boy* ten years later
chalked up 476 performances. Between them came the second
world war. Rattigan enlisted in the R.A.F. and saw active
service as a rear-gunner, but this did not prevent him from
sending back several plays which enlivened the wartime
theatre. After the war he decided to resuscitate the then dormant form of the one-act play (it had fallen into disuse after
its function as a curtain-raiser had been made unnecessary by
the conditions of modern theatre-going). Wise, commercial
heads were shaken at this seemingly regressive move on the
part of the playwright. His favourite management H. M. Ten-
nent under the sway of the formidable Hugh 'Binkie' Beau-
mont temporarily deserted him. But the playwright's instinct
proved to be sound. *Playbill*—as the two one-acters, *The
Browning Version* and *Harlequinade*, were called—pleased
critics and public alike and ran for almost a year.

Initial success led to continual revival. For several decades
there were very few evenings when one or other of the plays
printed here was not in production somewhere or other. All,
with the exception of *Harlequinade*, have been made into successful movies. And, after a sharp decline in his popularity in
the mid-1950s, the National Theatre revival of *Playbill* in 1980
may prove to be something of a landmark in Rattigan's
posthumous fortunes.

Rattigan appears to have known what he was going to be

while still at Harrow School in the 1920s. When not practising in the nets, he would be ensconced in the Vaughan Library reading the works of J. M. Barrie, A. W. Pinero, John Galsworthy, H. Granville Barker, Somerset Maugham, and George Bernard Shaw. The plays of most of these writers were to be seen on the London stage in Rattigan's youth. A seat in the gallery cost one shilling (5p) and he could meet that out of his pocket-money. It was from this lofty vantage-point that he first saw some of the early work of Noël Coward, often mistakenly thought of as a direct contemporary and with whom his name was frequently to be paired by historians of the modern theatre.

After Harrow came Oxford. He went up to Trinity College in 1930 to read History. 'I am fascinated by History,' he once said to me, 'and have read a good deal of it, but not at Oxford.' There was pressure from Frank, his father, whose career was in the Diplomatic Service, for his son to pursue the same secure occupation. He knew Terry was keen on writing, but he did not see how he was going to make a living out of that. Didn't Harold Nicolson manage to combine Diplomacy with literature quite happily? Now there was a model for Terry to copy. Rattigan played along with this for a while but always knew it was playwriting and not the Diplomatic Service to which he was going to devote his life.

For the moment he appeared to acquiesce in his father's plans and this meant preparing himself to pass the language requirement for candidates to the Diplomatic Service. He spent a part of his summer vacation in 1931 in the villa at Wimereux, near Boulogne, belonging to a French martinet, called appropriately Martin, who put young English gentlemen through their linguistic paces. He insisted that they spoke French at all times while in the villa. Again it was an experience whose artistic rewards were to come later.

Like many undergraduates consumed by theatrical ambition Rattigan intended to use Oxford as a springboard from which to take the plunge into the deep end of the professional theatre. The play of which he was co-author went (while he was still 'up') into production at the Q theatre, a tryout venue, at Kew in Surrey, and actually transferred for a time to the West End. After that there was no holding him. He abandoned his History Honours course, quitted the University, dropped the pretence that he would follow his father into the Diplomatic Service and came to London with the firm resolve to live by writing plays.

Once the shock to the parental system had been absorbed and his beautiful mother Vera had mediated on his behalf, Frank generously agreed to make him an allowance of £2 a week while he tried to establish himself in his chosen career. The only drawback was Frank Rattigan put a term to it. If Terry had not succeeded in supporting himself by his plays within two years then the money would cease and he would have to take a job. Afterwards Rattigan attributed some of the emphasis on box-office success that coloured his career to this bargain struck with his father. At any rate he set about the task of playwriting with great energy and purpose. He wrote six plays within two years, of which *French Without Tears* was probably the third.

In 1935 Rattigan and John Gielgud made an adaptation of *A Tale of Two Cities* which Bronson Albery, whose family owned the Wyndham's, Criterion and New (now the Albery) theatres, wanted to produce. Production seemed imminent. But the actor-manager Martin-Harvey, who had toured for years in another adaptation, *The Only Way*, claimed that it gave him the virtual stage copyright in Dickens' novel. Although this was nonsense, Albery after some deliberations with his friends at the Garrick Club gave in, and the Rattigan version was called off. The only consolation was that Albery did say he would read very carefully anything else of his that Rattigan cared to send him. What to send? A powerful drama of gloom and doom? Vera Rattigan dissuaded him from doing that and suggested he send the finespun comedy then called *Gone Away*.

By this time Frank's deadline had expired and Rattigan was sitting at an office stool, as it were, working for a film studio in Teddington belonging to Warner Brothers, churning out scripts, almost by the hour, for a pittance. One of his fellow-

scribes with whom he shared an office and collaborated on a
story with a lot of laughs among themselves but not much
result was the future author of *The Music of Time*, Anthony
Powell. Mr. Powell remembered Rattigan at this period in
Faces in My Time (1980):

Although he had sidestepped his father's efforts to put him into the
Diplomatic Service, Rattigan was outwardly very much like the
popular notion (as opposed to the usual reality) of a young diplomat;
tall, good-looking, elegant in turnout, somewhat chilly in manner.
He had been a cricketer of some eminence at Harrow. His homo-
sexuality, of which he made no particular secret, probably un-
swerving, was not at all obvious on the surface.

Rattigan's hour of liberation was nigh. A couple of Albery's
productions had run into trouble, and he required something
he could put on rapidly while he re-deployed his forces. Albery
appointed Harold French to direct Rattigan's comedy at the
Criterion Theatre and they started at once on casting it:

Now, after two years of hawking it around to every management in
the telephone book, and a total of nine rejections [said Rattigan], it
was at last to be done. In the West End. With real actors.

French had some changes to suggest. The first was the title,
which Rattigan, remembering an old nursery primer, agreed
to change to *French Without Tears*, and the second was the
setting which Rattigan had made, as in life, in Northern
France. French said it needed more romantically to be in the
South. Rattigan happily complied. He also wrote in one little
scene during rehearsal where Alan (Rex Harrison) says, 'you
must never leave me alone with Diana' (Kay Hammond).
There was no time for a pre-London tour; the play had to open
'cold'. Harold French invited a few friends to the dress rehearsal who gave it indeed a rather chilly reception. Roland
Culver, who played the Commander, recalled in a radio
programme in 1976 the deep gloom of the cast at the end, with
Jessica Tandy, who played the French girl, saying they could
not possibly open tomorrow. However, the first night on
November 6, 1936 was a triumph. The curtain went up and
down a dozen times with the audience still applauding after

it was finally lowered. 'You just couldn't stop them,' Mr. Culver remembered. 'I don't think Terry made a speech. I don't like to suggest such a thing but I'm not sure he was capable of making a speech, partly through emotion, and partly because he'd had to strengthen himself during the course of the evening.'

Happily the daily and evening newspaper critics were just as enthusiastic about the play as the first-nighters. 'A scream from start to finish,' declared the *Daily Sketch*. 'Should make London laugh for a year,' hazarded the *Evening News*. As we have seen, it did—for three. The anonymous critic of *The Times* (who was in fact the novelist Charles Morgan) hit the nail squarely when he said, '. . . what we are concerned with is a world in which nothing matters except to be entertained.' He then apportioned generous helpings of praise all round:

The entertainment, in its own frothy kind, is beyond question. Mr. Rattigan writes a sly, cool and delightfully opportune dialogue; Mr. Rex Harrison has most of it to manipulate and manipulates it with casual adroitness . . . A very amusing game it is, and the more remarkable in that its excursions into sentiment, for which Miss Jessica Tandy is responsible, are so smooth and carefully proportioned that they do not break the form.

French Without Tears is a brilliant amalgam of straight autobiography and delicate fantasy. At Martin's, which became Maingot's, there was no Diana Lake (so exquisitely played in the original by Kay Hammond) to entice the young men away from their studies. She was a triumphant invention of the author's. But the young men themselves are taken, I gather, largely from the life. Alan's dilemma between the Diplomatic Service and authorship, resolved during the play, directly reflects Rattigan's at that time, and the plot of his much-rejected novel represents his political awareness which emerged more fully in other plays he wrote before the war including a satire against Hitler, *Follow My Leader*, which was banned by the Lord Chamberlain on the grounds that it might give offence to a foreign power. On the other hand *French Without Tears* gave offence to no-one, save perhaps M. Martin if he ever saw it. It transmitted with easy assurance that peculiarly English mood of insouciance, which may have misled one of the play's admirers, the German Ambassador, Herr von Ribbentrop, into advising Hitler that Britain would not readily resort to arms against Nazi aggression. Looking at the play purely as a piece of stagecraft it is remarkable how well distributed and proportioned the comedy is among the different characters. Although it is full of gloriously showy parts it is essentially an ensemble work. Rattigan himself discerned the influence, at first glance incongruous, of Chekhov here, whose technique he had studied with the same assiduousness he had devoted to more indigenous models.

When Rattigan returned home after the war he was no longer the dazzling young playwright of promise. He was a professional dramatist at the top of his profession who had done more than anyone to keep the legitimate London theatre alive and reflecting the spirit of the time during the war. He had somehow managed to recreate the insouciant mood, transposed to rationed wartime London, where it was by no means out of place, in a later comedy, *While The Sun Shines* (1943), which also greatly pleased the public; and he had captured the stoical courage and high-spirits of an R.A.F. bomber squadron based somewhere in England in *Flare Path* (1942). Again, he caught something of the social disruption and political undercurrents produced by the wartime coalition government in the play he wrote for the husband and wife team of Alfred Lunt and Lynn Fontanne, *Love in Idleness* (1944). But although he was now rich and successful, and assured of an audience, he remained ambitious. He had various unfulfilled artistic yearnings. One was to place a vast historical canvas on the stage in a play about Alexander the Great; another was to revive the highly emotive spirit of the Edwardian theatre of his youthful reading and playgoing with its tear-jerking climaxes and stirring curtain-lines. Many of these Edwardian plays were concerned with cases of injustice, often to a woman who had been compromised in some way; others such as Galsworthy's *Justice* were about an individual who had fallen foul of the law and involved putting the whole rigmarole of courtroom procedure on the stage.

Rattigan had always been interested in the Law. It was in his
blood. His forbears had been lawyers; his brother was a
solicitor. In his youth he would haunt the law-courts eaves-
dropping from the public gallery, alert for material for yet
to be written plays. He enjoyed reading accounts of famous
trials, among them the Archer-Shee affair.

Rattigan was too young actually to remember the furore
about Cadet George Archer-Shee being asked to leave the
Royal Naval College at Osborne for allegedly stealing a postal
order, because it began in 1908 before he was born. But the
chain of events, by which the ultimately sucessful attempt to
clear the name of one small boy had become a burning public
issue debated in the House of Commons, had lodged in his
consciousness. The vindication of the individual's right to a
fair hearing when victimised by a bureaucratic organisation
in control of his destiny seemed not without relevance to post-
war Britain.

The notion of dramatising the famous affair (a kind of
minor Dreyfus Case in which the anti-semitism was replaced
by anti-Catholicism) began in discussions Rattigan had with
the film director 'Puffin' Asquith (son of one of the Prime
Ministers of the period), with whom he had worked on a
number of films during the war, and Anatole de Grunwald,
the producer. When de Grunwald took against the Archer-
Shee case as a subject for a film, Rattigan turned his mind to
dramatising it for the stage. Michael Darlow and Gillian
Hodson in their *Terence Rattigan: The Man and His Work*
(Quartet Books, 1979) recall a bet Rattigan had with Asquith
that he would be able to put the affair on the stage without
resorting to a court-room scene or any costly changes of set.
Rattigan's rapid progress with the writing once he got going
may be charted by reference to the Diary of the Conservative
M.P. Sir Henry 'Chips' Channon for 1945. Rattigan was engaged in a love-affair with Chips at the time and read him
the work-in-progress noting his suggestions for its improve-
ment. It is to discussions with Chips we owe the name Winslow,
and it was to Chips's son Paul (as I write, Minister for the Arts
in Mrs. Thatcher's Government) that the play was dedicated.

'In the hope that he will live to see a world in which this play will point no moral.' It was finished within six weeks.

The Winslow Boy is the first of Rattigan's plays which has a historical 'source'. Later ones were *Adventure Story* (Alexander), *Man and Boy* (Ivar Kreuger), *A Bequest to the Nation* (Nelson), *Cause Célèbre* (Alma Rattenbury) and the unfinished play about Haig and Asquith which Rattigan was writing when he died in 1977. In the Archer-Shee case the historical ingredients suited Rattigan to perfection. The world of the English professional class at its most assured with a schoolboy in the centre of the picture; the world which threw up such compelling and flamboyant performers at the bar as Edward Carson and Rufus Isaacs.

However much Rattigan may have altered characters and setting to conform to his technical requirements of staging, he does stick fairly closely to the main facts of the case, as may be seen most conveniently by reference to Rodney M. Bennett's *The Archer-Shees Against the Admiralty* (Robert Hale 1973.) The one interesting fact that does not emerge from the play at all is that the Archer-Shees were Catholics of Irish origin, and there was strong anti-Catholic prejudice among the officers at the Royal Naval College at Osborne at that time. After his disgrace Cadet George was readmitted as a pupil at Stonyhurst and the naval authorities were piqued that they took him back so easily, so much so that, according to Mr. Bennett, at least one boy wishing to enter the navy from Stonyhurst went to the length of transferring to another school for two terms so that he could put its name on his application form.

The most celebrated moment in the play, the speech at the end of Act Two when after ruthlessly grilling the boy and completely shattering his composure, Sir Robert says, 'Oh yes. The boy is plainly innocent. I accept the brief,' does have a parallel in history. George, who was a remarkably good witness when under pressure, was strenuously cross-examined for a long time by Carson before he agreed to act as the boy's lawyer. The cross-examination took place in Carson's office, with George's M.P. brother present behind a curtain, not in the drawing-room of the family home in London.

What is remarkable in the play is not merely the way the playwright manages to sustain the tense excitememt of the case within the confines of that room and to convey all the essential information to the audience, but also how he manages to communicate its complexity, the long period of time it took to unfold, totally changing the lives of its main participants, beginning with a parent protesting against the summary action of college authorities, culminating in a Petition of Right in the House of Commons.

Sir John Gielgud was an obvious choice for the lawyer but he turned it down and it went eventually to Emlyn Williams. 'I had the privilege and great joy of being in *The Winslow Boy*, the best part I've ever played,' Mr. Williams once told me. 'I wasn't really the immediate casting for it by any means because I was really much too un-English being Welsh because you see Terry is the most English playwright one knows . . . he has this tremendous quality of understatement and economy which I don't naturally have.'

Many of Rattigan's most convincing plays have a boy, or a young man at a testing moment in his life, at the middle of them. His need in the period after Oxford to justify his choice of career to his father by becoming a success seems to have left him with what, in a less urbane, a less self-controlled and self-effacing writer, we might be inclined to call an obsession with father-son relationships. As Rattigan became more mature in his art he began to see that the strength in this equation was not necessarily always on the side of the father and the weakness on the side of the son. In *Man and Boy* (1963) a play about high finance set during the Depression the balance of power between son and father becomes very finely poised with, as Rattigan once said, 'the father having a weakness for weakness, as it were, and the son having a weakness for strength'. In *The Browning Version* there is no father and son as such; the parents of the boy at the middle of things, young Taplow, are mentioned once or twice as being rather grand, but never seen. Instead as a substitute father we have the figure of the elderly schoolmaster on the point of retirement,

Andrew Crocker-Harris, known throughout the school as 'the Crock'.

Taplow needs the approval of the Crock (in order to get his Remove) but so does the Crock need the admiration of Taplow, if his entire life is not to be accounted a failure. The Crock's favourite saying when asked in advance if someone will be promoted, 'He will get what he deserves. No more. No less,' takes on new levels of irony each time it is repeated. Although the play only lasts for slightly more than an hour it has the concentration of the Greek tragedy that becomes such a highly emotive gift in the course of it. Rattigan was remembering his old classics master, Coke Norris, and the ambience of Harrow School when he sketched in the detail with its thinly disguised reference to the Eton and Harrow match at Lord's (in which he himself once took part). This detail is all brought forward in time to cover the period in which the play was written, with the wounding reference to the Crock as 'the Himmler of the Lower Fifth'. However the insights of the play are such that it remains timeless and will, I hazard, out-last even the system of privileged private education, and the compulsory study of classics, on which it is founded.

It was that fine actor Eric Portman who created the part of the Crock when *Playbill* was presented originally at the Phoenix Theatre in 1948. T. C. Worsley, the dramatic critic of the *New Statesman*, wrote:

Mr. Eric Portman as the schoolmaster gives one of the brilliant performances of the year. He keeps and holds very exactly the details of the personality, the tics of speech and the uncontrollable jerks of mannerism which a lifetime has stamped on the mask; then when he reaches for the moment for the real man to break through (his dazed repetition, for instance, as if he simply can't believe it, of 'the Himmler of the Lower Fifth') he triumphantly avoids the mawkish.

Managements contemplating a revival of *The Browning Version* have always fought shy of its original stable-mate, *Harlequinade*, on the grounds that it smacked too much of the wartime provincial touring theatre under the auspices of the Council for the Encouragement of Music and the Arts (CEMA, the ancestor of the Arts Council), and that nowadays the jokes would have lost all their fizz. But when the National Theatre presented it in 1980 as the second item in their re-creation of the original pairing this proved not to be the case. True it is rooted in those tatty tours that brightened many a blacked-out or austerity-grey evening, and it also, as we have seen, contains a flashback to the author's undergraduate acting experience; but the real subject is the Coward-like one that theatrical people—'pros', if you like—are a happy breed, set apart from ordinary mortals in their own sealed-off world, subject to a different set of motivations from the rest of us. This was the only time he ever wrote a play about actors. The Gosports who 'are the theatre' owe not a little to the Lunts, whom he had observed at close range when they were re-hearsing *Love in Idleness* (a play they had not wholly liked); and their elderly aunt Dame Maud, still with the company playing the Nurse, contains more than a suggestion of Dame Sibyl Thorndike.

However, their prototypes are legion in the profession and exist anywhere the dream of performance takes over from the reality it is said to mirror. Rattigan's gift of invention and surprise was never more fluent and delightful as he piles one episode upon another, from the senile mediocre actor who leaves the stage for good at the beginning of the play (only to return at the end) to Arthur Gosport's discovery of his own unwitting bigamy with a grandchild from his first marriage howling in the wings. None of this, however trivial or catas-trophic, must be allowed to interrupt the creative process. This was the faith by which Terence Rattigan lived. I said at the beginning of this introduction that when you read these texts you must visualise them in performance. Nowhere in the book is this more necessary than when you read *Harlequinade*.

ANTHONY CURTIS

FRENCH WITHOUT TEARS

French Without Tears was first produced at the Criterion Theatre, London, on November 6th, 1936, with the following cast:

KENNETH LAKE	...	*Trevor Howard*
BRIAN CURTIS	...	*Guy Middleton*
HON. ALAN HOWARD ...	...	*Rex Harrison*
MARIANNE	...	*Yvonne Andre*
MONSIEUR MAINGOT ...	...	*Percy Walsh*
LT.-CMDR. ROGERS ...	...	*Roland Culver*
DIANA LAKE...	...	*Kay Hammond*
KIT NEILAN	...	*Robert Flemyng*
JACQUELINE MAINGOT	...	*Jessica Tandy*
LORD HEYBROOK ...	...	*William Dear*

Directed by HAROLD FRENCH

ACT I	JULY 1ST. MORNING
ACT II SCENE 1	JULY 14TH. AFTERNOON
SCENE 2	THE SAME EVENING
ACT III SCENE 1	LATER THE SAME NIGHT
SCENE 2	THE FOLLOWING MORNING

The action passes in the living-room at 'Miramar', a villa in a small seaside town on the west coast of France.

ACT I

SCENE: *The living-room at 'Miramar', a villa in a small seaside town on the west coast of France.*

TIME: *July 1st, about 9 a.m.*

The room is rather bare of furniture. There is a large, plain table in the centre, surrounded by eight kitchen chairs. There are two dilapidated armchairs against the back wall. The wallpaper is grey and dirty-looking.

On the L., two french windows open out on to a small garden. They are open at the moment, and the sun is streaming through. There is a door back R. leading into the hall, and another down-stage R. leading into the kitchen.

The table is laid for breakfast, with an enormous coffee-pot in the middle and a quantity of rolls.

As the curtain rises KENNETH *is discovered sitting at the table. He is about twenty, good-looking in a rather vacuous way. At the moment he is engaged in writing in a notebook with one hand, while with the other he is nibbling a roll. A dictionary lies open before him.*

There is the sound of someone heavily descending the stairs. The door at the back opens and BRIAN *comes in. He is older than* KENNETH, *about twenty-three or twenty-four, large, thick-set, and red-faced. He wears an incredibly dirty pair of grey flannel trousers, a battered brown tweed coat, and a white sweater.*

BRIAN. Morning, Babe.

    KENNETH *doesn't look up.* BRIAN *goes to the table, picks up a letter, and opens it.*

KENNETH. (*Looking musingly ahead.*) She has ideas above her station.

BRIAN. What's that?

KENNETH. How would you say that in French?

BRIAN. What?

KENNETH. She has ideas above her station.

3

BRIAN. She has ideas above her station. She has ideas . . .
He stuffs his letter in his pocket and goes to kitchen door calling.
　Marianne!

VOICE. (*From the kitchen.*) Oui, Monsieur?

BRIAN. (*With an appalling accent.*) Deux œufs, s'il vous plaît.

VOICE. (*Off.*) Bien, Monsieur.

BRIAN. Avec un petit peu de jambon.

VOICE. (*Off.*) Oui, Monsieur. Des œufs brouillés, n'est-ce pas?

BRIAN. Brouillés? Ah, oui, brouillés. (*He closes the door.*) I'm
　getting pretty hot at this stuff, don't you think? You know,
　nowadays it's quite an effort for me to go back to English.

KENNETH. If you're so hot, you'd better tell me how to say she
　has ideas above her station.

BRIAN. Oh, yes, I forgot. It's fairly easy, old boy. Elle a des
　idées au-dessus de sa gare.

KENNETH. You can't do it like that. You can't say au-dessus de
　sa gare. It isn't that sort of station.

BRIAN. (*Pouring himself out a cup of coffee.*) Well, don't *ask* me.

KENNETH. I thought you were so hot at French.

BRIAN. Well, as a matter of fact, that wasn't strictly the truth.
　Now if a Frenchman asked me where the pen of his aunt
　was, the chances are I could give him a pretty snappy come-
　back and tell him it was in the pocket of the gardener.

KENNETH. Yes, but that doesn't help me much.

BRIAN. Sorry, old boy.

KENNETH. I suppose I'd better just do it literally. Maingot'll
　throw a fit.

BRIAN. That doesn't bother you, does it?

KENNETH. You're not going into the diplomatic. He doesn't
　really get worked up about you.

BRIAN. Well, I don't know about that. The whole of his beard
　came off yesterday when I was having my lesson.

KENNETH. No, but he doesn't really mind. It's absolute physical
　agony to him when I do something wrong. He knows as well
　as I do that I haven't got one chance in a thousand of
　getting in.

BRIAN. (*Cheerfully.*) Don't say that, old boy. You're breaking
　my heart.

KENNETH. (*Gloomily.*) Yes, but it's true. (*He starts to write again.*)

BRIAN. As a matter of fact, Alan told me you had a pretty good chance.

KENNETH. (*Looking up, pleased.*) Did he really?

BRIAN *nods.*

BRIAN. He ought to know, oughtn't he? Isn't he Maingot's red-hot tip for the diplomatic stakes?

KENNETH. If he was keener about getting in he'd walk it. He will anyway, I should think.

BRIAN. I think I'll make a book on the result this year. I'll lay evens on Alan—a class colt with a nice free action; will win if he can get the distance.

KENNETH. What about me?

BRIAN. I'll lay you threes about yourself.

KENNETH. Threes? More like twenties.

BRIAN. Oh, I don't know. Nice-looking colt—good stayer. Bit of a dog from the starting-gate, perhaps. Say seven to two, then.

Enter ALAN *through the door at the back. He is about twenty-three, dark and saturnine. He wears carefully creased grey flannel trousers and a German ' sport jacket'.*

Morning, Alan. We were just talking about you.

ALAN. Good morning, Brian. Good morning, Babe. (*He looks at his place at the head of the table.*) Not one blood-stained letter. What were you saying about me?

BRIAN. I'm making a book on the diplomatic stakes. I'm laying evens about you.

ALAN. (*Sitting down.*) That's not very generous.

BRIAN. Hell, you're the favourite

ALAN. What about the startling rumours that the favourite may be scratched.

KENNETH. (*Looking up quickly.*) Why, have they accepted your novel?

ALAN. Do I look as if they'd accepted my novel?

BRIAN. I don't know how you do look when they accept your novels.

ALAN. I hope, my dear Brian, that one day you'll have a chance of finding out.

KENNETH. Well, what's this talk about your scratching?

ALAN. Perhaps just to give you a better chance, ducky.

BRIAN. You're not serious about it though, old boy?

ALAN. Probably not.

KENNETH. But you must be mad, Alan. I mean even if you do want to write you could still do it in the diplomatic. Honestly, it seems quite crazy—

ALAN. You're giving a tolerably good imitation of my father.

BRIAN. What does His Excellency have to say about the idea, by the way?

ALAN. His Excellency says that he doesn't mind me choosing my own career a bit, provided always it's the one he's chosen for me.

BRIAN. Broad-minded, eh?

ALAN. That's right. Always sees two sides to every question— his own, which is the right one; and anyone else's, which is the wrong one.

KENNETH. But seriously, Alan, you can't really be thinking—

ALAN. Oh, stop it, child, for God's sake. I didn't say I was going to scratch.

KENNETH. You said you were thinking of it.

ALAN. Well, you know that. I'm always thinking of it. I very rarely think of anything else. But I won't do it, so don't worry your dear little head about it.

He taps KENNETH *on the head with a brioche.* KENNETH *sulkily returns to his work.*

Enter MARIANNE, *the maid, with a plate of scrambled eggs and bacon, placing them in front of* BRIAN.

BRIAN. Ah, mes œufs, as I live.

MARIANNE. (*To* ALAN.) Monsieur le Commandant, va-t-il aussi prendre des œufs avec son déjeuner, Monsieur?

BRIAN. Oh, well—er—(*To* ALAN.) She's talking to you, old boy.

ALAN. Je ne sais rien des habitudes de Monsieur le Commandant, Marianne.

MARIANNE. Bien, Monsieur. Alors voulez-vous lui demander s'il les veut, Monsieur, lorsqu'il descend?

ALAN. Bien.

Exit MARIANNE.

BRIAN. What did she want?

ALAN. She wanted to know if the Commander took eggs with his breakfast.

BRIAN. I meant to ask you. Did you see him when he arrived last night?

ALAN. Yes, I went to the station with Maingot to meet him.

BRIAN. What's he like?

ALAN. Very naval commander.

BRIAN. Yes, old boy, but what's that?

ALAN. You know. Carries with him the salty tang of the sea wherever he goes.

BRIAN. Pity he's carried it here. Paucot-sur-mer could do without any more salty tang than it's got already. Has he a rolling gait?

ALAN. He was sober when he arrived.

BRIAN. No, old boy, drunk or sober, all sailors have a rolling gait.

MONSIEUR MAINGOT *comes in hurriedly through the door at the back. He is about sixty, with a ferocious face and a white beard.*

MAINGOT. Bonjour—Bonjour—Bonjour!

All three rise. He shakes hands with each in turn, then sits down at the head of the table R. at the opposite end to the three boys.

Mon Dieu, que je suis en retard ce matin! (*He opens a letter.*)

BRIAN. (*Speaking in a whisper to Alan.*) What's he like, though, really?

ALAN. (*Also in a whisper.*) Pretty hellish, I thought.

BRIAN. Po-faced, I suppose?

MAINGOT. (*Roaring into his letter.*) Français! Voulez-vous parlez français, Messieurs, s'il vous plaît.

Pause.

(*Looking up from his letter.*) Qu'est-ce que c'est que ça, po-faced?

ALAN. Nous disions que Monsieur le Commandant avait une figure de vase de nuit, Monsieur.

MAINGOT. Ah! Mais c'est pas vrai.

ALAN. Nous exaggérons un peu.

MAINGOT. Je crois bien.

He returns to his letters.

> KENNETH *surreptitiously pushes his notebook towards* ALAN, *pointing at a certain sentence.* ALAN *reads it and shakes his head violently.* KENNETH *looks pleadingly at him.* ALAN *considers and is about to speak when* MAINGOT *looks up.*

Dîtes-moi, est-ce-que vous connaissez un Lord Heybrook? (*Looking at letter.*)

ALAN. Non, Monsieur.

MAINGOT. Il voudrait venir le quinze Juillet.

ALAN. (*To* BRIAN.) Do you know him?

BRIAN. Lord Heybrook? No, old boy. (*Confidentially.*) As a matter of fact, I knew a peer once, but he died. What about Lord Heybrook, anyway?

ALAN. He's coming here on the fifteenth.

MAINGOT. (*Roaring.*) Français, Messieurs—français!

Pause.

> MAINGOT *takes up the* Matin *and begins to read.* KENNETH *again pushes his notebook towards* ALAN, *and* ALAN *again is about to speak.*

(*Roaring.*) Ah! Ce Hitler! (*Throwing paper on floor.*) Quel phenomène!

> ALAN *closes his mouth and* KENNETH *pulls his notebook back quickly.*

(*To* BRIAN.) Aha, Monsieur Curtis, vous étiez saôul au Casino hier soir, n'est-ce pas?

BRIAN. (*Puzzled.*) Saôul?

ALAN. Drunk.

BRIAN. Oh, non, Monsieur. Pas ça. Un peu huilé, peut-être.

> COMMANDER ROGERS *comes in. He is about thirty-five, dark, small, very neat, rather solemn. All get up.*

MAINGOT. Ah, Bonjour, Monsieur le Commandant, et comment allez-vous? J'espère que vous avez bien dormi?

Ah, pardon! (*Introducing the others.*) Monsieur Curtis—Monsieur le Commandant Rogers. Monsieur Lake—Monsieur le Commandant Rogers. Monsieur Howard—vous connaissez déjà.

> BRIAN *and* KENNETH *shake hands.*

ALAN. Bonjour! (*To* ROGERS.)

ROGERS. Yes, we met last night. (*Indicating a chair.*) Shall I sit here?

ALAN. That's Kit Neilan's place, as a matter of fact. I think this is your place. (*He shows a place next to* MAINGOT.)

MAINGOT. (*Rising.*) Ah! Pardon, Monsieur le Commandant. Voilà votre place. Asseyez-vous donc et soyez à votre aise.

ROGERS. Thanks. (*He sits.*)

ALAN. I've been told to ask you if you like eggs with your breakfast.

MAINGOT. Oui, Monsieur. Mais voulez-vous parlez français, s'il vous plaît.

ROGERS. (*Smiling apologetically.*) I'm afraid I don't speak your lingo at all, you know.

MAINGOT. Lingo? Ah, oui, langue. C'est ça. Mais il faut essayer. You—must—try.

ROGERS. (*Turning to* MAINGOT, *then to* ALAN.) Oui—Non.

ALAN. What?

MAINGOT. Pardon?

ROGERS. Oui, je ne—want any eggs.

ALAN. Right, I'll tell Marianne. (*He gets up and goes into the kitchen.*)

MAINGOT. (*To* ROGERS.) Il faut dire: Je ne veux pas des œufs pour mon petit déjeuner.

ROGERS *smiles vaguely.* MAINGOT *laughs.*

Ça viendra, ça viendra.

Re-enter ALAN.

BRIAN. I say, sir, did you have a good crossing?

ROGERS. Pretty bad, as a matter of fact. Still, that didn't worry me.

BRIAN. You're a good sailor?

ALAN *laughs.*

Oh, of course you would be. I mean you are, aren't you?

MAINGOT *gets up.*

MAINGOT. Eh, bien. Par qui vais-je commencer?

KENNETH. Moi, Monsieur.

MAINGOT. *Par Moi.* (*Rising.*) Alors, allons dans le jardin. (*Bowing.*) *Messieurs!*

He goes out into garden, followed by KENNETH.

ALAN. Poor Babe! He's going to be slaughtered.

ROGERS. Really. Why?

ALAN. (*Shaking his head sadly.*) Elle a des idées au-dessus de sa gare.

ROGERS. What does that mean?

ALAN. It doesn't mean she has ideas above her station.

ROGERS. The Professor is pretty strict, I suppose.

ALAN. Where work is concerned, he's a sadist.

ROGERS. I'm glad to hear it. I want to learn as much French as I can, and I'm starting from scratch, you know.

BRIAN. Are you learning it for any special reason, sir?

ROGERS. Yes. Interpretership exam. in seven months' time.

ALAN. If you stay here for seven months you'll either be dead or a Frenchman.

ROGERS. How long have you been here?

ALAN. On and off for a year, but then, I have a way of preserving my nationality. I wear a special charm. (*He indicates his German coat.*)

ROGERS. Are you very pro-German, then?

BRIAN. He only wears that coat to annoy Maingot.

ROGERS. Oh, I see. What do you wear in Germany?

ALAN. A beret usually. Sabots are too uncomfortable.

ROGERS *laughs politely. There is a pause, broken suddenly by a roar coming from the garden.*

MAINGOT. (*Off.*) Aha, ça c'est formidable! Qu'est ce que vous me fichez là donc? 'Elle a des idées au-dessus de sa gare'. Idiot! Idiot! Idiot!

The noise subsides. ALAN *shakes his head.*

ALAN. Poor Babe. But he had it coming to him.

BRIAN. The Babe was having the horrors this morning before you came down. He said he hadn't one chance in a thousand of getting in.

ALAN. He hasn't.

ROGERS. Of getting in what?

ALAN. The diplomatic.

ROGERS. Oh, I suppose you're all budding diplomats?

BRIAN. All except me. I'm learning French for—er—commercial reasons.

ALAN. He's learnt a lot already. He can say 'How much?' in
French, and you know how valuable that phrase is in the
world of—er—commerce.

BRIAN. (*Laughing heartily.*) Yes, old boy, and that's not all. I can
say, 'Five francs? Do you think I'm made of money?'

ALAN. (*Laughing too.*) 'Cinq francs? Crois-tu que je sois con-
struit d'argent?'

They both suddenly become aware that ROGERS *isn't laughing. They
stop and there is rather an awkward pause.* ALAN *and* BRIAN
exchange a brief glance. BRIAN *silently frames the word 'Po-faced'
in his mouth.*

ROGERS. (*With a wooden face.*) Who else is staying here at the
moment?

ALAN. There's only Kit Neilan, I think, that you haven't met.

ROGERS. Oh! Is he going into the diplomatic, too?

ALAN. Yes. (*To* BRIAN.) By the way, Brian, what odds did you
lay against Kit in your book?

BRIAN. I didn't, but I should think five to two against would
about meet the case.

ALAN. I don't know. The odds must have lengthened considerably these last few weeks.

BRIAN. Why? Oh, you mean Diana. I say, old boy, I hadn't
thought of that. You don't think there's a chance of a well-
fancied colt being withdrawn before the big contest?

ALAN. No. She won't marry him. That is, not until she's
exhausted other possibilities.

ROGERS. Er—who is this girl?

BRIAN. Diana? She's Babe's—Kenneth Lake's sister. She's
staying here.

ROGERS. Oh! Is she learning French, too?

BRIAN. No. She just stops us from learning it. No, she's staying
here because her people live in India and she's got nowhere
else to go.

ROGERS. Pretty dull for her here, I should think.

ALAN. That girl wouldn't find it dull on a desert island.

BRIAN. Unless it *was* deserted.

ALAN. True. But one feels somehow it wouldn't be deserted long if she were on it.

ROGERS. What do you mean by that?

ALAN. I've no idea. She's a nice girl. You'll love her.

BRIAN *hides a smile.*

At least, it won't be her fault if you don't.

ROGERS. (*Politely.*) I don't quite follow you, I'm afraid.

ALAN. I'm sorry, sir. I was forgetting you're of an age to take care of yourself.

ROGERS. (*Testily.*) There's no need to call me 'sir', you know.

ALAN *raises his eyebrows.*

What you're implying is that this girl is—er—rather fast.

ALAN. I'm not implying it. I'm saying it. That girl is the fastest worker you're ever likely to see.

ROGERS. Oh! (*He goes back to his food.*)

BRIAN. (*Conciliatorily.*) What he means is that she's just naturally full of joie de vivre and all that. She's all right really. She just likes company.

ALAN. (*Under his breath.*) A battalion, you mean.

ROGERS. You sound embittered.

ALAN. Embittered? Oh, no. Oh, dear me, no. (*He breaks a roll open rather violently.*) Both Brian and I, for reasons that I won't go into now, are immune. Only I thought it just as well to let you know before you met her that Diana Lake, though a dear girl in many ways, is a little unreliable in her emotional life.

ROGERS. You mean she isn't in love with this chap Kit What's-his-name, who wants to marry her?

ALAN. The only reason I have for supposing she isn't is that she says that she is. But that's good enough for me.

Pause. BRIAN *gets up.*

BRIAN. Well, Maingot's simple French Phrases are calling me.

ROGERS. (*Evidently glad to change the subject.*) Maingot's Phrase-book. He's given me that to do, too.

BRIAN. Good. Then very soon now you will be able to walk into a chemist's and say in faultless French, 'Please, sir, I wish a toothpaste with a slightly stronger scent.'

ROGERS. Oh, really.

ALAN. Then think how nice it'll be if you're in a railway car-
riage, and you're able to inform a fellow traveller that the
guard has just waved a red flag to signify that the locomotive
has run off the line.

ROGERS. Sounds a bit out of date, I must say.

BRIAN. Maingot's grandfather wrote it, I believe.

The telephone rings. BRIAN *turns round.*

Do you know, I have a nasty feeling that's Chi-Chi.

ROGERS. Who's Chi-Chi?

BRIAN. That's not her real name.

MAINGOT's *voice is heard from the garden.*

MAINGOT. (*Off.*) Monsieur Howard.

ALAN. (*Getting up, calling.*) Oui, Monsieur?

MAINGOT. (*Off.*) Voulez-vous répondre au téléphone, je vous en
prie?

ALAN. Bien, Monsieur. (*He goes to telephone and takes off the
receiver.*) Hullo . . . Bien. (*He holds out the receiver to* BRIAN.)

BRIAN. Me? Hell! (*He takes the receiver.*) Hullo . . . Ah hullo,
Chi-Chi, comment ça va? Comment-allez-vous? . . . Quoi?
. . . Quoi? . . . Wait a moment, Chi-Chi. (*Lowers receiver.*)
(*To* ALAN.)

Take it for me, old boy. I can't hear a word the girl's saying.

ALAN *comes and takes it.*

ALAN. Hullo, Oui, il ne comprend pas . . . Bien. Je le lui
demanderai.

(*To* BRIAN.) Can you see her tonight at the Casino? She wants
you to meet her sister.

BRIAN. Ask her if it's the same one I met on Tuesday.

ALAN. (*In 'phone.*) Il voudrait savoir s'il a déjà rencontré votre
sœur. . . . Bon. (*To* BRIAN.) She says it's a different one.

BRIAN. Tell her it's O.K. I'll be there.

ALAN. (*In 'phone.*) Il dit qu'il sera enchanté. . . . Oui . . . au
revoir. (*He rings off.*)

BRIAN. I told that damn woman not to ring up here.

(MAINGOT *enters from window.*)

MAINGOT. Alors. Qui est ce qui vient de téléphoner?

BRIAN. (*Apologetically.*) C'était quelqu'un pour moi, Monsieur.

MAINGOT. Pour vous?

BRIAN. Oui, une fille que je connais dans la ville.

MAINGOT. Une fille. (*He bursts into a stentorian roar of laughter and goes back into the garden.*) Une fille qu'il connait! Ho! Ho!

BRIAN. Now what's bitten him?

ALAN. A fille doesn't mean a girl, Brian.

BRIAN. It says so in my dictionary. What does it mean, then?

ALAN. A tart.

BRIAN. Oh! (*He considers a second.*) Well, I hate to have to say it, old boy, but having a strict regard for the truth that's a fairly neat little description of Chi-Chi. See you two at lunch time.

He goes out.

ALAN. There in a nutshell you have the reason for Brian's immunity to the charms of Diana Lake.

ROGERS. (*Icily.*) Really?

ALAN. (*Easily.*) Yes. (*Pause. He takes a cigarette.*) This place is going to be rather a change for you after your boat, isn't it?

ROGERS. (*Stung.*) You mean my ship, don't you?

ALAN. Oh, is there a difference?

ROGERS. There is.

ALAN. Of course. It's a grave social error to say boat for ship, isn't it? Like mentioning a lady's name before the royal toast or talking about Harrow College.

ROGERS. Yes, that would be very wrong.

DIANA LAKE *comes in from the garden. She is in a bathing wrap which she wears open, disclosing a bathing dress underneath. She is about twenty, very lovely.*

DIANA. Good morning. (*She stops at the sight of* ROGERS, *and decorously pulls her wrap more closely about her.*)

ROGERS *and* ALAN *get up.*

ALAN. Good morning, Diana. I don't think you've met Commander Rogers.

DIANA *comes forward and shakes hands.*

DIANA. How do you do?

ROGERS. How do you do?

DIANA. (*To* ROGERS.) I didn't know you'd—you must have arrived last night, I suppose?

ALAN. Don't you remember? You asked me what train he was coming by.

DIANA *comes round the table; kisses him on the top of his head.*

DIANA. Do sit down, Commander Rogers. (*He sits.*) How are you this morning, Alan?

ALAN. (*Feeling her bathing dress.*) I'll bet you didn't go in the water.

DIANA. Yes, I did.

ALAN. Right in?

DIANA. Yes, right in. Ask Kit.

ALAN. (*Really surprised.*) Kit? You don't mean to say that you got Kit to go bathing with you?

DIANA. Yes, I did. He's fetching my towel. I left it behind.

ALAN. God! you women.

DIANA. What?

ALAN. Without the slightest qualm and just to gratify a passing whim, you force a high-souled young man to shatter one of his most sacred principles.

ROGERS. What principle is that, if I might ask?

DIANA. (*Emphatically.*) Never, under any circumstances, to do anything hearty.

ROGERS. (*Challengingly.*) Personally, I rather like an early morning dip.

ALAN. (*As if the words burnt his mouth.*) An—early—morning—dip?

ROGERS. Certainly. That's hearty, I suppose.

ALAN. Well—

DIANA. I quite agree with you, Commander Rogers. I don't think there's anything nicer than a swim before breakfast. Ashtray? (*Hands it to* ROGERS.)

ALAN. You'd like anything that gave you a chance to come down to breakfast in a bathing dress.

DIANA. Does it shock you, Alan?

ALAN. Unutterably.

DIANA. I'll go and dress then.

ALAN. No. There's no point in that. You've made one successful entrance. Don't spoil it by making another.

ROGERS. I don't think I quite understand you.

ALAN. Diana does, don't you, angel?

DIANA. (*Sweetly.*) Has another publisher refused your novel, Alan?

ALAN, *momentarily disconcerted, can find nothing to say. Pause.*

Enter KIT *through the french window. He is about twenty-two, fair and good-looking. He wears a dressing-gown over his bathing dress, and carries two towels over his arm.*

KIT. (*Sullenly.*) Morning.

ALAN. (*In gentle reproof.*) Well, well, well.

KIT. (*Shamefacedly.*) Well, why not?

ALAN *shakes his head sadly.*

ALAN. I don't think you've met Commander Rogers.

KIT. (*Shaking hands.*) How do you do? I heard you were coming. (*He begins to dry his hair on a towel, throwing the other one to* DIANA.)

ALAN. Did Diana go in the water?

KIT. No.

DIANA. Kit, you dirty liar.

KIT. I've done enough for you already this morning. I'm not going to perjure myself as well. (*He sits down gloomily and pours himself out a cup of coffee.*) I had hoped you wouldn't be here, Alan, to witness my shame.

ALAN. You of all people an early morning dipper.

KIT. (*Shuddering.*) Don't put it like that. You make it sound worse than it is. Say a nine o'clock bather. Oh, hell, this coffee's cold. Marianne!

ALAN. Mere toying with words can't hide the truth. Do you know I think that girl could make you go for a bicycle tour in the Pyrenees if she set her mind to it.

KIT. She could you know, Alan, that's the awful thing.

Slight pause.

ROGERS. I once went for a bicycle tour in the Pyrenees.

ALAN. Really?

KIT *splutters into his coffee simultaneously.*

JACQUELINE *comes out of the kitchen. She is about twenty-five or twenty-six, not unattractive, but nothing in looks to compare with* DIANA. *She wears an apron and has a handkerchief tied over her hair.*

JACQUELINE. Marianne's upstairs. Do you want anything? (*She speaks with only the barest trace of accent.*)

KIT. Hello, Jack.

ALAN. Good morning, darling.

JACQUELINE. (*Going to* ROGERS.) How do you do, Commander Rogers. I'm so glad you could come to us.

ROGERS. (*Shaking hands.*) Er——how do you do?

JACQUELINE. I hope you've found everything you want.

ROGERS. Yes, thank you.

JACQUELINE. Did Marianne ask you if you wanted eggs for breakfast?

ROGERS. I don't want any, thanks.

JACQUELINE. I see. Well, don't worry about asking for anything you need. By the way, do you drink beer at meals or do you prefer wine?

ROGERS. (*Sitting.*) Beer, please. Nothing like a can of beer.

ALAN. No, I suppose there isn't.

JACQUELINE. (*To* KIT.) What were you shouting about, by the way?

KIT. Jack, darling, the coffee's cold.

JACQUELINE. Of course it's cold. You're half an hour late for breakfast.

KIT. Yes, but . . .

JACQUELINE. You can't have any more because Marianne's doing the rooms.

KIT. I thought perhaps, Jack, darling, knowing how much you love me, you might be an angel and do something about it.

JACQUELINE. Certainly not. It's against all the rules of the house. Besides, you'd better go and get dressed. I'm giving you a lesson in five minutes.

KIT. In the near future, when I am Minister of Foreign Affairs, this incident will play a large part in my decision to declare war on France.

JACQUELINE *pushes him back into his chair and grabs the coffee-pot.*

JACQUELINE. Ooh! This is the last time I'm going to do this for you.

She goes back into the kitchen.

KIT. (*To* DIANA.) You see what a superb diplomat I should make.

ALAN. Rather the Palmerston tradition, wasn't it?

ROGERS. Was that Maingot's daughter.

KIT. Yes. Her name's Jacqueline.

ROGERS. Jacqueline? (*Brightly.*) I see. That's why you call her Jack.

KIT. (*Looking at him distastefully.*) Yes, that's why we call her Jack.

ROGERS. She speaks English very well.

KIT. She's been in England half her life. I believe she's going to be an English school-marm. You'll like her. She's amusing. (*He continues to dry himself.*) Hell! I still feel wet.

He glares at DIANA *who comes behind his chair and dries his hair with her own towel.*

DIANA. You've got such lovely hair, darling. That's why it takes so long to dry.

KIT. (*To* ALAN.) You know, Alan, this is a nice girl.

ALAN. (*Tilting his chair back and gazing at* DIANA.) Yes, she's nice. She's good, too.

ROGERS *gets up.*

ROGERS. Well, I must go upstairs. I want to get my room ship-shape.

ALAN. And above board?

ROGERS. (*Turning savagely on* ALAN.) Yes, and above board. Any objection?

ALAN. (*Airily.*) No, no objection at all. Make it as above board as you like.

ROGERS. (*Bowing stiffly.*) Thank you. I'm most grateful.

Exit ROGERS.

ALAN. (*Pensively.*) Do you know, I don't think he likes me.

KIT. Who does? I'm the only one who can stand you and then only in small doses.

DIANA. Kenneth adores you, anyway. He's quite silly the way he tries to imitate you.

ALAN. Your brother shows remarkable acumen sometimes.

DIANA. And then, of course, I adore you too. You know that.

KIT *swings his chair round and pulls her roughly down on to his knee.*

KIT. Hey! I'm not going to have you adoring anybody except me. Do you understand? (*He kisses her.*)

DIANA. Darling, you're not jealous of Alan, are you?

KIT. I'm jealous of anyone you even look at.

DIANA. All right, then in future I won't look at anyone except you.

KIT. That's a promise?

DIANA. That's a promise.

ALAN, *still leaning back in his chair, whistles a tune softly.*

(*Feeling* KIT's *hands.*) Darling, you *are* cold.

KIT. Yes, I know. I think I'll go and dress and not wait for the coffee. (*He gets up.*) You've probably given me pneumonia. But I don't mind. You could tear me up in little pieces and trample on them, and I'd still love you.

DIANA. Sweet little thing. Take these things upstairs, darling, will you? (*Gives him towels.*)

KIT *goes out.*

ALAN. That's no reason why you should, you know.

DIANA. Should what?

ALAN. Tear him up in little pieces and trample on them.

DIANA *crosses over to the window where she stands, looking out.*

So you're not going to look at anyone except Kit.

DIANA *doesn't answer.* ALAN *gets up and walks over to the window. He puts his arm round her waist and his cheek against her.*

(*After a pause.*) This doesn't mean I'm falling for you.

DIANA. (*Gently.*) Doesn't it, Alan?

ALAN. No, it doesn't.

He walks over to the armchair and sits.

DIANA. I *am* disappointed.

ALAN. What do you think of the Commander?

DIANA. I think he's quite nice.

ALAN. Yes. (*Gently.*) Yes. I want to tell you, it's no good starting anything with him.

DIANA. Don't be silly, Alan.

ALAN. It really isn't any good, darling, because you see I've warned him against you.

DIANA. You warned him? (*Coming to* ALAN.) What did you say?

ALAN. I told him what you are.

DIANA. (*Quietly.*) What's that?

ALAN. Don't you know?

DIANA. Alan, much as I like you there *are* times when I could cheerfully strangle you.

ALAN. Is this one of them, darling?

DIANA. Yes, ducky, it is.

ALAN. Good, that's just what I hoped.

DIANA. This is rather a new rôle for you, isn't it, playing wet nurse to the Navy?

ALAN. You don't think it suits me?

DIANA. No, darling, I'm afraid I don't. What are you doing it for?

ALAN. It's not because I'm fond of the Commander. As a matter of fact it would rather amuse me to see you play hell with the Commander. But I do like Kit, that's why. So no hanky-panky with the Navy or . . .

DIANA. Or what?

ALAN. Or I shall have to be rather beastly to you, darling, and you know you wouldn't like that.

DIANA. You don't understand me at all, Alan.

ALAN. I understand every little bit of you, Diana, through and through. That's why we get along so well together.

DIANA. (*Tearfully.*) I ought to *hate* you.

ALAN. Well, go on trying, darling, and you may succeed. (*He kisses her on the back of the neck.*) I've got to go and finish some stuff for Maingot. See you at lunch time. (*He goes to the door.*)

DIANA. Alan?

ALAN. (*Turning at door.*) Yes?

DIANA. What do you mean by hanky-panky?

ALAN. *I* should tell *you*.

He goes out.

    DIANA *kicks petulantly at the window. She goes to the table, opens her handbag, takes out a small mirror and looks at herself.*

Enter JACQUELINE *from the kitchen with the coffee-pot.*

DIANA. Oh, thank you so much.

JACQUELINE. Where's Kit?

DIANA. He's gone up to dress. He felt cold.

JACQUELINE. Isn't that like him. Well, you can tell him that I'm not going to make him any more coffee however loud he screams.

DIANA. Yes, I'll tell him, and I think you're quite right.

Enter ROGERS *through the door at the back.*

ROGERS. (*Nervously.*) Oh, hullo.

JACQUELINE *goes out into the kitchen.*

DIANA. (*Brightly.*) Hullo, Commander Rogers.

ROGERS *goes over to the bookcase at the back.*

Looking for something?

ROGERS. Yes, Maingot's Phrase Book, as a matter of fact. (*He bends down and pulls a book out.*) Here it is, I think. (*He looks at the title.*) No, it isn't.

DIANA. Let me help you. I think I know where it is.

ROGERS. Oh, that's very good of you.

DIANA *bends down at the bookcase and pulls a book out.*

DIANA. Here. (*She hands it to him.*)

ROGERS. Oh, thanks most awfully.

DIANA. (*Going back to the table.*) Well, what are your first impressions of Monsieur Maingot's establishment?

ROGERS. Oh, I—er—think it ought to be very cheery here.

DIANA. I'm sure you'll love it.

ROGERS. Yes, I'm sure I will.

DIANA. The boys are so nice, don't you think?

ROGERS. Er—yes, I think they are—some of them. (*He makes a tentative move towards the door.*)

DIANA. (*Quickly.*) I suppose you find Alan a bit startling, don't you?

ROGERS. Alan?

DIANA. The one with the German coat.

ROGERS. Oh, yes. Yes, he is a bit startling. Well, I ought to be getting along.

DIANA. Why? You've got your room pretty well shipshape by now, haven't you?

ROGERS. Oh, thanks, yes, I have.

DIANA. Well, don't go for a bit. Stay and talk to me while I have my coffee. Have you got a cigarette?

ROGERS. (*Coming to her.*) Yes, I have. (*Offers her one.*)

DIANA. (*Takes one.*) Thanks. I was saying about Alan——

ROGERS. Match?

DIANA. Thanks. (*He lights it.*) What was I saying?

ROGERS. About Alan.

DIANA. Oh, yes, about Alan—he's really very nice but you mustn't take everything he says seriously.

ROGERS. Oh. Oh, I see. No, I won't.

DIANA. He's just the tiniest bit—you know (*she taps her forehead significantly*) unbalanced.

ROGERS. Oh, really.

DIANA. I thought it as well to warn you.

ROGERS. Yes. Thank you very much.

DIANA. Otherwise it might lead to trouble.

ROGERS. Yes, it might.

Pause.

DIANA. Poor Alan. I'm afraid he's got it very badly.

ROGERS. Er—got what?

DIANA. Well—(*She leans back and blows a puff of smoke into the air.*) Of course I oughtn't to say it. (*Pause. She throws him a quick glance to see if he has caught her meaning. Evidently he hasn't.*)

ROGERS. Oh.

DIANA. I'm awfully sorry for him of course.

ROGERS. (*Puzzled, but polite.*) Of course.

DIANA. It's so funny, because from the way he behaves to me and the things he says about me, you'd think he hated me, wouldn't you?

ROGERS. Yes, you would. (*Pause.*) Doesn't he?

DIANA. (*Laughing.*) No. Oh no. Far from it.

ROGERS. (*The light of understanding in his face at last.*) Oh, I see. You mean he's rather keen on you?

DIANA. I mustn't give him away. It wouldn't be fair. But if he ever talks to you about me, as he probably will, and tries to give you the impression that I'm a (*smiling*) scheming wrecker of men's lives, you needn't necessarily believe him.

ROGERS. No—no, I won't, of course. But I don't see why he should, you know.

DIANA. (*Embarrassedly.*) Well, you see, Commander Rogers, I like Alan, but I don't like him as much as perhaps he wants me to, and I suppose that makes him feel rather embittered.

ROGERS. Ah, yes. I see.

DIANA. (*Gaily.*) Well, don't let's talk any more about it, because it's not a very pleasant subject. Tell me about yourself. Tell me about the Navy. I'm always thrilled to death by anything to do with the sea.

ROGERS. Really, that's splendid.

Pause.

DIANA. It must be a wonderful life.

ROGERS. Yes, it's a pretty good life on the whole.

DIANA. Marvellously interesting, I should think.

ROGERS. Yes, pretty interesting.

DIANA. I bet you've had any amount of wildly exciting experiences.

ROGERS. Oh, well, you know, things have a way of happening in the Navy.

DIANA. Yes, I'm sure they have. (*Pause.*) You naval people never talk about yourselves, do you?

ROGERS. Well, you know, silent service and all that.

DIANA. Yes, I know, but I do hope you're not going to be too silent with me, because honestly, I am so terribly interested.

ROGERS. (*Smiling.*) I'll try not to be too silent then.

Pause.

DIANA. What are you doing this morning?

ROGERS. Nothing special. Why?

DIANA. How would you like to have a look round the town?

Enter JACQUELINE *from the kitchen.*

JACQUELINE. Hasn't Kit come down yet?

ROGERS. (*To* DIANA.) Oh, I'd love to.

DIANA. Good. I'll go and get dressed and we'll go for a little stroll.

ROGERS. But isn't it rather a bore for you?

DIANA. No, of course not. I'd love it. (*She goes to the door.*)

JACQUELINE. Diana?

DIANA. Yes?

JACQUELINE. (*Pouring out a cup of coffee.*) If you're going past Kit's room you might give him this. (*She hands her the cup.*)

DIANA. Right, I will. (*To* ROGERS.) Are you sure I'm not dragging you away from your work or anything?

JACQUELINE *goes back into the kitchen.*

ROGERS. Oh, no. That's quite all right. I haven't been given anything to do yet.

DIANA. Good. Well, I'll go and put some clothes on.

She turns to go. ALAN *comes in and almost collides with her in the doorway.*

(*Turning.*) I'll meet you down here then in about a quarter of an hour?

ROGERS. Right.

DIANA *smiles at* ROGERS, *walks past* ALAN *without glancing at him and goes out.*

ALAN. (*Going to the table and sitting.*) Going for a little constitutional, Commander? (*He has some books in his hands. He places them on the table in front of him and opens a notebook.*)

ROGERS. Yes. (*He turns his back.*)

ALAN. (*Taking a fountain pen from his pocket and unscrewing the top.*) You've got a nice day for it. (*Pause. He writes in his notebook and begins to sing the Lorelei. Without looking up.*) It's a lovely song, the Lorelei, don't you think?

ROGERS. It *could* be.

ALAN. True. (*He continues to write.*) It's a stupid fable anyway. I ask you, what sailor would be lured to his doom after he had been warned of his danger?

ROGERS. (*Turning quickly.*) If you think that's funny, I don't.

Enter KENNETH *through the window.*

KENNETH. Oh, Commander Rogers, Maingot wants to see you a moment.

Pause. ROGERS *is standing facing* ALAN *across the table, and* ALAN *is still writing.*

ROGERS. Right. Thank you. (*He marches out into the garden.*)

ALAN. (*After a pause.*) Well, Babe, I suppose you were murdered by the old man.

KENNETH. (*Wearily.*) More so than usual this morning.

Pause. ALAN *goes on writing.*

ALAN. (*Without looking up.*) Babe, I don't like your sister.

KENNETH. (*Walking round the table and looking over* ALAN's *shoulder at what he is writing.*) Don't you? I thought you did like her, rather a lot.

ALAN *looks up. Pause.*

Enter JACQUELINE *from the kitchen. She has taken off her apron and the handkerchief over her hair.*

JACQUELINE. Good morning, Kenneth.

KENNETH. Good morning, Mam'selle.

JACQUELINE. Had your lesson?

KENNETH. Yes. I've got to do the whole damn thing again. (*He goes to the door.*) Alan, I wish to God I had your brains.

He goes out.

ALAN *looks after him a moment, then goes back to his work.*

JACQUELINE. (*Looking at her watch.*) Kit is a monster. He's never been on time for his lesson yet. (*She goes to the window and looks out.*)

ALAN. (*Looking up from his work.*) What have you done to your hair, Jack?

JACQUELINE. (*Turning round.*) Do you like it? (*Her hair is done in the same way as* DIANA's.)

ALAN. (*He gets up and walks over to her, holding her out at arm's length and studying her hair. Doubtfully.*) No, it's a mistake, Jack. You won't beat her by copying the way she does her hair.

JACQUELINE. He'll like it, Alan, I'm sure he will.

ALAN. He won't notice it.

JACQUELINE. He will, you see.

ALAN. I'll bet you five francs he doesn't.

JACQUELINE. All right. That's a bet.

ALAN. Go and change it while there's still time. Make it look hideous like it used to.

JACQUELINE. (*Laughing.*) No, Alan.

Pause.

ALAN. Poor Jack. I must find you someone else to fall in love with.

JACQUELINE. So long as you don't tell him that I adore him, I don't mind what you do.

ALAN. Anyone less half-witted than Kit would have seen it years ago.

JACQUELINE. Am I very obvious, Alan? I don't want to bore him.

ALAN. Go and change that hair.

JACQUELINE. Do you think if Diana were out of the way I should stand a chance?

ALAN. You're not thinking of putting her out of the way, are you?

JACQUELINE. (*Smiling.*) I'd do it painlessly, Alan.

ALAN. Why painlessly?

JACQUELINE. I'm not jealous of her really, though.

ALAN. Oh, no. Not a bit.

JACQUELINE. Honestly, Alan, I wouldn't mind if she made him happy. But she doesn't. She seems to enjoy making him miserable. And now that the Commander's here it's going to be much worse. You know what I mean, don't you?

ALAN. I have an idea.

JACQUELINE. Can't we do anything about it, Alan?

ALAN. Yes. Go and change that hair, Jack. It's the only chance.

JACQUELINE. No, I won't do anything of the sort.

Enter KIT, *dressed.*

KIT. (*Walking right up to* JACQUELINE *and taking her hands earnestly.*) Jack, I have something to tell you. (*To* ALAN.) Go away, Alan, this is confidential.

ALAN *goes back to the table and his work.*

JACQUELINE. What is it, Kit?

KIT. I haven't done that work you set me.

JACQUELINE. Oh, Kit. Why not?

KIT. Well, I took Diana to the Casino last night, and——

JACQUELINE. Kit, really——

KIT. But as a great treat I'll translate you some La Bruyère this morning. Come on. (*He pulls her towards one of the arm-chairs.*)

JACQUELINE. I set you that work specially because I thought it would interest you, and anyway you can't afford to slack off just now before your exam.

KIT. (*Hands a her book.*) Now sit down and read your nice La Bruyère and be quiet. Are you comfortable? (*Opening his own book.*) Page one hundred and eight. Listen, Alan. You can learn a lot from hearing French beautifully translated. Chapter four. (*Translating.*) Of the heart . . .

JACQUELINE. Of love.

KIT. Of love, then. (*Translating.*) There is a fragrance in pure love . . .

JACQUELINE. In pure friendship.

KIT. (*Translating.*) Friendship can exist between people of different sexes.

ALAN. You don't say.

KIT. I don't. La Bruyère does. (*Translating.*) Friendship can exist between people of different sexes, quite exempt from all grossness.

JACQUELINE. Quite free from all . . .

ALAN. Hanky-panky.

JACQUELINE. Quite free from all unworthy thoughts.

KIT. Quite exempt from all grossness. (*Looking up.*) I know what it is. It's been bothering me all the time. You've changed your hair, haven't you, Jack?

JACQUELINE. (*Giving* ALAN *a quick glance.*) Yes, Kit, I've changed my hair.

KIT. Alan, do look at Jack. She's changed her hair.

ALAN. (*Looking up.*) So she has. Well—well—well.

KIT. I knew you'd done something to yourself. (*He studies her.*) It's queer, you know. It makes you look quite . . .

JACQUELINE. (*Eagerly.*) Quite what, Kit?

KIT. I was going to say alluring.

He laughs as if he'd made a joke; JACQUELINE *laughs, too.*

JACQUELINE. You do like it, anyway, Kit?

KIT. Yes, I do. I think it's very nice.

JACQUELINE. You think I ought to keep it like this?

Before KIT *can answer,* ROGERS *has appeared from garden.*

ROGERS. Sorry, Maingot wants to take me now, so would one of you mind telling Diana—er—I mean Miss Lake, that we'll have to postpone our walk?

Pause.

ALAN. Yes, I'll tell her.

ROGERS. Thank you.

He goes back into garden.

JACQUELINE. (*Breaking a silence.*) You think I ought to keep it like this?

KIT. (*Turning slowly.*) Keep what?

JACQUELINE. My hair.

KIT. Oh, don't be such a bore about your hair, Jack. Yes, keep it like that. It'll get a laugh anyway.

He goes out quickly. Pause. JACQUELINE *closes her book with a slam and rises.*

JACQUELINE. Five francs please, Alan.

CURTAIN

ACT II

SCENE 1

SCENE: *Same as Act I.*

TIME: *A fortnight later, about 2 p.m.*

Lunch is just finished. All the characters seen in Act I are still sitting at the table. MAINGOT *sits at one end,* ALAN *facing him at the other end. On* MAINGOT'S *right are* ROGERS, DIANA, *and* KIT, *in that order, facing the audience. On his left are* BRIAN, KENNETH, *and* JACQUELINE, *also in that order, with their backs to the audience.*

On the rise of the CURTAIN *conversation is general.* ALAN *is talking to* JACQUELINE, BRIAN *to* MAINGOT, *and* ROGERS *to* DIANA. *After a few seconds conversation lapses and* ROGERS' *voice can be heard.*

ROGERS. Oh, yes, Tuppy Jones. Yes, he's in Belligerent. I know him quite well. Cheery cove. (*He chuckles.*) There's an amusing story about him as a matter of fact. He got a bit tight in Portsmouth, and broke seven Belisha Beacons with an air pistol.

MAINGOT. (*Turning politely to* ROGERS.) Eh, bien, Monsieur le Commandant, voulez-vous raconter votre petite histoire en français? Please to tell your little story in French.

ROGERS. (*Confused.*) Oh, no, sir. That's a bit unfair. I don't know enough.

MAINGOT. You should have learnt enough, my Commander.

ROGERS. But, dash it, sir, I've only been here a few days.

MAINGOT. Two weeks, my Commander. After two weeks my pupils are usually enough advanced to tell me little stories in French.

ROGERS. Well, I'm afraid I can't tell this one, sir. It wasn't a story anyway.

ALAN. (*Leaning forward malevolently.*) Au contraire, Monsieur, l'histoire de Monsieur le Commandant était excessivement rigolo.

29

MAINGOT. Bien. Alors, racontez-la vous même.

ALAN. Il paraît qu'il connait un type qui s'appelle Tuppy Jones. Alors ce bonhomme, se promenant un soir par les rues de Portsmouth, et ayant un peu trop bu, a brisé, à coups de pistolet à vent, sept Belisha Beacons.

MAINGOT. (*Who has been listening attentively, his ear cupped in his hand.*) Et puis?

ALAN. C'est tout, Monsieur.

MAINGOT. C'est tout?

KIT. Vous savez que ce Tuppy Jones était d'un esprit le plus fin du monde.

MAINGOT. Je crois bien. Au même temps, je n'ai pas tout à fait compris. Qu'est-ce que ça veut dire—Belisha Beacons?

ALAN. Ah, ça c'est un peu compliqué.

BRIAN. (*Showing off his French.*) Belisha Beacons sont des objets——(*He stops.*)

ALAN. Qui se trouvent actuellement dans les rues de Londres——

KIT. Et qui sont dédiés au salut des passants.

MAINGOT. Aha. Des emblèmes religieux?

ALAN. C'est ça. Des emblèmes religieux.

MAINGOT. (*To* ROGERS.) So one finds it funny in England to break these religious emblems with a wind pistol?

ROGERS. (*Not having understood.*) Well—(MAINGOT *shrugs his shoulders sadly.*)

(*Angrily to* ALAN.) Damn you, Howard.

BRIAN. That's not fair.

ALAN. It was a very good story, I thought.

MAINGOT. (*Rising, having finished his wine.*) Bien, Messieurs, Mesdames, la session est terminée. (*He gets up.* ALL *get up after him.*)

(*Holding up his hand.*) One moment please. I speak in English for those who cannot understand. How many of you are going tonight to the Costume Ball and great battle of flowers at the Casino? Please hold up your hands.

KIT. (*To* ALAN.) Good lord! Is it July the fourteenth? I'd no idea.

All hold up their hands.

MAINGOT. All of you! Good. The festivities commence at eight o'clock; there will be no dinner 'ere. All right.

MAINGOT moves to window and stops.

One moment, please. I give my history lecture at two-thirty, that is to say in twenty minutes' time. All right.

He goes out into garden.

ROGERS and DIANA are moving towards the french windows. KIT catches them up.

KIT. (*To* DIANA.) What about a game of Japanese billiards, Diana?

DIANA. (*Indicating* ROGERS.) Bill's just asked me to play, Kit. I'll play you afterwards. Come on, Bill.

ROGERS. Sorry, Neilan.

ROGERS and DIANA go out together. KIT goes to an armchair and sits sulkily. BRIAN has pulled out a wallet and is fumbling inside it. ALAN is going out through the window when KENNETH catches him up.

KENNETH. Alan, will you help me with that essay now? You said you would.

ALAN. Oh hell! Can't you do it yourself?

KENNETH. Well, I could, but it might mean missing this dance tonight, and I'd hate that. Do help me. It's on Robespierre, and I know nothing about him.

ALAN. There's a chapter on him in Lavisse. Why don't you copy that out? The old man won't notice. He'll probably say that it isn't French, but still——

He goes out.

KENNETH. (*Shouting after him.*) Alan, be a sportsman.

ALAN. (*Off.*) Nothing I should hate more.

KENNETH. Oh, hell!

KENNETH turns sadly and goes past KIT to the door at the back.

KIT. (*Moodily.*) What Alan wants is a good kick in the pants.

KENNETH. (*At door.*) Oh, I don't know.

He goes out. BRIAN *puts his wallet back in his pocket.*

BRIAN. I say, old boy, I suppose you couldn't lend me fifty francs, could you?

KIT. No, I couldn't. At any rate, not until you've paid me back that hundred you owe me.

BRIAN. Ah, I see your point. (*Cheerfully.*) Well, old boy, no ill feelings. I'll have to put off Chi-Chi for tonight, that's all.

KIT. You weren't thinking of taking her to this thing at the Casino, were you?

BRIAN. Yes.

KIT. What do you think Maingot would have said if he'd seen her?

BRIAN. That would have been all right. I told him I was taking the daughter of the British Consul.

KIT. But she doesn't exactly look like the daughter of the British Consul, does she?

BRIAN. Well, after all, it's fancy dress. It's just possible the daughter of the British Consul might go dressed as Nana of the Boulevards. Still, I admit that if he'd actually met her he might have found it odd that the only English she knew was 'I love you, Big Boy'.

KIT. How do you manage to talk to her, then?

BRIAN. Oh, we get along, old boy, we get along. (*Going to window.*) You couldn't make it thirty francs, I suppose?

KIT. No, and I don't suppose Chi-Chi could either.

BRIAN. Oh, well, you may be right. I'd better pop round in the car and tell her I won't be there tonight.

KIT. Oh, listen, Brian, if you want someone to take, why don't you take Jack?

BRIAN. Isn't anyone taking her?

KIT. Yes, I'm supposed to be, but——

BRIAN. (*Surprised.*) You, old boy? What about Diana?

KIT. Oh, she's being taken by the Commander.

BRIAN. Oh.

Pause.

As a matter of fact, I don't think I'll go at all. I don't fancy myself at a battle of flowers.

KIT. Nor do I, if it comes to that.

BRIAN. Oh, I don't know. I think you'd hurl a prettier bloom than I would. Well, so long.

He goes out. KIT *sits biting his nails. The ferocious din of a sports car tuning up comes through the window.* KIT *jumps up.*

KIT. (*Shouting through the window.*) Must you make all that noise?

BRIAN. (*Off, his voice coming faintly above the din.*) Can't hear, old boy.

The noise lessens as the car moves off down the street. JACQUELINE *and* MARIANNE *come in, the latter bearing a tray.*

KIT. (*Turning.*) God knows why Brian finds it necessary to have a car that sounds like—like five dictators all talking at once.

JACQUELINE. (*Helping* MARIANNE *clear.*) It goes with his character, Kit. He'd think it was effeminate to have a car that was possible to sit in without getting cramp and that didn't deafen one.

KIT. (*Sitting again.*) I wonder what it's like to be as hearty as Brian?

JACQUELINE. Awful, I should think.

KIT. No, I should think very pleasant. Have you ever seen Brian bad-tempered?

JACQUELINE. No, but then I think he's too stupid to be bad-tempered.

KIT. It doesn't follow. Cats and dogs are bad-tempered, sometimes. No, Brian may be stupid but he's right-minded. He's solved the problem of living better than any of us.

MARIANNE *goes out with a loaded tray.*

It seems a simple solution, too. All it needs, apparently, is the occasional outlay of fifty francs. I wish I could do the same.

JACQUELINE. I expect you could if you tried.

KIT. I have tried. Often.

JACQUELINE *is folding up the table-cloth.*

Does that shock you?

JACQUELINE. Why should it?

KIT. I just wondered.

JACQUELINE. I'm a woman of the world.

KIT. (*Smiling.*) That's the last thing you are. But I'll tell you this, Jack. I like you so much that it's sometimes quite an effort to remember that you're a woman at all.

JACQUELINE. Oh.

She puts the table-cloth in a drawer of the table and shuts it with something of a slam.

I thought you liked women.

KIT. I don't think one likes women, does one? One loves them sometimes, but that's a different thing altogether. Still, I like you. That's what's so odd.

JACQUELINE. (*Brightly.*) Thank you, Kit. I like you, too.

KIT. Good. That's nice for both of us, isn't it?

He returns his gaze to the window. JACQUELINE, *in a sudden fit of temper, kicks the leg of the table.*

Clumsy!

JACQUELINE. (*Limping over to the other armchair and sitting.*) Have you found anything to wear tonight?

KIT. Supposing I didn't go, would you mind?

JACQUELINE. Well, I have been rather looking forward to to-night.

KIT. Alan could take you. He's a better dancer than I am.

JACQUELINE. (*After a pause.*) Why don't you wear that Greek dress of my brother's?

KIT. Jack, you know, I don't think I could cope with a battle of flowers. (*He turns and meets her eyes.*) Could I get into this dress of your brother's?

JACQUELINE. Yes, easily. It may be a bit tight.

ALAN *comes in through the window.*

KIT. That reminds me. I hope there'll be plenty to drink at this affair.

ALAN. (*Morosely.*) There's nothing else for it. I shall have to murder that man.

JACQUELINE. Who?

ALAN. The Commander.

KIT. Surely that's my privilege, isn't it?

ALAN. I've just been watching him play Japanese billiards with Diana. Now you would think, wouldn't you, that Japanese billiards was a fairly simple game? You either roll wooden balls into holes or you don't. That should be the end of it. But as played by the Commander it becomes a sort of naval battle. Every shot he makes is either a plunging salvo or a blasting broadside, or a direct hit amidships.

KIT. At least he has the excuse that it amuses Diana. (*He gets up.*) Will you explain to me, Alan, as an impartial observer, how she can bear to be more than two minutes in that man's company?

ALAN. Certainly. He's in the process of falling in love with her.

KIT. Yes, that's obvious, but—

ALAN. When one hooks a salmon one has to spend a certain amount of time playing it. If one doesn't, it escapes.

KIT. Is that meant to be funny?

ALAN. Of course. When the salmon is landed, all that's necessary is an occasional kick to prevent it slipping back into the water.

KIT. (*Angrily.*) Don't be a damned fool.

ALAN. Tomorrow a certain Lord Heybrook is arriving. Diana is naturally rather anxious to bring the Commander to the gaff as quickly as possible, so that she can have two nice fat fish gasping and squirming about on the bank, before she starts to fish for what'll be the best catch of all of you, if she can bring it off.

Pause. KIT *suddenly bursts out laughing.*

KIT. No wonder you can't get anyone to take your novel.

ALAN. (*Hurt.*) I can't quite see what my novel has got to do with the machinations of a scalp-hunter.

JACQUELINE *rises in alarm.*

KIT. (*Walking over to* ALAN.) Listen, Alan. One more crack like that——

JACQUELINE. (*Hurriedly, to* ALAN.) Kit's quite right. You shouldn't say things like that.

KIT. (*Turning to her savagely.*) What do you know about it, anyway?

JACQUELINE. Nothing, only——

KIT. Well, please go away. This is between Alan and me.

JACQUELINE. Oh, I'm sorry.

JACQUELINE *goes into garden.*

KIT. Now. Will you please understand this. I am in love with Diana, and Diana is in love with me. Now that's not too hard for you to grasp, is it? Because I'll repeat it again slowly if you like.

ALAN. (*Genially.*) No, no. I've read about that sort of thing in books. The Commander, of course, is just an old friend who's known her since she was so high.

KIT. The Commander's in love with her, but you can't blame Diana for that.

ALAN. Of course I don't. It was a very smart piece of work on her part.

KIT. (*Swallowing his anger.*) She's too kind-hearted to tell him to go to hell——

ALAN. I suppose it's because she's so kind-hearted that she calls him 'darling', and plays these peculiar games with him all over the place.

Pause.

KIT. I called you an impartial observer a moment ago. Well, you're not. I believe you're in love with Diana yourself.

ALAN. My dear Kit! As a matter of fact, I admit it's quite possible I shall end by marrying her.

KIT. You'll what?

ALAN. But that'll only be——to take another sporting metaphor ——like the stag who turns at bay through sheer exhaustion at being hunted.

Pause.

KIT. (*Aggressively.*) God! Alan, I've a good mind to——

ALAN. I shouldn't. It'd make us both look rather silly.

DIANA *and* ROGERS *heard off in garden.*

Besides, you know how strongly I disapprove of fighting over a woman.

DIANA *appears at window,* ROGERS *following.*

ROGERS. (*Coming in through window.*) Well, of course, there was only one thing to do. So I gave the order—all hands on deck—— (*Stops at sight of* KIT *and* ALAN).

ALAN. And did they come?

ROGERS. (*Ignoring* ALAN, *to* DIANA.) Let's go out in the garden, Diana.

DIANA. (*Languidly throwing herself into an armchair.*) It's so hot, Bill. Let's stay here.

KIT. Aren't you going to play me a game of Japanese billiards, Diana?

DIANA. You don't mind, do you, Kit? I'm quite exhausted as a matter of fact.

KIT. (*Furious.*) Oh, no. I don't mind a bit.

He goes out into the garden. Pause. ALAN *begins to hum the Lorelei.* ROGERS *walks towards window.*

ALAN. Don't leave us, Commander. If one of us has to go, let it be myself.

ROGER *stops.* ALAN *walks to door at back.*

I shall go aloft.

He goes out.

ROGERS. Silly young fool. I'd like to have him in my ship. Do him all the good in the world.

DIANA. Yes. It might knock some of the conceit out of him.

ROGERS. Y-e-s. Has he been—bothering you at all lately?

DIANA. (*With a gesture of resignation.*) Oh, well. I'm awfully sorry for him, you know.

ROGERS. I find it hard to understand you sometimes, Diana.

He sits in chair beside her. She pats his hand.

At least I think I do understand you, but if you don't mind me saying it, I think you're too kind-hearted—far too kind-hearted.

DIANA. (*With a sigh.*) Yes, I think I am.

ROGERS. For instance—I can't understand why you don't tell Kit.

DIANA. (*Rising.*) Oh, Bill, please——

ROGERS. I'm sorry to keep on at you about it, Diana, but you don't know how much I resent him behaving as if you were still in love with him.

DIANA. But I can't tell him—not yet, anyway. (*Gently.*) Surely you must see how cruel that would be?

ROGERS. This is a case where you must be cruel only to be kind.

DIANA. Yes, Bill, that's true. Terribly true. But you know, cruelty is something that's physically impossible to me. I'm the sort of person who's miserable if I tread on a snail.

ROGERS. You must tell him, Diana. Otherwise it's so unfair on him. Tell him now.

DIANA. (*Quickly.*) No, not now.

ROGERS. Well, this evening.

DIANA. Well, I'll try. It's a terribly hard thing to do. It's like
—it's like kicking someone when he's down.

ROGERS *puts his arms round her.*

ROGERS. I know, old girl, it's a rotten thing to have to do. Poor
little thing, you mustn't think I don't sympathize with you,
you know.

DIANA. (*Laying her head on his chest.*) Oh, Bill, I do feel such a
beast.

ROGERS. Yes, yes, of course. But these things happen, you know.

DIANA. I can't understand it even yet. I loved Kit—at least I
thought I did, and then you happened—and—and—Oh,
Bill, do you do this to all the women you meet?

ROGERS. Er—do what?

DIANA. Sweep them off their feet so that they forget everything
in the world except yourself.

ROGERS. Diana, will you give me a truthful answer to a question I'm going to ask you?

DIANA..Yes, of course, Bill.

ROGERS. Is your feeling for me mere—infatuation, or do you
really, really love me?

DIANA. Oh, you know I do, Bill.

ROGERS. (*He kisses her.*) Oh, darling. And you really don't love
Kit any more?

DIANA. I'm still fond of him.

ROGERS. But you don't love him?

DIANA. No, Bill, I don't love him.

JACQUELINE *comes in through the window.* ROGERS, *his back to
her, doesn't see her.* DIANA *breaks away.*

ROGERS. And you *will* tell him so?

DIANA. Hullo, Jacqueline.

JACQUELINE. Hullo, Diana. Rather warm, isn't it?

She walks across the room and into the kitchen.

DIANA. (*Alarmed.*) You don't think she saw anything, do you?

ROGERS. I don't know.

DIANA. She may have been standing outside the window the
whole time. I wouldn't put it past her.

ROGERS. What does it matter anyway? Everyone will know
soon enough.

DIANA. (*Thoughtfully.*) She's the sort of girl who'll talk.

ROGERS. Let her.

DIANA. (*Turning to him.*) Bill, you don't understand. Our feelings for each other are too sacred to be soiled by vulgar gossip.

ROGERS. Er—yes, yes. But, dash it, we can't go on keeping it a secret for ever.

DIANA. Not for ever. But don't you find it thrilling to have such a lovely secret just between us and no one else? After all, it's our love. Why should others know about it and bandy it about?

ROGERS. Yes, I know, but——

KIT *comes in through window. He glances moodily at* DIANA *and* ROGERS *and throws himself into an armchair, picking up a paper and beginning to read.* ROGERS *points significantly at him and frames the words 'Tell him now' in his mouth.* DIANA *shakes her head violently.* ROGERS *nods his head urgently.* KIT *looks up.*

DIANA. (*Hurriedly.*) You people have got a lecture now, haven't you?

KIT. In about five minutes.

DIANA. Oh. Then I think I'll go for a little walk by myself. (*Going to window.*) We'll have our bathe about four, don't you think, Bill?

ROGERS. Right.

DIANA *goes out. Pause.*

(*Breezily.*) Well, Neilan, how's the world treating you these days.

KIT. Bloodily.

ROGERS. I'm sorry to hear that. What's the trouble?

KIT. Everything. (*He takes up a paper.*)

ROGERS. (*After a pause.*) This show tonight at the Casino ought to be rather cheery, don't you think?

KIT *lowers his paper, looks at him, and raises it again.*

Who are you taking?

KIT. (*Into the paper.*) Jacqueline.

ROGERS. Jacqueline?

KIT. (*Loudly.*) Yes, Jacqueline.

ROGERS. Oh. (*Cheerfully.*) That's a charming girl, I think.

Clever. Amusing. Pretty. She'll make somebody a fine wife.

KIT *emits a kind of snort.*

Did you say anything?

KIT *doesn't answer.*

She's what the French call a sympathetic person.

KIT. Do they? I didn't know.

ROGERS. Oh, yes they do. Much nicer than most modern girls. Take some of these English girls, for instance——

KIT. You take them. I want to read.

He turns his back. ROGERS, *annoyed, shrugs his shoulders.* BRIAN'S *car is heard outside in the road.* ROGERS *goes to the bookcase and takes out his notebook.*

BRIAN'S *voice can be heard in the garden singing ' Somebody Stole my Girl'.*

KIT *gets up.*

(*Shouting through the window.*) Blast you, Brian.

BRIAN. (*Appearing at window.*) What's the matter, old boy? Don't you like my voice?

KIT. No, and I don't like that song.

BRIAN. 'Somebody Stole my Girl'? Why, it's a—— (*He looks from* KIT *to* ROGERS.) Perhaps you're right. It's not one of my better efforts. (*He puts a parcel on the table.*) This has just come for Alan. It feels suspiciously like his novel. (*He goes to bookcase and takes out his notebook.*) You won't believe it, but I used to sing in my school choir. Only because I was in the rugger fifteen, I admit. (*Sits next* KIT.) What's the old boy lecturing on today?

KIT. The Near East, I suppose. He didn't finish it yesterday.

BRIAN. Good lord! Was it the Near East yesterday? I thought it was the Franco-Prussian War.

KIT. You must get a lot of value out of these lectures.

BRIAN. Well, I only understood one word in a hundred.

ROGERS. It's rather the same in my case.

BRIAN. Give me your notes in case the old boy has the impertinence to ask me a question.

He takes KIT'S *notes and starts to read them.* ALAN *comes in through door at the back, followed by* KENNETH.

ALAN. (*Going to table and picking up parcel.*) Ah, I see the novel has come home to father again.

BRIAN. Open it, old boy. There may be a marvellous letter inside.

ALAN. There'll be a letter all right. But I don't need to read it.
He sits down at table and pushes the parcel away.

BRIAN. Bad luck, old boy.

KENNETH *grabs the parcel and unties the string.*

You mustn't give up hope yet, though. First novels are always refused hundreds of times. I know a bloke who's been writing novels and plays and things all his life. He's fifty now, and he's still hoping to get something accepted.

ALAN. Thank you, Brian. That's very comforting.

KENNETH *has extracted a letter from the parcel and is reading it.*

ROGERS. (*Amicably.*) Will you let me read it some time?

ALAN. (*Pleased.*) Would you like to? I'm afraid you'd hate it.

ROGERS. Why? What's it about?

KENNETH *hands down the letter to* ALAN.

ALAN. (*Glancing over letter. He crumples the letter up and throws it away.*) It's about two young men who take a vow to desert their country instantly in the case of war and to go and live on a farm in Central Africa.

ROGERS. (*Uncomfortably.*) Oh.

ALAN. War breaks out and they go. One of them takes his wife. They go, not because they are any more afraid to fight than the next man, but because they believe violence in any circumstances to be a crime and that, if the world goes mad, it's their duty to remain sane.

ROGERS. I see. Conchies.

ALAN. Yes. Conchies. When they get to their farm one of them makes love to the other's wife and they fight over her.

ROGERS. Ah. That's a good point.

ALAN. But in fighting for her they are perfectly aware that the motive that made them do it is as vile as the impulse they feel to go back and fight for their country. In both cases they are letting their passions get the better of their reason —becoming animals instead of men.

ROGERS. But that's nonsense. If a man fights for his country or his wife he's—well, he's a man and not a damned conchie.

ALAN. The characters in my book have the honesty not to rationalize the animal instinct to fight, into something noble like patriotism or manliness. They admit that it's an ignoble instinct—something to be ashamed of.

ROGERS. (*Heated.*) Ashamed of! Crikey!

ALAN. But they also admit that their reason isn't strong enough to stand out against this ignoble instinct, so they go back and fight.

ROGERS. Ah. That's more like it. So they were proved wrong in the end.

ALAN. Their ideal wasn't proved wrong because they were unable to live up to it. That's the point of the book.

KIT. (*From his corner, morosely.*) What's the use of an ideal if you can't live up to it?

ALAN. In a hundred years' time men may be able to live up to our ideals even if they can't live up to their own.

KENNETH. (*Excitedly.*) That's it. Progress.

KIT. Progress my fanny.

ROGERS. But look here, are you a pacifist and all that?

ALAN. I am a pacifist and all that.

ROGERS. And you're going into the diplomatic?

ALAN. Your surprise is a damning criticism of the diplomatic. Anyway, it's not my fault. My father's an ambassador.

ROGERS. Still, I mean to say—— Look here, supposing some rotter came along and stole your best girl, wouldn't you fight him?

KIT. (*Looking up.*) You'd better ask me that question, hadn't you?

ROGERS. (*Swinging round.*) What the devil do you mean?

KIT. (*Getting up.*) And the answer would be yes.

ROGERS. (*With heavy sarcasm.*) That's very interesting, I'm sure.

ALAN. (*Enjoying himself.*) By the way, I forgot to tell you, in my novel, when the two men go back to fight for their country they leave the woman in Central Africa. You see after fighting over her they come to the conclusion that she's a bitch. It would have been so much better, don't you think, if they had discovered that sooner?

KIT. All right, you asked for it.

He raises his arm to hit ALAN, *who grapples with him and holds him.*
ALAN. Don't be a damned fool.

    ROGERS *strides over and knocks* ALAN *down.*

KIT. (*Turning furiously on* ROGERS.) What the hell do you think
you're doing?

    KIT *aims a blow at* ROGERS, *who dodges it, overturning a chair.*
    KENNETH *runs in to attack* ROGERS. BRIAN, *also running in, tries*
    to restrain both KENNETH *and* KIT.

BRIAN. Shut up, you damned lot of fools. (*Shouting.*) Kit, Babe,
show some sense, for God's sake! Look out—Maingot!

    ALAN *gets up and is about to go for* ROGERS *when* MAINGOT *comes*
    in from the garden, carrying a large notebook under his arm. KIT,
    KENNETH, *and* BRIAN *sit down.* ROGERS *and* ALAN *stand glaring*
    at each other. MAINGOT *picks up the chair that has been knocked*
    over, pulls it to the table, sits down, and spreads his notebook out
    on the table.

MAINGOT. Alors, asseyez-vous, Messieurs. Le sujet cet après-
midi sera la crise de mille huit cent quarante en Turquie.

    ALAN *and* ROGERS *sit down, still glaring at each other.*

Or la dernière fois je vous ai expliqué comment le gouver-
neur ottoman d'Egypte, Mehemet Ali, s'était battu contre
son souverain, le Sultan de Turquie. Constatons donc que la
chute du Sultanat . . .

CURTAIN

ACT II

Scene 2

SCENE: *The same.*
TIME: *About six hours later.*

    DIANA *is discovered sitting in one armchair, her feet up on the other.*
She is smoking a cigarette and gazing listlessly out of the window.
JACQUELINE *comes in through door at back, dressed in a Bavarian*
costume.

JACQUELINE. Hullo! Aren't you getting dressed?

DIANA. (*Turning her head. She gets up and examines* JACQUELINE.)
Darling, you look too lovely.

JACQUELINE. Do you like it?

DIANA. I adore it. I think it's sweet. (*She continues her examination.*) If I were you, dear, I'd wear that hat just a little more on the back of the head. Look, I'll show you. (*She arranges* JACQUELINE's *hat.*) No, that's not quite right. I wonder if it'd look better without a hat at all. (*She removes hat.*) No, you must wear a hat.

JACQUELINE. I suppose my hair's wrong.

DIANA. Well, it isn't quite Bavarian, is it, darling? Very nice, of course. (*Pulling* JACQUELINE's *dress about.*) There's something wrong here. (*She kneels down and begins to rearrange the dress.*)

Pause.

JACQUELINE. I've got something to say to you, Diana. Do you mind if I say it now?

DIANA. Of course not. (*Tugging dress.*) Oh, lord, there's a bit of braid coming off here.

JACQUELINE. Oh!

DIANA. I'll fix it for you.

JACQUELINE. If you look in that basket over there you'll find a needle and thread. (*She points to a work-basket which is lying on the seat of one of the chairs.*)

DIANA. Right. (*She goes to basket.*)

JACQUELINE. But you needn't trouble——

DIANA. (*Extracting needle and thread.*) That's all right. It's no trouble. I enjoy doing this sort of thing. (*Threading needle.*) Well, what was it you wanted to say to me?

JACQUELINE. I overheard your conversation with the Commander this afternoon.

DIANA. (*Making a bad shot with the thread. She turns to the light.*) All of it, or just a part of it?

JACQUELINE. I heard you say that you were in love with the Commander and that you didn't love Kit.

DIANA. Oh! (*Kneeling at* JACQUELINE's *feet.*) Now, scream if I stick a needle into you, won't you? (*She begins to sew.*) Is that what you wanted to tell me?

JACQUELINE. I wanted to know if you were going to tell Kit that you didn't love him.

DIANA. (*Sewing industriously.*) Why?

JACQUELINE. Because if you don't tell him, I will.

DIANA. (*After a slight pause.*) My poor Jacqueline, I never knew you felt like that about Kit.

JACQUELINE. Yes, you did. You've known for some time, and you've had a lot of fun out of it.

DIANA. Well, I wish you the best of luck.

JACQUELINE. Thank you. (*Starting.*) Ow!

DIANA. Sorry, darling, did I prick you?

JACQUELINE. Are you going to tell him?

DIANA. I don't think so.

JACQUELINE. I shall, then.

DIANA. My dear, I think that would be very silly. He won't believe you, it'll make him very unhappy, and, worst of all, he'll be furious with you.

JACQUELINE. (*Thoughtfully.*) Yes, that's true, I suppose.

DIANA. (*Biting off the thread and standing up.*) There. How's that?

JACQUELINE. Thank you so much. That's splendid. So you won't leave Kit alone?

DIANA. Now, let's be honest, for a moment. Don't let's talk about love and things like that, but just plain facts. You and I both want the same man.

JACQUELINE. But you don't——

DIANA. Oh yes, I do.

JACQUELINE. But what about the Commander?

DIANA. I want him too.

JACQUELINE. Oh!

DIANA. Don't look shocked, darling. You see, I'm not like you. You're clever—you can talk intelligently, and you're nice.

JACQUELINE. That's a horrid word.

DIANA. Now I'm not nice. I'm not clever and I can't talk intelligently. There's only one thing I've got, and I don't think you'll deny it. I have got a sort of gift for making men fall in love with me.

JACQUELINE. Oh, no. I don't deny that at all.

DIANA. Thank you, darling. I didn't think you would. Well, now, you have been sent into the world with lots of gifts, and you make use of them. Well, what about me, with just my one gift? I must use that too, mustn't I?

JACQUELINE. Well, what you call my gifts are at any rate social. Yours are definitely anti-social.

DIANA. Oh, I can't be bothered with all that. The fact remains that having men in love with me is my whole life. It's hard for you to understand, I know. You see, you're the sort of person that people *like*. But nobody *likes* me.

JACQUELINE. Oh, I wish you wouldn't keep harping on that. I wouldn't mind if everybody hated me, provided Kit loved me.

DIANA. You can't have it both ways, darling. Kit looks on you as a very nice person.

JACQUELINE. (*With sudden anger.*) Oh, God! What I'd give to be anything but nice!

DIANA. In a way, you know, I envy you. It must be very pleasant to be able to make friends with people.

JACQUELINE. You could be friends with Kit if you were honest with him.

DIANA. Darling! And I called you intelligent! Kit despises me. If he didn't love me he'd loathe me. That's why I can't let him go.

JACQUELINE. (*Pleadingly.*) Oh, Diana, I do see your point of view. I do see that you must have men in love with you, but couldn't you, please, couldn't you make the Commander do?

DIANA. No—I always act on the principle that there's safety in numbers.

JACQUELINE. Well, there's this Lord Heybrook arriving to-morrow. Supposing I let you have the Commander and him.

DIANA. No, darling. I'm sorry. I'd do anything else for you, but if you want Kit, you must win him in fair fight.

JACQUELINE. (*A shade tearfully.*) But I don't stand a chance against you.

DIANA. To be perfectly honest, I agree with you, darling.

JACQUELINE. I only hope you make some awful blunder, so that he finds out the game you're playing.

DIANA. (*With dignity.*) I don't make blunders. He's taking you to the Casino tonight, isn't he?

JACQUELINE. Yes, but he's so furious because you're going with
the Commander that he'll give me the most dreadful evening.

DIANA. That's all right. I'm not going. I don't feel like it, as a
matter of fact.

JACQUELINE. But have you told the Commander?

DIANA. Yes; he's furious, poor poppet, but it's very good for
him.

JACQUELINE. (*After a pause.*) I wonder if you realize the trouble
you cause? You know there was a fight about you this
afternoon?

DIANA. Yes. I hear Alan was in it. That's *very* interesting.

JACQUELINE *is surprised.* DIANA *smiles.* KIT'S *voice is heard off,*
calling 'Jack, where are you?' JACQUELINE *turns to* DIANA *in*
sudden fright.

JACQUELINE. Does Kit know you're not going tonight?

KIT *comes in through door at back. His lower half is enclosed in the*
frilly skirt of a Greek Evzone, beneath which can be seen an ordinary
pair of socks with suspenders. In addition he wears a cricket shirt
and tie. He carries the tunic over his arm.

KIT. Jack, I can't get into this damned coat.

DIANA *bursts into a shriek of laughter.*

DIANA. Kit, you look angelic! I wish you could see yourself.

KIT. You shut up.

JACQUELINE. I told you it might be rather a tight fit.

KIT. But it's miles too small. Your brother must be a pygmy.

JACQUELINE. Take that shirt off and then try.

KIT. Jack, would you mind terribly if I didn't come? I can't
go dressed as an inebriated danseuse.

DIANA *shrieks with laughter again.*

JACQUELINE. Don't be silly, Kit. It's going to look lovely.

KIT. Honestly, though, I don't think I'll come. You wouldn't
mind?

JACQUELINE. I'd mind—awfully.

KIT. Alan's not going. I don't think I can face it really. I've
asked Babe if he'll take you, and he says he'd love to.
(*Turning to* DIANA—*offhandedly.*) I hear you're not going,
Diana.

DIANA. No. I feel rather like you about it.

KIT. (*To* DIANA.) You know, they have dancing in the streets tonight. We might get rid of the others later and go out and join in the general whoopee—what do you say?

DIANA. Yes, that's a lovely idea, Kit.

KIT. (*Turning to* JACQUELINE.) I'm awfully sorry, Jack, but honestly——

JACQUELINE. It's all right. I'll have a lovely time with Kenneth. (*She goes out quickly through door at back.*)

KIT. She seems rather odd. You don't think she minds, do you?

DIANA. Well, how on earth should I know?

KIT. Darling, if we go out tonight, you will get rid of the Commander, won't you? If he comes I won't be answerable for the consequences.

DIANA. He's not so easy to get rid of. He clings like a limpet. Still, I'll do my best.

KIT. I can't understand why you don't just tell him to go to hell.

DIANA. (*Gently.*) That'd be a little—cruel, wouldn't it, Kit?

KIT. As someone said once, why not be cruel only to be kind?

DIANA. Yes, that's true, but, you know, Kit, cruelty is something that's physically impossible to me. I'm the sort of person who's miserable if I tread on a snail.

KIT. But can't you see, darling? It's unfair on him to let him go on thinking he's got a hope.

DIANA. Poor old Bill. Oh, well, darling, come and give me a kiss and say you love me.

ROGERS *comes in through garden door.*

KIT. With pleasure. (*He kisses her, although she tries to push him away.*) I love you.

ROGERS. (*To* KIT) What the devil do you think you're doing?

KIT. I'll give you three guesses.

ROGERS. I've had enough of this. I'm going to give this young puppy a good hiding.

DIANA. (*Trying to separate them.*) Don't be silly, Bill.

ROGERS. Out of the way, Diana.

KIT. Do what the Commander says, Diana.

DIANA. (*Still separating them.*) You're both quite mad.

MAINGOT *comes in through door at back dressed in Scottish High-*
land costume. BRIAN *and* ALAN *follow, gazing at him with rapture.*
KIT *and* ROGERS *and* DIANA *break apart.*

ALAN. (*Clasping his hands in admiration.*) Mais c'est exquis,
Monsieur! Parfait!

MAINGOT. N'est-ce pas que c'est beau? Je l'ai choisi moi-même.
Ça me va bien, hein?

ALAN. C'est tout ce qu'il y a de plus chic.

BRIAN. Vous ne pouvez pas dire le différence entre vous et un
réel Highlander.

MAINGOT. Mais oui. Ça—c'est un véritable costume écossais.

DIANA. Oh, yes, that is formidable.

MAINGOT. (*Crossing to* DIANA) Vous croyez? Et aussi je connais
quelques pas du can-can écossais.

ALAN. Amusez-vous bien, Monsieur.

MAINGOT. Merci.

BRIAN. J'espère que vous baiserez beaucoup de dames, Monsieur.

MAINGOT. (*Turning appalled.*) Ha? Qu'est qu'il dit, ce garçon là?

BRIAN. Ai-je dit quelque chose?

MAINGOT. Une bétise, Monsieur. On ne dit j'amais baiser—
embrasser. Il ne faut pas me donner des idées.

He goes out chuckling. ALAN, BRIAN, *and* DIANA *go to the window*
to watch him go down the street. KIT *and* ROGERS *stand looking at*
each other rather sheepishly.

ALAN. My God! What *does* he look like?

DIANA. He looks perfectly sweet.

JACQUELINE *comes in, followed by* KENNETH, *in sailor costume.*

BRIAN. Your father's just gone off, Jack. If you hurry you can
catch him.

JACQUELINE. Right. (*Gaily.*) Goodbye, everyone. You're all
fools not to be coming. We're going to have a lovely time.

KENNETH. (*To* ALAN.) Alan, do change your mind and come.

ALAN. No, thank you, Babe—have a good time.

KENNETH. Alan——

ALAN. Well, I'm going to have a drink. Anyone coming with
me?

BRIAN. I'm ahead of you, old boy.

DIANA. Yes, I'm coming.

ALAN. I suppose that means I'll have to pay for both of you.

DIANA. Yes, it does.

ALAN. Are you two coming?

ROGERS *and* KIT *look at each other and then shake their heads.*

ROGERS AND KIT. No.

DIANA *and* BRIAN, KENNETH *and* JACQUELINE *all go out, talking.*

ALAN. Oh, no. I see you're going to have a musical evening!
(*He follows the other two out.*)

KIT. Now we can have our little talk.

ROGERS. I don't mean to do much talking.

KIT. But I do. Diana has just this minute given me a message
to give you. She wants you to understand that she knows
what you feel about her, and she's sorry for you. But she
must ask you not to take advantage of her pity for you to
make her life a burden.

ROGERS. Right. Now that you've had your joke, let me tell
you the truth. This afternoon Diana asked me to let you
know, in as kindly a way as possible, that her feelings for
you have changed entirely, and that she is now in love with
me.

KIT. (*Astounded.*) God! What nerve! Do you know what she's
just said about you? (*Shouting.*) She called you a silly old
bore, who stuck like a limpet and weren't worth bothering
about.

ROGERS. Oh, she did, did she?

KIT. Yes, she did, and a lot more besides that wouldn't bear
repeating.

ROGERS. All right, you lying young fool. I've felt sorry for you
up to this, but now I see I've got to teach you a lesson. Put
your hands up.

KIT. (*Putting up his fists.*) It's a pleasure.

They stand facing each other, ready for battle. Pause. ROGERS *suddenly
begins to laugh.*

ROGERS. (*Collapsing, doubled up with laughter, into a chair.*) You
look so damned funny in that get-up.

KIT. (*Looking down at his legs, and beginning to giggle.*) A little
eccentric, I admit.

ROGERS. Like a bedraggled old fairy queen.

KIT. I'll go and change.

ROGERS. (*Becoming serious.*) No, don't. If you do I'll have to fight you. I can't when you're looking like that, and if you go on looking like that it'll save us from making idiots of ourselves.

KIT. You know, that's rather sensible. I am surprised.

ROGERS. You know, I'm not quite such a damned fool as you youngsters seem to think. As a matter of fact, I'm a perfectly rational being, and I'm prepared to discuss this particular situation rationally. Now, I'm ready to admit that you have a grievance against me.

KIT. But I haven't—speaking rationally.

ROGERS. Oh, yes. Rationally speaking, you might say that I've alienated the affections of your sweetheart.

KIT. (*Smiling.*) But you haven't done anything of the sort.

ROGERS. (*Raising his hand.*) Please don't interrupt. Now, I'm perfectly ready to apologize for something that isn't altogether my fault. I hope you will accept it in the spirit in which it is offered.

KIT. (*Incredulous.*) But do you really think Diana's in love with you?

ROGERS. Certainly.

KIT. Why do you think that?

ROGERS. She told me so, of course.

KIT. (*Laughing.*) My poor, dear Commander——

ROGERS. I thought we were going to discuss this matter rationally?

KIT. Yes, but when you begin with a flagrant misrepresentation of the facts——

ROGERS. You mean, I'm a liar?

KIT. Yes, that's exactly what I do mean.

ROGERS. (*Jumping to his feet.*) Come on. Get up. I see I've got to fight you, skirt or no skirt.

KIT. No, no. Let reason have one last fling. If that fails we can give way to our animal passions. Let me tell you my side of the case.

ROGERS. (*Sitting.*) All right.

KIT. I've just had a talk with Diana. She said you were in love with her. I suggested to her that it was only fair to you to let you know exactly where you stood—in other words, that she was in love with me and that you had no chance. She answered that, though what I'd said was the truth——

ROGERS. She never said that.

KIT. (*Raising his hand.*) Please don't interrupt. (*Continuing.*) Though what I'd said was the truth, she couldn't tell you because it would be too cruel.

ROGERS *starts slightly*.

I then said, rather aptly, that this was a case where she should be cruel only to be kind.

ROGERS. You said what?

KIT. Cruel only to be kind.

ROGERS. What did she say?

KIT. She said she found it physically impossible to be cruel. She said she was the sort of person who was miserable if she trod on a snail.

ROGERS. What? You're sure of that?

KIT. Certainly.

ROGERS. She said she was miserable if she trod on a snail?

KIT. Yes.

ROGERS. (*With a world of feeling.*) Good God!

KIT. What's the matter?

ROGERS. It's awful! (*Rising and walking about.*) I can't believe it. I don't believe it. This is all a monstrous plot. (*Swinging round.*) I believe you listened in to my conversation with Diana this afternoon.

KIT. Why?

ROGERS. Because I also told her she ought to be cruel only to be kind, and she made precisely the same answer as she made to you.

KIT. (*After a pause.*) You mean about the snail?

ROGERS. Yes, about the snail.

KIT. In other words she's been double-crossing us. No, you've made all that up.

ROGERS. I only wish I had.

KIT. How do I know you're telling the truth?

ROGERS. You'll have to take my word for it.

KIT. Why should I?

ROGERS. Do you want to make me fight you?

KIT. Yes, I do.

Pause.

ROGERS. Well, I'm not going to.

KIT. (*Sitting down suddenly.*) I wonder why it's such a comfort to get away from reason.

ROGERS. Because in this case reason tells us something our vanity won't let us accept.

KIT. It tells us that Diana's a bitch.

ROGERS *half moves out of his chair.*

Reason! Reason!

ROGERS *subsides.*

ROGERS. You're right. We'd better face it. Diana's in love with neither of us, and she's made a fool out of both of us.

KIT. We don't know that—I mean that she's in love with neither of us. She may be telling lies to one and the truth to the other.

ROGERS. Is that what your reason tells you?

KIT. No.

Pause. They are both sunk in gloom.

I feel rather sick.

ROGERS. I must have a stronger stomach than you.

Pause.

I suppose you loved her more than I did?

KIT. Loved her? I still do love her, damn it.

ROGERS. But you can't, now that you know what you do.

KIT. What difference does that make? I love her face, I love the way she walks, I love her voice, I love her figure. None of that has changed.

ROGERS. (*Sympathetically.*) Poor boy. It's simpler for me though it's far more of a shock. You see, what I loved about her was her character.

Pause.

KIT. You used to kiss her, I suppose?

ROGERS. (*Sadly.*) Oh, yes.

KIT. You didn't—you didn't——?

ROGERS. (*Severely.*) I loved her for her character. (*After a pause.*) Did you?

KIT. Well, no, not really.

ROGERS. I see.

Pause.

KIT. What are we going to do?

ROGERS. We'd better face her together. We'll ask her point-blank which of us she really does love.

KIT. If she says me, I'm done for.

ROGERS. But you won't believe her?

KIT. I'll know she's lying, but I'll believe her all the same.

ROGERS. Well, supposing she says me?

KIT. That's my only hope.

ROGERS. Then, for your sake, I hope she says me.

KIT. That's terribly kind of you, Bill. I say, I may call you Bill, mayn't I?

ROGERS. Oh, my dear Kit.

Pause.

You know, what I feel like doing is to go out and get very drunk.

KIT. Suppose we go and throw ourselves into the sea instead.

ROGERS. I think my idea is better.

KIT. Yes, perhaps you're right. Then let's start now.

ROGERS. You can't go out like that, my dear Kit.

KIT. Then let's go to the Casino.

ROGERS. I haven't got anything to wear.

KIT. (*Holding out tunic.*) Wear this over your flannels.

ROGERS. All right. Help me put it on.

ALAN *and* BRIAN *come in.* KIT *is buttoning up* ROGERS' *tunic. They both stop in amazement.*

ALAN. What on earth——?

KIT. (*Excitedly.*) Bill and I are going to the Casino, Alan. You've got to come, too.

ALAN. Bill and you? What is this? Some new sort of game?

KIT. Go and put something on. You come, too, Brian.

BRIAN. No, old boy. Not me.

KIT. Go on, Alan. We want to get out of the house before Diana arrives. Where is she, by the way?

ROGERS. Who cares!

KIT *laughs.*

ALAN. (*Scratching his head.*) Let me get this straight. You want me to come to the Ball with you and the Commander——

KIT. Don't call him the Commander, Alan. His name is Bill.

ALAN. Bill?

KIT. Yes, Bill. He's one of the best fellows in the world.

ROGERS. We're going to get drunk together, aren't we, Kit?

ALAN. Kit?

KIT. Screaming drunk, Bill.

ALAN. (*Dashing to door.*) I won't be a minute.

Exit ALAN.

BRIAN. This sounds like a party.

KIT. Brian, tell me how I can get hold of your Chi-Chi? Is she going to the Casino tonight?

BRIAN. Yes, old boy.

KIT. How can I recognize her?

BRIAN. I don't think you can miss her. She's not likely to miss you, anyway, if you go into the bar alone.

KIT. Has she got a good figure.

BRIAN. I like it, but I'm easy to please. From sideways on it's a bit S-shaped, if you know what I mean.

ALAN *comes down, wearing his German coat.*

ALAN. I shall probably be lynched in this thing.

KIT. Come on. Let's go.

They go to the window. KIT *with his arm across* ROGERS' *shoulder.*

BRIAN. Hi! Wait a minute. What am I to tell Diana?

They stop.

ROGERS. Tell her we're being cruel only to be kind.

KIT. Tell her to be careful she doesn't go treading on any snails.

ALAN. Just tell her to go to hell. That leaves no room for doubt.

They go out. BRIAN *gazes after them as the*

CURTAIN FALLS

ACT III

Scene 1

SCENE: *The same.*

TIME: *A few hours later.*

The curtain rises to disclose ALAN *on the sofa,* KIT *in the armchair,* ROGERS *on the floor by the end of the sofa, each smoking a cigar. They are still in the clothes in which they had gone to the Casino.* ROGERS *is half asleep.*

KIT. (*Drowsily.*) I don't agree with you. I don't agree with you at all. You can't judge women by our standards of Right and Wrong.

ALAN. They have none of their own, so how can you judge them.

KIT. Why judge them at all. There they are—all of them, I grant you, behaving absolutely nohow—still, that's what they're for, I mean they're built that way, and you've just got to take them or leave them. I'll take them.

ROGERS. (*Murmuring dreamily.*) I'll take vanilla.

KIT. Now, you tell me that Diana's a cow. All right, I shan't deny it. I shall only say that I, personally, like cows.

ALAN. But you can like them without loving them. I mean, love is only sublimated sex, isn't it?

ROGERS. (*Rousing himself a little.*) Devilish funny thing—my old friend Freud, the last time I met him, said *exactly* the same thing. Bill, old man, he said, take my word for it, love is only sublimated sex. (*Composing himself for sleep again.*) That's what Old Freudie said.

ALAN. I fear that Bill is what he'd describe himself as half seas over.

KIT. He's lucky. The more I drank up at that foul Casino the more sober I became. What were you saying about sublimated sex?

56

ALAN. Only that if that's what you feel for Diana, why subli-
mate?

KIT. Ah! Because she's clever enough to give me no choice.

ALAN. How simple everything would be if that sort of so-called
virtue were made illegal—if it were just a question of will
you or won't you.

ROGERS' *head falls back on to the chair.*

No one ought to be allowed to get away with that—'I'd
like to but I mustn't'. It's that that leads to all the trouble.
The Commander has now definitely passed out. You know
(*excitedly*) I like him, Kit. It's quite amazing how pleasant
he is when you get to know him.

A slight smile appears on ROGERS' *face.*

KIT. Yes, I know.

ALAN. Do you realize that if it hadn't been for Diana, we'd
probably have gone on disliking him for ever?

KIT. Yes. We've got to be grateful to her for that.

ALAN. I wonder *why* we disliked him so much before tonight.

ROGERS. (*From a horizontal position.*) I'll tell you.

ALAN. Good lord! I thought you'd passed out.

ROGERS. Officers in the Royal Navy never pass out.

ALAN. They just fall on the floor in an alcoholic stupor, I
suppose?

ROGERS. Exactly.

KIT. Well, tell us why we disliked you so much.

ROGERS. Right.

ALAN *helps him to a sitting position.*

Because you all made up your mind to dislike me before I
ever came into this house. All except Diana, that's to say.
From the moment I arrived, you all treated me as if I were
some interesting old relic of a bygone age. I've never known
such an unfriendly lot of blighters as you all were.

ALAN. We thought you were a bumptious bore.

ROGERS. Oh, I may have seemed a bortious bump, but that
was only because I was in a blue funk of you all. Here was
I who'd never been away from my ship for more than a few
days at a time, suddenly plumped down in a house full of
strange people, all talking either French, which I couldn't

understand, or your own brand of English, which was almost as hard, and all convinced I was a half-wit. Of course I was in a blue funk.

ALAN. Well, I'm damned.

ROGERS. As a matter of fact, I liked you all.

ALAN. Oh, that's very gratifying.

ROGERS. I didn't agree with most of your opinions, but I enjoyed listening to them. I wanted to discuss them with you, but I was never given the chance. You all seemed to think that because I was in the Navy I was incapable of consecutive thought—I say, whisky doesn't half loosen the old tongue.

ALAN. But you always seemed so aggressive.

ROGERS. I was only defending myself. You attacked first, you know.

ALAN. (*Contritely.*) I'm terribly sorry.

ROGERS. That's all right. As a matter of fact it's done me a lot of good being here. One gets into a bit of a rut, you know, in the Service. One's apt to forget that there are some people in the world who have different ideas and opinions to one's own. You'll find the same in the diplomatic.

ALAN. I know. That's one of the reasons I want to chuck it.

ROGERS. Will you let me give you a bit of advice about that? I've been wanting to for a long time, but I've always been afraid you'd bite my head off if I did.

ALAN. Of course.

ROGERS. Well, chuck it. Go and do your writing.

ALAN *looks surprised. He takes a deep puff at his cigar.*

ALAN. I'd go back to England tomorrow, only—— (*He stops.*)

ROGERS. Only what?

ALAN. I don't know if I can write, for one thing.

ROGERS. It's ten to one you can't, but I shouldn't let that stop you. If it's what you want to do, I should do it.

ALAN. That isn't the real reason.

ROGERS. You haven't got the guts, is that it?

ALAN. That isn't quite my way of putting it, but I suppose it's true. I can't bring myself to make a definite decision. I'm afraid of my father, of course. But it's not only that. I admit that there are a dozen things I'd rather do than the diplomatic. It's an exciting world at the moment. Do you know, sometimes I think I'll go and fight. There must be a war on somewhere.

ROGERS. I thought you were a pacifist?

ALAN. Oh, what the hell?—I shall become a diplomat.

ROGERS. You'll be a damned bad one.

ALAN. I can adapt myself.

ROGERS. (*Rising, yawning.*) Well, I've given you my advice for what it's worth. I shall now go to bed to sleep the sleep of the very drunk.

ALAN. You mustn't go yet. You've got to wait for Diana.

ROGERS. (*With a magnificent gesture.*) Diana—pooh!

ALAN. It's all very well for you to say 'Diana—pooh', but this weak-kneed, jelly-livered protoplasm here is still in her clutches.

KIT. (*Who has been musing.*) Are you referring to me?

ALAN. Diana's only got to raise her little finger and he'll go rushing back to her, screaming to be forgiven.

ROGERS. Then we must stop her raising her little finger.

ALAN. Exactly. That's why we must face her together.

ROGERS. (*Sitting heavily.*) The United Front. We must scupper her with a plunging salvo.

ALAN. Oh, no, don't let's do that.

KIT. (*Dismally.*) She's only got to say she still loves me.

ALAN. My dear Kit, if she has to choose between you and Bill, she'll choose you. You're younger, you're better-looking, and you've got more money. Don't you agree, Bill?

ROGERS. He's certainly younger and he's certainly got more money.

ALAN. (*To* KIT.) You must be firm, you must be strong. If you show any weakness, you'll be a traitor to our sex.

ROGERS. By jove, yes. We must put up a good show in this engagement.

KIT. It's all very well for you to talk. You don't know——

ALAN. Haven't I resisted her attacks for a whole month?

KIT. They were only little skirmishes. You don't know what it is to receive the whole brunt of her attack. It's quite hope-

less. You can help me as much as you like, but if she attacks
me directly, I shall go under, I know that.

ALAN. Do you hear that, Commander? I submit that he be
tried for Extreme Cowardice in the face of the Enemy.

ROGERS. The Court finds the prisoner guilty. (*Rising with dignity.*) Mr. Neilan, I must call upon you to surrender your
trousers. Ah? I see you have come into court without them.
Very well, I have no option but to ask you for your skirt.

KIT. Come and get it.

ROGERS. I've been longing to get my hands on that damn thing
all the evening. Come on, Alan.

KIT *leaps out of his chair, and runs across the room pursued by*
ROGERS *and* ALAN. *He is cornered and there is a scuffle.* DIANA,
*stately and sad, comes through the french windows. She stands in
the doorway for some five seconds before* ROGERS *sees her.*

ROGERS. Crikey! (*He taps the two others on the shoulders and they
straighten themselves.*)

There is a rather nervous silence.

DIANA. (*Coming into the room.*) Well—I hope you all enjoyed
yourselves at the Casino.

ROGERS. (*After glancing at the others.*) Oh, yes. Thanks very much.

DIANA. Brian gave me a message from you which I found rather
hard to understand. Perhaps you'd explain it now.

Pause. ALAN *looks inquiringly from* KIT *to* ROGERS. ROGERS *looks
appealingly at* ALAN.

ALAN. Well, who is to fire the first shot of the salvo?

No answer.

Come, come, gentlemen.

No answer.

Very well, I must engage the enemy on your behalf. Diana,
these two gentlemen have good reason to believe that you
have been trifling with their affections. You have told Kit
that you are in love with him and are bored by Bill, and you
have told Bill that you are in love with him and are bored
by Kit. So now they naturally want to know who exactly
you are in love with and who exactly you are bored by.

ROGERS. (*Nodding vigorously.*) Yes, that's right.

DIANA. (*With scorn.*) Oh, do they?

ALAN. Are you going to answer their question?

DIANA. Certainly not. Whom I love and whom I don't love is
entirely my own affair. I've never heard such insolence.

ALAN. (*Turning to* ROGERS *and* KIT, *chuckling*.) Insolence! She's
good, this girl, she's very good.

DIANA. (*Patiently*.) May I please be allowed to go to my room?

ALAN. (*Barring her way*.) Not until you've answered our question.

DIANA. I think you'd better let me go.

ALAN. Just as soon as you've given a straight answer to a
straight question.

Pause. DIANA *at length takes a step back.*

DIANA. All right. You want to know who I'm in love with.
Well, I'll tell you. (*To* ALAN.) I'm in love with you.

ALAN *recoils. There is a dead silence.*

DIANA *brushes past* ALAN. *He seizes her wrist.*

DIANA. Good night!

ALAN *drops his hands and steps back. He falls limply into a chair.*
DIANA *goes out.*

ROGERS. (*Scratching his head.*) Now will someone tell me, was
our engagement a success?

ALAN. (*Bitterly*.) A success? (*Groaning*.) Oh, what a girl, what a
girl!

KIT. (*Gloomily*.) It was a success as far as I'm concerned.

Pause.

ALAN. I'm frightened. I'm really frightened.

ROGERS. What? (*Sternly*.) Alan, I never thought to hear such
words from you.

ALAN. I can't help it. I shall fall. Oh, God! I know it, I shall fall.

ROGERS. You must be firm. You must be strong. The United
Front must not be broken.

ALAN. I want you to promise me something, you two. You must
never, never leave me alone with that girl.

ROGERS. That sounds like rank cowardice.

ALAN. Cowardice be damned! You don't realize the appalling
danger I'm in. If I'm left alone with her for a minute, I
shudder to think what might happen. She might even (*in a
whisper*) marry me.

ROGERS. Oh, not that.

ALAN. It's true. God help me. I think she may easily try to
marry me. (*Turning imploringly to the others.*) So you see, you
can't desert me now. Don't let me out of your sight for a
second. Even if I beg you on my knees to leave me alone
with her, don't do it. Will you promise?

ROGERS. I promise.

ALAN. And you, Kit?

KIT. (*Nods.*) All right.

ALAN. Thank you. I've only got three weeks before the exam.,
but that's a long time with Diana in the house.

ROGERS. I think your hope lies in this Lord Heybrook fellow
who's coming tomorrow. She may easily find that a peer in
hand is worth more than one in the vague future. (*Getting up.*)
I shall go to bed. Good night, Alan. You have my best
wishes. (*At door.*) Don't go down to breakfast tomorrow until
I come and fetch you. Good night, Kit. (*He goes out.*)

ALAN. There's a real friend. I hope you're going to show the
same self-sacrifice.

KIT. I don't know what you're making all the fuss about. You
ought to be very happy.

ALAN. Happy? (*Sarcastically.*) I've noticed how happy you've
been these last few weeks.

KIT. I have in a way.

ALAN. That's not my way. Damn it, Kit, I'm a man with
principles and ideals. I'm a romantic. Let me give you a
little word-picture of the girl I should like to fall in love
with. Then you can tell how far it resembles Diana. First
of all, she must not be a cow.

KIT. (*Shrugging indifferently.*) Oh, well, of course——

ALAN. Secondly, she will be able to converse freely and intelligently with me on all subjects—Politics—Philosophy—
Religion—— Thirdly, she will have all the masculine virtues
and none of the feminine vices. Fourthly, she will be physically unattractive enough to keep her faithful to me, and
attractive enough to make me desire her. Fifthly, she will
be in love with me. That's all, I think.

KIT. You don't want much, do you? I admit it isn't a close

description of Diana, but where on earth do you expect to find this love-dream?

ALAN. They do exist, you know. There's someone here, in this house, who answers to all the qualifications, except the last.

KIT. (*Sitting forward.*) Good lord! You don't mean Jack, do you?

ALAN. Why not?

KIT. But—but you couldn't be in love with Jack.

ALAN. I'm not, but she's exactly the sort of girl I should like to be in love with.

KIT. (*Smiling.*) Love and Jack. They just don't seem to connect. I'm frightfully fond of her, but somehow—I don't know—I mean you couldn't kiss her or make love to her.

ALAN. Why not try it and see?

KIT. Who? Me? Good lord, no.

ALAN. Don't you think she's attractive?

KIT. Yes, I suppose she is, in a way, very attractive. But don't you see, Alan, I know her far too well to start any hanky-panky. She'd just scream with laughter.

ALAN. Really? She'd just scream with laughter? (*Turning on him.*) You poor idiot, don't you realize the girl's been madly in love with you for two months now?

KIT. (*After a pause, derisively.*) Ha, ha!

ALAN. All right. Say ha, ha! Don't believe it and forget I ever said it. I promised her I'd never tell you.

Pause.

KIT. What did you have to drink up at the Casino?

ALAN. Less than you.

KIT. Are you stone-cold sober?

ALAN. As sober as ten Lady Astors.

KIT. And you sit there and tell me——

Voices heard outside.

KIT. (*Getting up in alarm.*) Oh, lord!

MAINGOT *comes in, followed by* JACQUELINE *and* KENNETH.

MAINGOT. Aha! Le Grec et l'Allemand. Vous vous êtes bien amusés au Casino?

JACQUELINE. Hello, Kit.

ALAN. Très bien, Monsieur. Et vous?

KIT *is gaping open-mouthed at* JACQUELINE.

MAINGOT. Ah, oui! C'était assez gai, mais on y a mangé excessivement mal, et le champagne était très mauvais et m'a couté les yeux de la tête. Quand même le quartorze ne vient qu'une fois par an. Alors je vais me coucher. Bonsoir, bonne nuit et dormez bien.

ALL. Bonsoir.

MAINGOT *goes out through door at back, carrying his Highland shoes which he has changed for slippers.*

JACQUELINE. Why did you all leave so early?

KIT. (*Gaping.*) Oh, I don't know.

JACQUELINE. Your costume caused a sensation, Kit. Everyone was asking me what it was meant to be.

KIT. (*Nervously.*) Really.

ALAN. Did you have a good time, Kenneth?

KENNETH. Oh, all right. I'll say good night. I've got an essay to finish before tomorrow.

JACQUELINE. Good night, Kenneth, and thank you.

KENNETH. Good night.

KENNETH *goes out, looking sulky, through door at back.*

ALAN. You must have had a wonderful time with the Babe in that mood.

JACQUELINE. What's the matter with him, Alan?

ALAN. He's angry with me for not doing his essay for him. I think I'd better go and make my peace with him. (*At door.*) Don't go to bed for a few minutes. I want to talk to you, Jack.

He goes out. There is a pause. KIT *is plainly uncomfortable.*

KIT. Jack?

JACQUELINE. Yes?

KIT. Did you have a good time tonight?

JACQUELINE. (*Puzzled.*) Yes, thank you, Kit.

KIT. Good. I—er—I'm sorry I couldn't take you.

JACQUELINE. That's all right. (*Smiling.*) That was Brian's girl you and Alan were dancing with, wasn't it? What's she like?

KIT. Pretty hellish.

Pause.

Jack?

JACQUELINE. Yes?

KIT. Oh, nothing. (*He gets up and wanders forlornly about the room.*) Was it raining when you came back?

JACQUELINE. No, it wasn't raining.

KIT. It was when we came back.

JACQUELINE. Really?

Pause.

KIT. Yes, quite heavily.

JACQUELINE. It must have cleared up, then.

Pause. KIT *is fiddling with a box of matches.*

KIT. (*Turning with sudden decision.*) Jack, there's something I must—— (*In turning he upsets matches.*) Damn, I'm sorry.

JACQUELINE. I've never seen a clumsier idiot than you, Kit. (*She goes on her knees.*) I seem to spend my life cleaning up after you. There!

She gets up. KIT *kisses her suddenly and clumsily on the mouth. She pushes him away. They are both embarrassed and puzzled.*

(*After a long pause.*) You smell of whisky, Kit.

Enter ALAN.

ALAN. Oh!

KIT. I'm going to bed. Good night. (*He goes out.*)

JACQUELINE. What's the matter with him? Is he drunk?

ALAN. No, Jack, but I've a confession to make to you.

JACQUELINE. (*In alarm.*) You haven't told him?

ALAN. I couldn't help it.

JACQUELINE. Oh, Alan, no.

ALAN. Will you forgive me?

JACQUELINE. I'll never forgive you. It's ruined everything. (*A shade tearfully.*) He's just been talking to me about the weather.

ALAN. Well, he's a bit embarrassed. That's natural.

JACQUELINE. But he'll spend all his time running away from me now, and when he is with me he'll always be wondering if I want him to kiss me, and he'll go on talking about the weather, and—(*turning away*)—oh, it's awful!

ALAN. I'm sorry, Jack. I meant well.

JACQUELINE. Men are such blundering fools.

ALAN. Yes, I suppose we are. Will you forgive me?

JACQUELINE. (*Wearily.*) Of course I forgive you. (*After a pause.*) I'm going to bed.

ALAN. All right. We'll talk about it in the morning. I may be able to persuade Kit I was joking.

JACQUELINE. (*At door.*) No. Please don't say anything more to Kit. You've done enough harm as it is. (*Relenting.*) Good night, Alan. You're just a sentimental old monster, aren't you?

ALAN. Who, me?

JACQUELINE. Yes, you. Good night.

She goes out. ALAN, *left alone, lights a cigarette. Then he goes to door at back and opens it.*

ALAN. (*Calling.*) Jack?

JACQUELINE. (*Off.*) Yes?

ALAN. Will you see if Brian's in his room. I want to lock up.

JACQUELINE. (*Off.*) Right. (*After a pause.*) No, he must still be out.

ALAN. I'll leave a note for him.

He closes the door, takes an envelope from his pocket, and unscrews his pen. While he is writing DIANA *comes in softly and stands behind him. He doesn't hear her.*

DIANA. (*Gently.*) Alan.

ALAN. (*Jumping up.*) Oh, God!

DIANA. Do you mind if I speak to you for a moment?

ALAN. (*Pointing vaguely at the ceiling.*) Well, I was just going to bed. (*Dashes to garden door.*)

DIANA. (*Inexorably.*) I suppose you didn't believe what I told you just now. (*She catches him.*)

ALAN. (*Looking despairingly round for help.*) No, I didn't believe it.

DIANA. (*With quiet resignation.*) No. I knew you wouldn't, and, of course, after what's happened I couldn't expect you to. But, whether you believe me or not, I just want to say this.

ALAN. (*Wildly.*) In the morning, Diana, say it in the morning. I'm frightfully tired and——

DIANA. Please listen to me. I just wanted to say that it's been you from the first moment we met. Kit and Bill never meant a thing to me. I let them think I was in love with them. But it was only because I had some idea it might make you jealous.

ALAN. It's a pity you didn't succeed.

DIANA. Oh, I know what you think of me, and you're quite right, I suppose. (*Pathetically.*) I've told so many lies before that I can't expect you to believe me when I'm telling the truth.

ALAN. Poor little Matilda.

DIANA. (*Comes back to* ALAN.) But this is the truth, now. This is the only completely sincere feeling I've ever had for anyone in all my life. (*Simply.*) I *do* love you, Alan. I always have and suppose I always will.

ALAN. (*In agony.*) Oh, go away. Please go away.

DIANA. All right. I know you have every right to think I'm lying, but I'm not, Alan, really, I'm not. That's what's so funny.

ALAN. (*Imploringly.*) Oh, God help me!

DIANA. (*At door.*) Good night, Alan. (*Simply.*) I do love you.

She smiles tearfully at him. He throws away his cigarette, and walks over to her.

ALAN. Say that again, blast you!

DIANA. I love you.

He embraces her fervently.

DIANA. (*Emerging from embrace, ecstatically.*) I suppose this is true.

ALAN. You know damn well it is.

DIANA. Say it, darling.

ALAN. (*Hedging.*) Say what?

DIANA. Say you love me.

ALAN. Must I? Oh, this is hell! (*Shouting.*) I love you.

DIANA. (*Turning back rapturously.*) Alan, darling——

BRIAN *comes in through window.*

BRIAN. Hello, Alan, hello, Diana, old thing.

DIANA *looks through* BRIAN *and turns hurriedly to the door.*

DIANA. (*Softly.*) Good night, Alan. I'll see you in the morning.

She goes out. ALAN *sinks into a chair.*

BRIAN. Did you see that, old boy? She cut me dead. She's furious with me. I must tell you about it, because it's a damned funny story. After you boys had gone I took Diana

to have a bite of dinner with me. Well, we had a bottle of
wine and got pretty gay, and all the time she was giving me
the old green light.

ALAN. The green light?

BRIAN. Yes. The go-ahead signal. Well, after a bit I rather
handed out an invitation to the waltz, if you follow me.

ALAN. Yes. I follow you.

BRIAN. I mean, everybody being out, it seemed an opportunity not to be missed. Well, do you know what she did
then, old boy?

ALAN. No.

BRIAN. She gave me a sharp buffet on the kisser.

ALAN. What did you do?

BRIAN. I said, well, if that isn't what you want, what the hell
do you want? Then she got up and left me. I never laughed
so much in all my life.

ALAN. (*Dazedly*.) You laughed?

BRIAN. Wouldn't you, old boy?

ALAN *gazes at him with amazed admiration.*

Well, I'm for bed. I say, I met the most charming little girl
just now on the front—fantastic piece she was. She gave me
her card—yes, here it is. Colette, chez Mme Pontet, Rue
Lafayette, 23. Bain 50 francs. I think I shall pop round
tomorrow and have a bain.

ALAN. (*Rising and gazing at* BRIAN *with awe*.) Oh, Brian! How
right-minded you are!

BRIAN. Me?

ALAN. Thank God you came in when you did. You don't
know what you've done for me with your splendid, shining
example. I now see my way clear before me. A great light
has dawned.

BRIAN. I say, old boy, are you feeling all right?

ALAN. Listen, Brian. You weren't the only person to get the
old green light from Diana tonight. I got it, too.

BRIAN. Doesn't surprise me. I should think she's pretty stingy
with her yellows and reds.

ALAN. Yes, but I didn't respond to it in the same glorious way
as you. However, what's done can be undone. (*Going to*

door.) I am now going upstairs to put the same question to
Diana that you did earlier in the evening.

BRIAN. I shouldn't, old boy. She'll say no, and believe me,
she's got rather a painful way of saying it.

ALAN. If she says no, then, lacking your own sterling qualities,
I shan't pay a visit to Rue Lafayette 23. No. I shall run
away. I shall go back to London tomorrow.

BRIAN. But what about your exam. and so forth?

ALAN. I shall chuck that. Well (*opening door*) I am now about to
throw my future life into the balance of fate. Diplomat or
writer. Which shall it be? Diana shall choose.

ALAN *goes out.*

BRIAN. (*To himself.*) Crackers!

*He shakes his head wonderingly. After a bit he rises, crosses to table,
and stops to think.*

BRIAN. (*Musing*). Bain 50 francs! (*Fumbles for money and starts
to count.*) Ten, twenty—thirty—forty—forty-one, forty-two
—forty-three—forty-three—— Damn.

Slamming of door is heard. ALAN *comes in.*

ALAN. I'm going to be a writer. Come and help me pack.

He disappears. BRIAN *follows him out murmuring expostulations as the*

CURTAIN FALLS

ACT III

SCENE 2

SCENE: *The same.*

TIME: *The next morning.*

MARIANNE *is clearing away the breakfast,* JACQUELINE *helping her.*
KENNETH *enters from window,* MAINGOT *following. They have evidently just finished a lesson.*

MAINGOT. (*At window.*) Dîtes à Monsieur Curtis que je l'attends.
Il ne vaut pas la peine de continuer. Vous n'en saurez j'amais
rien.

KENNETH. (*Sadly.*) Oui, Monsieur.

MAINGOT. Je serai dans le jardin. Oh, ma petite Jacqueline, que j'ai mal à la tête ce matin.

JACQUELINE. Pauvre, papa! Je suis bien fâchée.

MAINGOT. Ça passera—ça passera. Heuresement le quatorz ne vient qu'une fois par an.

He goes back into garden.

KENNETH. (*Calling.*) Brian.

BRIAN. (*Off.*) Yes, old boy?

KENNETH. Your lesson.

BRIAN. (*Off.*) Won't be a second.

KENNETH *closes the door and wanders mournfully over to the bookcase.*

JACQUELINE. Why so sad this morning, Kenneth?

KENNETH. You've heard the news about Alan.

JACQUELINE. Yes, my father told me.

KENNETH. Don't you think it's awful?

JACQUELINE. No. For one thing, I don't believe for a moment he's serious.

KENNETH. Oh, he's serious all right. What a damn fool! If I had half his chance of getting in the diplomatic I wouldn't go and chuck it up.

Enter BRIAN, *carrying a notebook.*

BRIAN. 'Morning all. Where's Maingot Père?

KENNETH. He's waiting for you in the garden.

BRIAN. Oh. (*Anxiously.*) Tell me, old boy, how is he this morning? Gay, happy—at peace with the world?

KENNETH. No. He's got a bad headache, and he's in a fiendish temper. (*He goes out.*)

BRIAN. Tut, tut. Couple of portos too many last night, I fear.

JACQUELINE. Why this tender anxiety for my father's health, Brian?

BRIAN. Well, Jack, I'm afraid I may have to deliver a rather rude shock to his nervous system. You see, I'm supposed to have done an essay on the Waterloo campaign, and what with one thing and another I don't seem to have got awfully far.

JACQUELINE. How far?

BRIAN. (*Reading.*) La bataille de Waterloo était gagnée sur les champs d'Eton.

JACQUELINE. And that's the essay, is it?

BRIAN *nods.*

Well, if I were you, I shouldn't show it to him. I'd tell him you did one of five pages and it got lost.

BRIAN. (*Doubtfully.*) Yes, but something seems to tell me he won't altogether credit that story.

Enter MAINGOT.

MAINGOT. Eh bien, Monsieur Curtis, qu'est-ce qu'on attend? Vous êtes en retard.

BRIAN. (*Affably.*) Ah, Monsieur, vous êtes bon—ce matin, j'espère?

MAINGOT. Non, j'ai affreusement mal à la tête.

BRIAN. (*Sympathetically.*) Oh. C'est trop mauvais. A trifle hungover, peut-être? Un tout petit peu suspendu?

MAINGOT. Vous êtes fou ce matin?

They go out together, MAINGOT *heard expostulating.*

BRIAN. (*Off, his voice coming faintly through the window.*) Il est très triste, Monsieur. J'ai perdu mon essai . . .

JACQUELINE *smiles. Having finished her clearing away, she takes off her apron and the handkerchief that covers her hair. She looks at herself in a pocket-mirror. The door at the back opens very slowly and* ALAN'S *head appears.*

ALAN. (*Whispering.*) Jack!

JACQUELINE. (*Turning.*) Hallo, Alan.

ALAN. Is Diana about?

JACQUELINE. She's in the garden. She wants to speak to you.

ALAN. I bet she does. But I'm taking good care she doesn't get a chance.

He comes cautiously into the room. He is dressed in a lounge suit preparatory for going away.

I want to get my books together. (*He goes to bookcase.*)

JACQUELINE. Alan, you're not serious about this, are you?

ALAN. Never more serious in my life, Jack. (*He is collecting books from the bookcase.*)

JACQUELINE. You're breaking Diana's heart, you know.

ALAN. Ha! Is that what she told you?

JACQUELINE. Oh, no. She wouldn't give herself away to me, but I honestly think she is rather in love with you, Alan.

ALAN. Yes, that's just what I'm afraid of.

JACQUELINE. You know, you're the only man in the world who's ever got away from Diana unscathed.

ALAN. (*Turning quickly.*) Don't say that! It's unlucky. I'm not out of the house yet.

He turns back to the bookcase as DIANA *comes quietly into the room from the garden.*

JACQUELINE. (*Quickly.*) Look out, Alan.

ALAN. (*Seeing* DIANA.) Oh, my God!

He darts out of the room, dropping all his books as he does so. DIANA *follows him out purposefully, but is too late. After a second she re-appears.*

DIANA. It's no good, he's sure to have locked the door of his room. (*She sits down mournfully.*) I'm afraid he's quite determined to go. I feel dreadfully bad about it, because I'm responsible for the whole thing. All this talk of writing is just nonsense. He's only running away from me.

JACQUELINE. I don't altogether blame him.

DIANA. I suppose it's a wonderful compliment for a man to throw up his career just for my sake, but I can't see it that way. I'm really frightfully upset.

JACQUELINE. You don't look it.

DIANA. But I am, honestly I am. You see, I can't understand why he should want to run away from me. I can't see what he's got to be frightened of.

JACQUELINE. Can't you?

DIANA. If only I could get a chance to talk to him alone, I'm sure I could persuade him not to go.

JACQUELINE. I'm sure you could, too. So is Alan. But I don't think you'll get the chance.

Enter MARIANNE *from kitchen.*

MARIANNE. (*To* JACQUELINE.) S'il vous plaît, M'mselle, voulez vous venir voir la chambre de Lord Heybrook? Je l'ai préparée.

JACQUELINE. Bien, Marianne. Je viens tout de suite.

Exit MARIANNE, *and* JACQUELINE *follows her to the door.*

DIANA. Oh, does this Lord Heybrook arrive this morning?

JACQUELINE *has turned back to the kitchen door as the other door opens and* ALAN *comes in.* JACQUELINE *is momentarily alarmed for his safety, but sees* ROGERS, *who strolls in behind* ALAN, *and is re-assured. She smiles and goes out.*

ALAN, *studiously avoiding looking at* DIANA, *goes over to the book-case and picks up the books he has dropped.* ROGERS *takes a position between him and* DIANA, *nonchalantly looking up at the ceiling.*

DIANA. (*Quietly.*) Bill, please go away. I want to talk with Alan alone.

ROGERS. Well, it's . . .

DIANA. (*Shortly.*) Bill, did you hear me? I asked you to go.

ROGERS. (*Firmly.*) I'm sorry, I can't.

DIANA. (*Realizing the situation, steps back with dignity.*) Do you think it's necessary to behave like this?

ALAN. You can say anything you want to say in front of Bill.

DIANA. No, thank you. I'd rather not.

ALAN. Then you don't say it.

DIANA. (*After a slight pause.*) All right, if you're determined to be so childish. This is all I want to say. (*With great sincerity.*) Alan, you know your own mind. If you feel you must run away from me, go ahead. I won't try to stop you. I only hope you'll be happy without me. I know I shan't be happy without you.

ALAN. (*Beginning to fall.*) You'll get over it.

DIANA. Oh, I expect so. You'll write to me occasionally, won't you?

ALAN. Oh, yes, every day, I expect.

DIANA. I'd like to know how you're getting on in your new career. I wish you the very, very best of luck.

ALAN. Thank you.

DIANA. I'll be thinking of you a lot.

ALAN. That's very kind of you.

DIANA. Well, that's really all I wanted to say, only . . . (*falteringly*) I would rather like to say goodbye, and that's a bit hard with Bill standing there like the Rock of Gibraltar.

There is a long pause.

ALAN. (*Suddenly.*) Bill, get out.

ROGERS *doesn't budge.*

ALAN. Get out, Bill.

ROGERS *seems not to have heard.* ALAN *approaches him menacingly.*
Get out, blast you!

ROGERS. (*Slowly.*) Is that the voice of reason, my dear fellow?
ALAN *stares at him and suddenly collects himself.*

ALAN. Oh, thank you, Bill. Come on, help me carry these books
upstairs, and don't leave my side until I'm in that damned
train.

They go towards the door.

DIANA. So you don't want to say goodbye?

ALAN. (*At door.*) Yes, I do. Goodbye.

He goes out, followed by ROGERS.

DIANA, *in a sudden rage, hurls some books through the door after
them.*

DIANA. You forgot some.

She goes to kitchen door.

(*Calling.*) Marianne, à quelle heure arrive ce Lord Heybrook?

JACQUELINE. (*Calling from the kitchen.*) Lord Heybrook's arriving
at ten-fifteen. (*She appears in the doorway.*) He'll be here any
moment now.

DIANA. (*Annoyed.*) Oh, thank you very much.

JACQUELINE. Well, any luck with Alan?

DIANA. (*Shortly.*) No.

JACQUELINE. He wouldn't listen to reason?

DIANA. Do you mind, Jacqueline? I'm really too upset to talk
about it.

JACQUELINE. Why don't you go to England with him, if you
feel like that?

DIANA. How can I go chasing him across half a continent? One
has a little pride after all.

JACQUELINE. Yes, I suppose one has.

DIANA. Besides, if Alan really feels he'll be happier without me,
there's nothing I can do about it.

JACQUELINE. No, I suppose there isn't. (*Inconsequentially.*) Poor
Lord Heybrook!

DIANA. What's Lord Heybrook got to do with it?

JACQUELINE. Nothing. (*She wanders over to the window.*) It's a

lovely morning for a bathe, don't you think? There's a cold
wind and the sea is rough, but I shouldn't let that stop you.

DIANA. Really, Jacqueline, you're becoming quite nice and
catty in your old age. (*Defiantly.*) As a matter of fact, I think
I will have a bathe. Why don't you come with me?

JACQUELINE. Oh, no. My bathing dress isn't nearly attractive
enough. Besides, I'm giving lessons all the morning. (*Looking at her watch.*) I'm supposed to be giving one now. Kit's
late as usual.

DIANA. By the way, how are you getting on in that direction?

JACQUELINE. Not very well, I'm afraid.

DIANA. Oh, I'm sorry. I suppose Kit's terribly upset about me?

JACQUELINE. You needn't worry. I shall do my best to console
him.

DIANA. I've been horribly unkind to him. After Alan's gone I
shall have to be specially nice to him to make up for it.

JACQUELINE. (*Alarmed.*) Oh, no.

DIANA *raises her eyebrows.*

Oh, why don't you go to England with Alan? Heaven
knows Alan's never done me any harm, but I can feel quite
ruthless about anything that will get you out of this house.

DIANA. Excitable race, you French—I always say.

Enter KIT.

KIT. (*Ignoring* DIANA.) Sorry, Jack. I'm late.

JACQUELINE. All right, Kit.

DIANA. Well, I don't want to disturb you. (*Going to door.*) I'm
going to have a bathe.

DIANA *goes out.* KIT *stands shyly, holding a notebook.*

JACQUELINE. (*Adopting a schoolmistress manner.*) Sit down, Kit.
Have you done that stuff?

They sit at table. KIT *hands her his notebook.*

Good. You must have worked quite hard.

She bends her head over the notebook. KIT *gazes at her.*

KIT. (*Suddenly.*) Jack, I want to say——

JACQUELINE. (*Hurriedly.*) This is wrong. (*She underlines a word.*)
You can't say that in French. You have to turn it. (*She writes
something in the book.*) Do you see?

KIT. (*Looking over her shoulder.*) Yes, I see.

JACQUELINE *continues to read.*

JACQUELINE. My dear Kit—— (*Reading.*) Une pipe remplie avec du tabac. What ought it to be?

KIT. Remplie de tabac, of course.

JACQUELINE. Why didn't you write it, then? (*She underlines another word.*) Kit, this whole exercise is terrible. What on earth were you thinking of when you did it?

KIT. You.

JACQUELINE. Well, you'd better do it again.

KIT. (*Annoyed.*) What! Do it all again?

JACQUELINE. Yes. (*Weakening.*) Why were you thinking of me?

KIT. Not the whole damn thing?

JACQUELINE. Certainly. Why were you thinking of me?

KIT. (*With dignity.*) Shall I translate you some 'La Bruyère'?

JACQUELINE. All right.

KIT. Page one hundred and eight.

They take up their books in a dignified silence.

JACQUELINE. If I let you off, will you tell me?

KIT. I might.

JACQUELINE. Very well. You're let off. Only mind you, if you do another exercise as bad as that I'll make you do it again, and three more besides. Now, why were you thinking of me?

KIT. I was wondering whether I ought to tell you I was sorry for—for what happened last night, or whether I ought to pass it off with a gay laugh and a shrug of the shoulders.

JACQUELINE. Which did you decide?

KIT. I decided to leave it to you.

JACQUELINE. I think I'd rather have the gay laugh and the shrug of the shoulders.

KIT. You shall have it. (*He gets up.*)

JACQUELINE. No, you needn't bother. We'll take the gay laugh, etcetera, for granted.

KIT. (*Sitting.*) Very well. The incident is now closed, permanently and perpetually closed. (*He opens his book.*) Chapter four. Of love. There is a fragrance in pure friendship——

JACQUELINE. (*Puzzled at his attitude.*) I don't know why you should have thought I wanted you to apologize. After all, what's a kiss between friends?

KIT. Alan told me this morning that you were in a steaming
fury with me about it, so I thought——

JACQUELINE. Oh, I see. Alan's been talking to you about me
this morning, has he? Come on, tell me, what's he been
saying now?

KIT. I don't see why I shouldn't tell you. You see, last night,
when Alan was a bit drunk, he played a stupid practical
joke on me. He told me (*covering his face with his hands*)—
this is a bit embarrassing, but it's a good laugh—he told
me that you had been madly in love with me for two
months. (*He uncovers his face and waits for the laugh, which
doesn't come.*) Well, I, being also rather drunk, believed him,
and so, as I was feeling rather sentimental, I—kissed you,
as you remember; and of course I couldn't understand why
you didn't fall into my arms and say, 'At last, at last!' or
some such rot. However, this morning Alan told me the
whole thing had been a joke, and that you were really
rather angry with me for—well—spoiling a beautiful friendship, and all that nonsense. So that's why I thought I'd
better apologize.

JACQUELINE. (*With sudden violence.*) What a blasted fool Alan is!

KIT. Yes, it was a damn silly trick to play. Not at all like him.

JACQUELINE. Kit—supposing I—had fallen into your arms and
said, 'At last, at last!' or some such rot, what would you
have done?

KIT. Oh, I should have kissed you again and said: 'I've loved
you all the time without knowing it,' or some such idiocy.

JACQUELINE. Oh, Kit. You wouldn't.

KIT. (*Apologetically.*) Well, I told you I was feeling sentimental
last night, and what with seeing what a fool I'd been over
Diana and trying to forget her, and suddenly hearing that
you were in love with me, and being drunk——

JACQUELINE. You don't feel sentimental this morning, do you?

KIT. Lord, no. You don't have to worry any more. I'm quite
all right now.

He takes up his book and tries to concentrate.

JACQUELINE. Isn't there any chance of your feeling sentimental
again, some time?

KIT. Oh, no. You're quite safe.

JACQUELINE. If I gave you a drink or two, and told you that what Alan said last night was the truth? And that I *have* been in love with you for two months and that I've been longing for you to kiss me every time I'm with you, would that make you feel sentimental?

KIT. There's no knowing what it mightn't make me feel.

Pause.

JACQUELINE. I haven't got any drink, Kit. Or must you have drink?

She stands up and KIT *embraces her.*

(*A little hysterically.*) At last! At last!

KIT. I've loved you all the time without knowing it.

JACQUELINE. Or some such idiocy.

KIT. I mean that, Jack.

JACQUELINE. Don't get serious, please, Kit. This is only a joke. It's only because we are both feeling a bit sentimental at the same time. (*Holding him away.*) Or are you?

KIT. Would I be behaving like this if I weren't?

JACQUELINE. I don't know. I wouldn't like to have played a sort of Diana trick on you. You haven't got that trapped feeling, have you?

KIT. I've got a peculiar feeling in the stomach, and an odd buzzing noise in the head. I think that must mean I'm in love with you.

JACQUELINE. You mustn't talk about love.

KIT. But you do.

JACQUELINE. I've got two months' start of you. I'm not going to let you mention the word 'love' for two months. Oh, Kit, do you think there's a chance you may be feeling sentimental in two months' time?

KIT. I'll take ten to one.

JACQUELINE. Well, go on being beastly to me in the meanwhile, because I should hate it if you didn't.

KIT. I'll try, but it won't be easy.

ALAN *pokes his head cautiously round the door.*

ALAN. Is Diana about?

JACQUELINE. Come in, Alan. You're quite safe, and I've got some news.

ALAN *comes in, followed by* ROGERS.

ALAN. What news?

JACQUELINE. I don't want the Commander to hear it. (*To* ROGERS.) Do you mind awfully?

ROGERS. Oh, no. Not at all. Tell me when you're finished.

He goes out.

ALAN. Well, what's the news?

JACQUELINE. Kit says it's just possible that in two months' time he may feel quite sentimental about me.

ALAN. Well, well, well. You could knock me over with a feather.

KIT. You've got a lot to explain, Alan. What the hell do you mean by telling me a whole packet of lies?

ALAN. Is that the proper way to speak to one, who, by a series of tortuous ruses, has at last brought you two love-birds together?

JACQUELINE. We're not love-birds. We're friends.

KIT. Sentimental friends.

JACQUELINE. No. Friends who sometimes feel sentimental.

ALAN. Well, make up your minds what you are, and I'll give you my blessing. Time presses. I came in to say goodbye.

ROGERS. (*Appearing in doorway.*) I can come in now, can't I?

JACQUELINE. How did you know?

ROGERS. Male intuition as opposed to female. I listened at the keyhole.

ALAN. Do you know, Jack, the only reason I'm sorry to be going is having to leave Bill just when I'd discovered him.

ROGERS. We'll see each other again, don't you worry. We're brothers under the skin.

ALAN. Tell me, Jack, did Diana say anything about coming to England with me?

JACQUELINE. No, she's definitely staying here. She says your happiness comes first.

ALAN. For my happiness read Lord Heybrook. Thank God for his lordship.

Enter KENNETH.

KENNETH. Alan, must you go?

ALAN. Yes, Babe, I must. There's a load off my mind, and I don't only mean Diana.

KENNETH. I don't think you know what you're doing.

ALAN. Oh, yes, I do.

A car noise is heard outside. MAINGOT *appears at window.*

MAINGOT. Jacqueline! Jacqueline! Je crois que c'est Lord Heybrook qui arrive. Es-tu-prête?

JACQUELINE. Oui, Papa.

MAINGOT. Bien! (*He darts out again.*)

JACQUELINE. (*Excitedly.*) Lord Heybrook! Oh, go and tell Diana, someone, or she'll miss her entrance.

KIT. (*Running to door.*) Diana, Lord Heybrook!

JACQUELINE. What does he look like, Kenneth?

KENNETH. I can't see. Your father is in the light.

ALAN. Oh, sit down, all of you. Give the man a chance.

MAINGOT. (*Calling off.*) Marianne! Les bagages!

Enter DIANA, *in her bathing dress. She takes up a position of nonchalance, with her back to the garden door.*

MAINGOT. (*Off.*) Par ici, Milord!

Enter LORD HEYBROOK *and* MAINGOT *from window.* LORD HEYBROOK *is a bright young schoolboy, about fifteen years old.*

(*Escorting* LORD HEYBROOK *across the room.*) Alors vous êtes arrivé. J'espère que vous avez fait bon voyage . . . etc.

LORD HEYBROOK, *after smiling around shyly, goes out followed by* MAINGOT. JACQUELINE *collapses with laughter on* KIT's *chest. The others begin to laugh also.*

DIANA. Come and help me pack, someone. I'm going to catch that London train or die.

She disappears through door at back.

ALAN. (*Pursuing her despairingly.*) No, no, oh, God, no! (*Turning at door.*) Stop laughing, you idiots. It isn't funny. It's a bloody tragedy.

But they only laugh the louder as the

CURTAIN FALLS

THE WINSLOW BOY

The Winslow Boy was first produced at the Lyric Theatre, London, on May 23rd, 1946, with the following cast:

RONNIE WINSLOW	*Michael Newell*
VIOLET	*Kathleen Harrison*
ARTHUR WINSLOW	*Frank Cellier*
GRACE WINSLOW	*Madge Compton*
DICKIE WINSLOW	*Jack Watling*
CATHERINE WINSLOW	*Angela Baddeley*
JOHN WATHERSTONE ...	... *Alastair Bannerman*
DESMOND CURRY	*Clive Morton*
MISS BARNES	*Mona Washbourne*
FRED	*Brian Harding*
SIR ROBERT MORTON	*Emlyn Williams*

The play directed by GLEN BYAM SHAW

ACT I   A SUNDAY MORNING IN JULY

ACT II   AN EVENING IN APRIL
            (NINE MONTHS LATER)

ACT III AN EVENING IN JANUARY
            (NINE MONTHS LATER)

ACT IV   AN AFTERNOON IN JUNE
            (FIVE MONTHS LATER)

The action of the play takes place in Arthur Winslow's house in Kensington, London, and extends over two years of a period preceding the war of 1914–1918.

ACT I

SCENE: *The drawing-room of a house in Courtfield Gardens, South Kensington, on a morning in July, at some period not long before the war of 1914–1918.*

The furnishings betoken solid but not undecorative upper middle-class comfort.

On the rise of the curtain A BOY of about fourteen, dressed in the uniform of an Osborne naval cadet, is discovered. There is something rigid and tense in his attitude, and his face is blank and without expression.

There is the sound of someone in the hall. As the sound comes nearer, he looks despairingly round, as if contemplating flight. An elderly maid (VIOLET) comes in, and stops in astonishment at sight of him.

VIOLET. Master Ronnie!

RONNIE. (*With ill-managed sang-froid.*) Hello, Violet.

VIOLET. Why, good gracious! We weren't expecting you back till Tuesday.

RONNIE. Yes, I know.

VIOLET. Why ever didn't you let us know you were coming, you silly boy? Your mother should have been at the station to meet you. The idea of a child like you wandering all over London by yourself. I never did. However did you get in? By the garden, I suppose.

RONNIE. No. The front-door. I rang and cook opened it.

VIOLET. And where's your trunk and your tuck box?

RONNIE. Upstairs. The taximan carried them up——

VIOLET. Taximan? You took a taxi?

RONNIE *nods.*

All by yourself? Well, I don't know what little boys are coming to, I'm sure. What your father and mother will say, I don't know——

RONNIE. Where are they, Violet?

83

VIOLET. Church, of course.

RONNIE. (*Vacantly.*) Oh, yes. It's Sunday, isn't it?

VIOLET. What's the matter with you? What have they been doing to you at Osborne?

RONNIE. (*Sharply.*) What do you mean?

VIOLET. They seem to have made you a bit soft in the head, or something. Well—I suppose I'd better get your unpacking done—Mr. Dickie's been using your chest of drawers for all his dress clothes and things. I'll just clear 'em out and put 'em on his bed—that's what I'll do. He can find room for 'em somewhere else.

RONNIE. Shall I help you?

VIOLET. (*Scornfully.*) I know *your* help. With *your* help I'll be at it all day. No, you just wait down here for your mother and father. They'll be back in a minute.

RONNIE *nods and turns hopelessly away.* VIOLET *looks at his retreating back, puzzled.*

Well?

RONNIE. (*Turning.*) Yes?

VIOLET. Don't I get a kiss or are you too grown up for that now?

RONNIE. Sorry, Violet.

He goes up to her and is enveloped in her ample bosom.

VIOLET. That's better. My, what a big boy you're getting!

She holds him at arm's length and inspects him.

Quite the little naval officer, aren't you?

RONNIE. (*Smiling forlornly.*) Yes. That's right.

VIOLET. Well, well—I must be getting on——

She goes out. RONNIE, *left alone, resumes his attitude of utter dejection. He takes out of his pocket a letter in a sealed envelope. After a second's hesitation, he opens it, and reads the contents. The perusal appears to increase his misery.*

He makes for a moment as if to tear it up; then changes his mind again, and puts it back in his pocket. He gets up and takes two or three quick steps towards the hall door. Then he stops, uncertainly.

There is the sound of voices in the hall. RONNIE *jumps to his feet; then, with a strangled sob runs to the garden door, and down the iron steps into the garden.*

The hall door opens and the rest of the Winslow family file in. They are ARTHUR *and* GRACE—*Ronnie's father and mother*—*and* DICKIE *and* CATHERINE—*his brother and sister. All are carrying prayer-books, and wear that faintly unctuous after-church air.*

ARTHUR *leans heavily on a stick. He is a man of about sixty, with a rather deliberately cultured patriarchal air.* GRACE *is about ten years younger, with the faded remnants of prettiness.* DICKIE *is an Oxford undergraduate, large, noisy, and cheerful.* CATHERINE, *approaching thirty, has an air of masculinity about her which is at odd variance with her mother's intense femininity.*

GRACE. (*As she enters.*) —But he's so old, dear. From the back of the church you really can't hear a word he says——

ARTHUR. He's a good man, Grace.

GRACE. But what's the use of being good, if you're inaudible?

CATHERINE. A problem in ethics for you, Father.

ARTHUR *is standing with his back to fireplace. He looks round at the open garden door.*

ARTHUR. There's a draught, Grace.

GRACE *goes to the door and closes it.*

GRACE. Oh, dear—it's coming on to rain.

DICKIE. I'm on Mother's side. The old boy's so doddery now he can hardly finish the course at all. I timed him today. It took him seventy-five seconds dead from a flying start to reach the pulpit, and then he needed the whip coming round the bend. I call that pretty bad going.

ARTHUR. I don't think that's very funny, Richard.

DICKIE. Oh, don't you, Father?

ARTHUR. Doddery though Mr. Jackson may seem now, I very much doubt if he failed in his pass mods. when he was at Oxford.

DICKIE. (*Aggrieved.*) Dash it—Father—you promised not to mention that again this vac——

GRACE. You did, you know, Arthur.

ARTHUR. There was a condition to my promise—if you remember—that Dickie should provide me with reasonable evidence of his intentions to work.

DICKIE. Well, haven't I, Father? Didn't I stay in all last night —a Saturday night—and work?

ARTHUR. You stayed in, Dickie. I would be the last to deny that.

GRACE. You *were* making rather a noise, dear, with that old gramophone of yours. I really can't believe you could have been doing much work with that going on all the time——

DICKIE. Funnily enough, Mother, it helps me to concentrate——

ARTHUR. Concentrate on what?

DICKIE. Work, of course.

ARTHUR. That was not what you appeared to be concentrating on when I came down to fetch a book—sleep, may I say, having been rendered out of the question by the hideous sounds emanating from this room.

DICKIE. Edwina and her father had just looked in on their way to the Graham's dance—they only stayed a minute——

GRACE. What an idiotic girl that is! Oh, sorry, Dickie—I was forgetting. You're rather keen on her, aren't you?

ARTHUR. You would have had ample proof of that fact, Grace, if you had seen them in the attitude I caught them in last night.

DICKIE. We were practising the Bunny Hug.

GRACE. The what, dear?

DICKIE. The Bunny Hug. It's the new dance.

CATHERINE. (*Helpfully.*) It's like the Turkey Trot—only more dignified.

GRACE. I thought that was the tango.

DICKIE. No. More like a Fox Trot, really. Something between a Boston Glide and a Kangaroo Hop.

ARTHUR. We appear to be straying from the point. Whatever animal was responsible for the posture I found you in does not alter the fact that you have not done one single stroke of work this vacation.

DICKIE. Oh. Well, I do work awfully fast, you know—once I get down to it.

ARTHUR. That assumption can hardly be based on experience, I take it.

DICKIE. Dash it, Father! You are laying in to me this morning.

ARTHUR. It's time you found out, Dickie, that I'm not spending two hundred pounds a year keeping you at Oxford, merely to learn to dance the Bunny Hop.

DICKIE. Hug, Father.

ARTHUR. The exact description of the obscenity is immaterial.

GRACE. Father's quite right, you know, dear. You really have been going the pace a bit, this vac.

DICKIE. Yes, I know, Mother—but the season's nearly over now——

GRACE. (*With a sigh.*) I wish you were as good about work as Ronnie.

DICKIE. (*Hotly.*) I like that. That's a bit thick, I must say. All Ronnie ever has to do with his footling little homework is to add two and two.

ARTHUR. Ronnie is at least proving a good deal more successful in adding two and two than you were at his age.

DICKIE. (*Now furious.*) Oh, yes. *I* know. *I* know. *He* got into Osborne and *I* failed. That's going to be brought up again——

GRACE. Nobody's bringing it up, dear——

DICKIE. Oh, yes they are. It's going to be brought up against me all my life. Ronnie's the good little boy, I'm the bad little boy. You've just stuck a couple of labels on us that nothing on earth is ever going to change.

GRACE. Don't be so absurd, dear——

DICKIE. It's not absurd. It's quite true. Isn't it, Kate?

CATHERINE *looks up from a book she has been reading in the corner.*

CATHERINE. I'm sorry, Dickie. I haven't been listening. Isn't what quite true?

DICKIE. That in the eyes of Mother and Father nothing that Ronnie does is ever wrong, and nothing I do is ever right?

CATHERINE. (*After a pause.*) If I were you, Dickie dear, I'd go and have a nice lie down before lunch.

DICKIE. (*After a further pause.*) Perhaps you're right.

He goes towards the hall door.

ARTHUR. If you're going to your room I suggest you take that object with you.

He points to a gramophone—1912 model, with horn—lying on a table. It's out of place in a drawing-room.

DICKIE, *with an air of hauteur, picks up the gramophone and carries it to the door.*

It might help you to concentrate on the work you're going to do this afternoon.

DICKIE *stops at the door, and then turns slowly.*

DICKIE. (*With dignity.*) That is out of the question, I'm afraid.

ARTHUR. Indeed? Why?

DICKIE. I have an engagement with Miss Gunn.

ARTHUR. On a Sunday afternoon? Escorting her to the National Gallery, no doubt?

DICKIE. No. The Victoria and Albert Museum.

He goes out with as much dignity as is consistent with the carrying of a very bulky gramophone.

GRACE. How stupid of him to say that about labels. There's no truth in it at all—is there, Kate?

CATHERINE. (*Deep in her book.*) No, Mother.

GRACE. Oh, dear, it's simply pelting. What are you reading, Kate?

CATHERINE. Len Rogers's Memoirs.

GRACE. Who's Len Rogers?

CATHERINE. A Trades Union Leader.

GRACE. Does John know you're a Radical?

CATHERINE. Oh, yes.

GRACE. And a Suffragette?

CATHERINE. Certainly.

GRACE. (*With a smile.*) And he still wants to marry you?

CATHERINE. He seems to.

GRACE. Oh, by the way, I've asked him to come early for lunch—so that he can have a few words with Father first.

CATHERINE. Good idea. I hope you've been primed, have you Father?

ARTHUR. (*Who has been nearly asleep.*) What's that?

CATHERINE. You know what you're going to say to John, don't you? You're not going to let me down and forbid the match, or anything, are you? Because I warn you, if you do, I shall elope——

ARTHUR. (*Taking her hand.*) Never fear, my dear. I'm far too delighted at the prospect of getting you off our hands at last.

CATHERINE. (*Smiling.*) I'm not sure I like that 'at last'.

GRACE. Do you love him, dear?

CATHERINE. John? Yes, I do.

GRACE. You're such a funny girl. You never show your feelings much, do you? You don't behave as if you were in love.

CATHERINE. How does one behave as if one is in love?

ARTHUR. One doesn't read Len Rogers. One reads Byron.

CATHERINE. I do both.

ARTHUR. An odd combination.

CATHERINE. A satisfying one.

GRACE. I meant—you don't talk about him much, do you?

CATHERINE. No. I suppose I don't.

GRACE. (*Sighing.*) I don't think you modern girls have the feelings our generation did. It's this New Woman attitude.

CATHERINE. Very well, Mother. I love John in every way that a woman can love a man, and far, far more than he loves me. Does that satisfy you?

GRACE. (*Embarrassed.*) Well, really, Kate darling—I didn't ask for anything quite like that—— (*To* ARTHUR.) What are you laughing at, Arthur?

ARTHUR. (*Chuckling.*) One up to the New Woman.

GRACE. Nonsense. She misunderstood me, that's all. (*At the window.*) Just look at the rain! (*Turning to* CATHERINE.) Kate, darling, does Desmond know about you and John?

CATHERINE. I haven't told him. On the other hand, if he hasn't guessed, he must be very dense.

ARTHUR. He *is* very dense.

GRACE. Oh, no. He's quite clever, if you really get under his skin.

ARTHUR. Oddly enough, I've never had that inclination.

GRACE. I think he's a dear. Kate darling, you *will* be kind to him, won't you?

CATHERINE. (*Patiently.*) Yes, Mother. Of course I will.

GRACE. He's really a very good sort——

She breaks off suddenly and stares out of the window.

Hullo! There's someone in our garden.

CATHERINE. (*Coming to look.*) Where?

GRACE. (*Pointing.*) Over there, do you see?

CATHERINE. No.

GRACE. He's just gone behind that bush. It was a boy, I think. Probably Mrs. Williamson's awful little Dennis.

CATHERINE. (*Leaving the window.*) Well, whoever it is must be getting terribly wet.

GRACE. Why can't he stick to his own garden?

There is a sound of voices outside in the hall.

GRACE. Was that John?

CATHERINE. It sounded like it.

GRACE. (*After listening.*) Yes. It's John. (*To* CATHERINE.) Quick! In the dining-room!

CATHERINE. All right.

She dashes across to the dining-room door.

GRACE. Here! You've forgotten your bag.

She darts to the table and picks it up.

ARTHUR. (*Startled.*) What on earth is going on?

GRACE. (*In a stage whisper.*) We're leaving you alone with John. When you've finished cough or something.

ARTHUR. (*Testily.*) What do you mean, or something?

GRACE. I know. Knock on the floor with your stick—three times. Then we'll come in.

ARTHUR. You don't think that might look a trifle coincidental?

GRACE. Sh!

She disappears from view as the hall door opens and VIOLET *comes in.*

VIOLET. (*Announcing.*) Mr. Watherstone.

JOHN WATHERSTONE *comes in. He is a man of about thirty, dressed in an extremely well-cut morning coat and striped trousers, an attire which, though excused by church parade, we may well feel has been donned for this occasion.*

ARTHUR. How are you, John? I'm very glad to see you.

JOHN. How do you do, sir?

ARTHUR. Will you forgive me not getting up? My arthritis has been troubling me rather a lot, lately.

JOHN. I'm very sorry to hear that, sir. Catherine told me it was better.

ARTHUR. It was, for a time. Now it's worse again. Do you smoke? (*He indicates a cigarette-box.*)

JOHN. Yes, sir. I do. Thank you. (*He takes a cigarette, adding hastily.*) In moderation, of course.

ARTHUR. (*With a faint smile.*) Of course.

Pause, while JOHN *lights his cigarette and* ARTHUR *watches him.*
Well, now. I understand you wish to marry my daughter.

JOHN. Yes, sir. That's to say, I've proposed to her and she's done me the honour of accepting me.

ARTHUR. I see. I trust when you corrected yourself, your second statement wasn't a denial of your first? (JOHN *looks puzzled.*) I mean, you do *really* wish to marry her?

JOHN. Of course, sir.

ARTHUR. Why, of course? There are plenty of people about who don't wish to marry her.

JOHN. I mean, of course, because I proposed to her.

ARTHUR. That, too, doesn't necessarily follow. However, we don't need to quibble. We'll take the sentimental side of the project for granted. As regards the more practical aspect, perhaps you won't mind if I ask you a few rather personal questions?

JOHN. Naturally not, sir. It's your duty.

ARTHUR. Quite so. Now, your income. Are you able to live on it?

JOHN. No, sir. I'm in the regular army.

ARTHUR. Yes, of course.

JOHN. But my army pay is supplemented by an allowance from my father.

ARTHUR. So I understand. Now, your father's would be, I take it, about twenty-four pounds a month.

JOHN. Yes, sir, that's exactly right.

ARTHUR. So that your total income—with your subaltern's pay and allowances plus the allowance from your father, would be, I take it, about four hundred and twenty pounds a year?

JOHN. Again, exactly the figure.

ARTHUR. Well, well. It all seems perfectly satisfactory. I really don't think I need delay my congratulations **any** longer. (*He extends his hand, which* JOHN, *gratefully, takes.*)

JOHN. Thank you, sir, very much.

ARTHUR. I must say, it was very good of you to be so frank and informative.

JOHN. Not at all.

ARTHUR. Your answers to my questions deserve an equal frankness from me about Catherine's own affairs. I'm afraid she's not—just in case you thought otherwise—the daughter of a rich man.

JOHN. I didn't think otherwise, sir.

ARTHUR. Good. Well, now——

He suddenly cocks his head on one side and listens. There is the sound of a gramophone playing 'Hitchy-koo' from somewhere upstairs.

Would you be so good as to touch the bell?

JOHN *does so.*

Thank you. Well, now, continuing about my own financial affairs. The Westminster Bank pay me a small pension—three hundred and fifty to be precise—and my wife has about two hundred a year of her own. Apart from that we have nothing, except such savings as I've been able to make during my career at the bank. The interest from which raises my total income to approximately eight hundred pounds per annum.

VIOLET *comes in.*

VIOLET. You rang, sir?

ARTHUR. Yes, Violet. My compliments to Mr. Dickie and if he doesn't stop that cacophonous hullaballoo at once, I'll throw him and his infernal machine into the street.

VIOLET. Yes, sir. What was that word again? Cac—something——

ARTHUR. Never mind. Say anything you like, only stop him.

VIOLET. Well, sir, I'll do my best, but you know what Master Dickie's like with his blessed old ragtime.

ARTHUR. Yes, Violet, I do.

VIOLET. I could say you don't think it's quite right on a Sunday.

ARTHUR. (*Roaring.*) You can say I don't think it's quite right on any day. Just stop him making that confounded din, that's all.

VIOLET. Yes, sir.

She goes out.

ARTHUR. (*Apologetically.*) Our Violet has no doubt already
   been explained to you?

JOHN. I don't think so, sir. Is any explanation necessary?

ARTHUR. I fear it is. She came to us direct from an orphanage
   when she was fourteen, as a sort of under-between-maid on
   probation, and in that capacity she was quite satisfactory;
   but I am afraid, as parlourmaid, she has developed certain
   marked eccentricities in the performance of her duties, due,
   no doubt, to the fact that she has never fully known what
   those duties were. Well, now, where were we? Ah, yes. I
   was telling you about my sources of income, was I not?

JOHN. Yes, sir.

ARTHUR. Now, in addition to the ordinary expenses of life, I
   have to maintain two sons—one at Osborne, and the other
   at Oxford—neither of whom, I'm afraid, will be in a position to support themselves for some time to come—one
   because of his extreme youth and the other because of—er
   —other reasons.

The gramophone stops suddenly.

   So, you see, I am not in a position to be very lavish as regards
   Catherine's dowry.

JOHN. No, sir. I quite see that.

ARTHUR. I propose to settle on her one-sixth of my total
   capital, which, worked out to the final fraction, is exactly
   eight hundred and thirty-three pounds six shillings and eight
   pence. But let us deal in round figures and say eight hundred and fifty pounds.

JOHN. I call that very generous, sir.

ARTHUR. Not as generous as I would have liked, I'm afraid.
   However—as my wife would say—beggars can't be choosers.

JOHN. Exactly, sir.

ARTHUR. Well, then, if you're agreeable to that arrangement, I
   don't think there's anything more we need discuss.

JOHN. No, sir.

ARTHUR. Splendid.

Pause. ARTHUR *takes his stick, and raps it, with an air of studied
   unconcern, three times on the floor. Nothing happens.*

JOHN. Pretty rotten weather, isn't it?

ARTHUR. Yes. Vile.

He raps again. Again nothing happens.

Would you care for another cigarette?

JOHN. No, thank you, sir. I'm still smoking.

ARTHUR *takes up his stick to rap again, and then thinks better of it. He goes slowly but firmly to the dining-room door, which he throws open.*

ARTHUR. (*In apparent surprise.*) Well, imagine that! My wife and daughter are in here of all places. Come in, Grace. Come in, Catherine. John's here.

GRACE *comes in, with* CATHERINE *behind.*

GRACE. Why, John—how nice! (*She shakes hands.*) My, you do look a swell! Doesn't he, Kate, darling?

CATHERINE. Quite one of the Knuts.

Pause. GRACE *is unable to repress herself*

GRACE. (*Coyly.*) Well?

ARTHUR. Well, what?

GRACE. How did your little talk go?

ARTHUR. (*Testily.*) I understood you weren't supposed to know we were having a little talk.

GRACE. Oh, you are infuriating! Is everything all right, John?

JOHN *nods, smiling.*

Oh, I'm so glad. I really am.

JOHN. Thank you, Mrs. Winslow.

GRACE. May I kiss you? After all, I'm practically your mother, now.

JOHN. Yes. Of course.

He allows himself to be kissed.

ARTHUR. While I, by the same token, am practically your father, but if you will forgive me——

JOHN. (*Smiling.*) Certainly, sir.

ARTHUR. Grace, I think we might allow ourselves a little modest celebration at luncheon. Will you find me the key of the cellars?

He goes out through the hall door.

GRACE. Yes, dear. (*She turns at the door. Coyly.*) I don't suppose you two will mind being left alone for a few minutes, will you?

She follows her husband out. JOHN *goes to* CATHERINE *and kisses her.*

CATHERINE. Was it an ordeal.

JOHN. I was scared to death.

CATHERINE. My poor darling——

JOHN. The annoying thing was that I had a whole lot of neatly turned phrases ready for him and he wouldn't let me use them.

CATHERINE. Such as?

JOHN. Oh—how proud and honoured I was by your acceptance of me, and how determined I was to make you a loyal and devoted husband—and to maintain you in the state to which you were accustomed—all that sort of thing. All very sincerely meant.

CATHERINE. Anything about loving me a little?

JOHN. (*Lightly.*) That I thought we could take for granted. So did your father, incidentally.

CATHERINE. I see. (*She gazes at him.*) Goodness, you do look smart!

JOHN. Not bad, is it? Poole's.

CATHERINE. What about *your* father? How did he take it?

JOHN. All right.

CATHERINE. I bet he didn't.

JOHN. Oh, yes. He's been wanting me to get married for years. Getting worried about grandchildren, I suppose.

CATHERINE. He disapproves of me, doesn't he?

JOHN. Oh, no. Whatever makes you think that?

CATHERINE. He has a way of looking at me through his monocle that shrivels me up.

JOHN. He's just being a colonel, darling, that's all. All colonels look at you like that. Anyway, what about the way your father looks at me! Tell me, are all your family as scared of him as I am?

CATHERINE. Dickie is, of course; and Ronnie, though he doesn't need to be. Father worships him. I don't know about Mother being scared of him. Sometimes, perhaps. I'm not—ever.

JOHN. You're not scared of anything, are you?

CATHERINE. Oh, yes. Heaps of things.

JOHN. Such as?

CATHERINE. (*With a smile.*) Oh—they're nearly all concerned
with you.

RONNIE *looks cautiously in at the window door. He now presents
a very bedraggled and woebegone appearance, with his uniform
wringing wet, and his damp hair over his eyes.*

JOHN. You might be a little more explicit——

RONNIE. (*In a low voice.*) Kate!

CATHERINE *turns and sees him.*

CATHERINE. (*Amazed.*) Ronnie! What on earth——

RONNIE. Where's Father?

CATHERINE. I'll go and tell him——

RONNIE. (*Urgently.*) No, don't. Please, Kate, don't!

CATHERINE, *halfway to the door, stops, puzzled.*

CATHERINE. What's the trouble, Ronnie?

RONNIE, *trembling on the edge of tears, does not answer her. She
approaches him.*

You're wet through. You'd better go and change.

RONNIE. No.

CATHERINE. (*Gently.*) What's the trouble, darling? You can
tell me.

RONNIE *looks at* JOHN.

You know John Watherstone, Ronnie. You met him last
holidays, don't you remember?

RONNIE *remains silent, obviously reluctant to talk in front of a
comparative stranger.*

JOHN. (*Tactfully.*) I'll disappear.

CATHERINE. (*Pointing to dining-room.*) In there, do you mind?

JOHN *goes out quietly.* CATHERINE *gently leads* RONNIE *further
into the room.*

Now, darling, tell me. What is it? Have you run away?

RONNIE *shakes his head, evidently not trusting himself to speak.*

What is it, then?

RONNIE *pulls out the document from his pocket which we have seen
him reading in an earlier scene, and slowly hands it to her.* CATHERINE
reads it quietly.

Oh, God!

RONNIE. I didn't do it.

CATHERINE *re-reads the letter in silence.*

RONNIE. Kate, I didn't. Really, I didn't.

CATHERINE. (*Abstractedly.*) No, darling. (*She seems uncertain what to do.*) This letter is addressed to Father. Did you open it?

RONNIE. Yes.

CATHERINE. You shouldn't have done that——

RONNIE. I was going to tear it up. Then I heard you come in from church and ran into the garden—I didn't know what to do——

CATHERINE. (*Still distracted.*) Did they send you up to London all by yourself?

RONNIE. They sent a petty officer up with me. He was supposed to wait and see Father, but I sent him away. (*Indicating letter.*) Kate—shall we tear it up, now?

CATHERINE. No, darling.

RONNIE. We could tell Father term had ended two days sooner——

CATHERINE. No, darling.

RONNIE. I didn't do it—really I didn't——

DICKIE *comes in from the hall. He does not seem surprised to see* RONNIE.

DICKIE. (*Cheerfully.*) Hullo, Ronnie, old lad. How's everything?

RONNIE *turns away from him.*

CATHERINE. You knew he was here?

DICKIE. Oh, yes. His trunks and things are all over our room. Trouble?

CATHERINE. Yes.

DICKIE. I'm sorry.

CATHERINE. You stay here with him. I'll find Mother.

DICKIE. All right.

CATHERINE *goes out by the hall door. There is a pause.*

DICKIE. What's up, old chap?

RONNIE. Nothing.

DICKIE. Come on—tell me.

RONNIE. It's all right.

DICKIE. Have you been sacked.

RONNIE *nods.*

Bad luck. What for?

RONNIE. I didn't do it!

DICKIE. (*Reassuringly.*) No, of course you didn't.

RONNIE. Honestly, I didn't.

DICKIE. That's all right, old chap. No need to go on about it. I believe you.

RONNIE. You don't.

DICKIE. Well, I don't know what it is they've sacked you for, yet——

RONNIE. (*In a low voice.*) Stealing.

DICKIE. (*Evidently relieved.*) Oh, is that all? Good Lord! I didn't know they sacked chaps for *that*, these days.

RONNIE. I didn't do it.

DICKIE. Why, good heavens, at school we used to pinch everything we could jolly well lay our hands on. All of us. I remember there was one chap—Carstairs his name was—captain of cricket, believe it or not—absolutely nothing was safe with him—nothing at all. Pinched a squash racket of mine once, I remember——

He has quietly approached RONNIE, *and now puts his arm on his shoulder.*
Believe me, old chap, pinching's nothing. Nothing at all. I say—you're a bit damp, aren't you?

RONNIE. I've been out in the rain——

DICKIE. You're shivering a bit, too, aren't you? Oughtn't you to go and change? I mean, we don't want you catching pneumonia——

RONNIE. I'm all right.

GRACE *comes in, with* CATHERINE *following.* GRACE *comes quickly to* RONNIE, *who, as he sees her, turns away from* DICKIE *and runs into her arms.*

GRACE. There, darling! It's all right, now.

RONNIE *begins to cry quietly, his head buried in her dress.*

RONNIE. (*His voice muffled.*) I didn't do it, Mother.

GRACE. No, darling. Of course you didn't. We'll go upstairs now, shall we, and get out of these nasty wet clothes.

RONNIE. Don't tell Father.

GRACE. No, darling. Not yet. I promise. Come along now.

She leads him towards the door held open by CATHERINE.
Your new uniform, too, What a shame!

She goes out with him.

DICKIE. I'd better go and keep 'cave' for them. Ward off the old man if he looks like going upstairs.

CATHERINE *nods.*

(*At door.*) I say—who's going to break the news to him eventually? I mean, someone'll have to.

CATHERINE. Don't let's worry about that now.

DICKIE. Well, you can count me out. In fact, I don't want to be within a thousand miles of that explosion.

He goes out. CATHERINE *comes to the dining-room door, which she opens, and calls 'John!'* JOHN *comes in.*

JOHN. Bad news?

CATHERINE *nods. She is plainly upset, and dabs her eyes with her handkerchief.*

That's rotten for you. I'm awfully sorry.

CATHERINE. (*Violently.*) How can people be so cruel!

JOHN. (*Uncomfortably.*) Expelled, I suppose?

He gets his answer from her silence, while she recovers herself.

CATHERINE. God, how little imagination some people have! Why should they torture a child of that age, John, darling? What's the point of it?

JOHN. What's he supposed to have done?

CATHERINE. Stolen some money.

JOHN. Oh.

CATHERINE. Ten days ago, it said in the letter. Why on earth didn't they let us know? Just think what that poor little creature has been going through these last ten days down there, entirely alone, without anyone to look after him, knowing what he had to face at the end of it! And then, finally, they send him up to London with a petty officer—is it any wonder he's nearly out of his mind?

JOHN. It does seem pretty heartless, I admit.

CATHERINE. Heartless? It's cold, calculated inhumanity. God, how I'd love to have that Commanding Officer here for just two minutes! I'd—I'd——

JOHN. (*Gently.*) Darling, it's quite natural you should feel angry about it, but you must remember, he's not really at school. He's in the Service.

CATHERINE. What difference does that make?

JOHN. Well, they have ways of doing things in the Service which may seem to an outsider horribly brutal—but at least they're always scrupulously fair. You can take it from me, that there must have been a very full inquiry before they'd take a step of this sort. What's more, if there's been a delay of ten days, it would only have been in order to give the boy a better chance to clear himself——

Pause. CATHERINE *is silent.*

I'm sorry, Catherine, darling. I'd have done better to keep my mouth shut.

CATHERINE. No. What you said was perfectly true——

JOHN. It was tactless of me to say it, though. I'm sorry.

CATHERINE. (*Lightly.*) That's all right.

JOHN. Forgive me?

He lays his arm on her shoulder.

CATHERINE. (*Taking his hand.*) Nothing to forgive.

JOHN. Believe me, I'm awfully sorry. (*After a pause.*) How will your father take it?

CATHERINE. (*Simply.*) It might kill him——

There is the sound of voices in the hall.

Oh, heavens! We've got Desmond to lunch. I'd forgotten——

JOHN. Who?

CATHERINE. Desmond Curry—our family solicitor. Oh, Lord! (*In a hasty whisper.*) Darling—be polite to him, won't you?

JOHN. Why? Am I usually so rude to your guests?

CATHERINE. No, but he doesn't know about us yet——

JOHN. Who does?

CATHERINE. (*Still in a whisper.*) Yes, but he's been in love with me for years—it's a family joke——

VIOLET *comes in.*

VIOLET. (*Announcing.*) Mr. Curry.

DESMOND CURRY *comes in. He is a man of about forty-five, with the figure of an athlete gone to seed. He has a mildly furtive manner, rather as if he had just absconded with his firm's petty cash, but hopes no one is going to be too angry about it.* JOHN, *when he sees him, cannot repress a faint smile at the thought of his loving* CATHERINE. VIOLET *has made her exit.*

CATHERINE. Hullo, Desmond. I don't think you know John Watherstone——

DESMOND. No—but, of course, I've heard a lot about him——

JOHN. How do you do?

He wipes the smile off his face, as he meets CATHERINE'S *glance. There is a pause.*

DESMOND. Well, well, well. I trust I'm not early.

CATHERINE. No. Dead on time, Desmond—as always.

DESMOND. Capital. Capital.

There is another pause, broken by CATHERINE *and* JOHN *both suddenly speaking at once.*

CATHERINE. ⎱ *(Simultaneously.)* ⎰ Tell me, Desmond——
JOHN. ⎰ ⎱ Pretty ghastly this rain——

JOHN. I'm so sorry——

CATHERINE. It's quite all right. I was only going to ask how you did in your cricket match yesterday, Desmond.

DESMOND. Not too well, I'm afraid. My shoulder's still giving me trouble——

There is another pause.

(At length.) Well, well. I hear I'm to congratulate you both——

CATHERINE. Desmond—you know?

DESMOND. Violet told me, just now—in the hall. Yes—I must congratulate you both.

CATHERINE. Thank you so much, Desmond.

JOHN. Thank you.

DESMOND. Of course, it's quite expected, I know. Quite expected. Still it was rather a surprise, hearing it like that —from Violet in the hall——

CATHERINE. We were going to tell you, Desmond dear. It was only official this morning, you know. In fact, you're the first person to hear it.

DESMOND. Am I? Am I, indeed? Well, I'm sure you'll both be very happy.

CATHERINE. ⎱ *(Murmuring* ⎰ Thank you, Desmond.
JOHN. ⎰ *together.)* ⎱ Thank you.

DESMOND. Only this morning? Fancy.

GRACE *comes in.*

GRACE. Hullo, Desmond, dear.

DESMOND. Hullo, Mrs. Winslow.

GRACE. (*To* CATHERINE.) I've got him to bed——

CATHERINE. Good.

DESMOND. Nobody ill, I hope?

GRACE. No, no. Nothing wrong at all——

ARTHUR *comes in, with a bottle under his arm. He rings the bell.*

ARTHUR. Grace, when did we last have the cellars seen to?

GRACE. I can't remember, dear.

ARTHUR. Well, they're in a shocking condition. Hullo, Desmond. How are you? You're not looking well.

DESMOND. Am I not? I've strained my shoulder, you know——

ARTHUR. Well, why do you play these ridiculous games of yours? Resign yourself to the onrush of middle age, and abandon them, my dear Desmond.

DESMOND. Oh, I could never do that. Not give up cricket. Not altogether.

JOHN. (*Making conversation.*) Are you any relation of D. W. H. Curry who used to play for Middlesex?

DESMOND. (*Whose moment has come.*) I am D. W. H. Curry.

GRACE. Didn't you know we had a great man in the room?

JOHN. Gosh! Curry of Curry's match?

DESMOND. That's right.

JOHN. Hat trick against the Players in—what year was it?

DESMOND. 1895. At Lord's. Twenty-six overs, nine maidens, thirty-seven runs, eight wickets.

JOHN. Gosh! Do you know you used to be a schoolboy hero of mine?

DESMOND. Did I? Did I, indeed?

JOHN. Yes. I had a signed photograph of you.

DESMOND. Yes. I used to sign a lot once, for schoolboys, I remember.

ARTHUR. Only for schoolboys, Desmond?

DESMOND. I fear so—yes. Girls took no interest in cricket in those days.

JOHN. Gosh! D. W. H. Curry—in person. Well, I'd never have thought it.

DESMOND. (*Sadly.*) I know. Very few people would nowadays——

CATHERINE. (*Quickly.*) Oh, John didn't mean that, Desmond——

DESMOND. I fear he did. (*He moves his arm.*) This is the main trouble. Too much office work and too little exercise, I fear.

ARTHUR. Nonsense. Too much exercise and too little office work.

VIOLET *comes in, in response to a bell rung by* ARTHUR *some moments before.*

VIOLET. You rang, sir?

ARTHUR. Yes, Violet. Bring some glasses, would you?

VIOLET. Very good, sir.

She goes out.

ARTHUR. I thought we'd try a little of the Madeira before luncheon—we're celebrating, you know, Desmond——

GRACE *jogs his arm furtively, indicating* DESMOND.

(*Adding hastily.*) —my wife's fifty-fourth birthday——

GRACE. Arthur! Really!

CATHERINE. It's all right, Father. Desmond knows——

DESMOND. Yes, indeed. It's wonderful news, isn't it? I'll most gladly drink a toast to the—er—to the——

ARTHUR. (*Politely.*) Happy pair, I think, is the phrase that is eluding you——

DESMOND. Well, as a matter of fact, I was looking for something new to say——

ARTHUR. (*Murmuring.*) A forlorn quest, my dear Desmond.

GRACE. (*Protestingly.*) Arthur, really! You mustn't be so rude.

ARTHUR. I meant, naturally, that no one—with the possible exception of Voltaire—could find anything new to say about an engaged couple——

DICKIE *comes in.*

Ah, my dear Dickie—just in time for a glass of Madeira in celebration of Kate's engagement to John——

VIOLET *comes in with a tray of glasses.* ARTHUR *begins to pour out the wine.*

DICKIE. Oh, is that all finally spliced up now? Kate definitely being entered for the marriage stakes. Good egg!

ARTHUR. Quite so. I should have added just now—with the

possible exception of Voltaire and Dickie Winslow. (*To* VIOLET.) Take these round, will you, Violet?

VIOLET *goes first to* GRACE, *then to* CATHERINE, *then to* JOHN, DESMOND, DICKIE, *and finally* ARTHUR.

CATHERINE. Are we allowed to drink our own healths?

ARTHUR. I think it's permissible.

GRACE. No. It's bad luck.

JOHN. We defy augury. Don't we, Kate?

GRACE. You mustn't say that, John dear. I know. You can drink each other's healths. That's all right.

ARTHUR. Are my wife's superstitious terrors finally allayed? Good.

The drinks have now been handed round.

ARTHUR. (*Toasting.*) Catherine and John!

All drink—CATHERINE *and* JOHN *to each other.* VIOLET *lingers, smiling, in the doorway.*

(*Seeing* VIOLET.) Ah, Violet. We mustn't leave you out. You must join this toast.

VIOLET. Well—thank you, sir.

He pours her out a glass.

Not too much, sir, please. Just a sip.

ARTHUR. Quite so. Your reluctance would be more convincing if I hadn't noticed you'd brought an extra glass——

VIOLET. (*Taking glass from* ARTHUR.) Oh, I didn't bring it for myself, sir. I brought it for Master Ronnie—— (*She extends her glass.*) Miss Kate and Mr. John.

She takes a sip, makes a wry face, and hands the glass back to ARTHUR.

ARTHUR. You brought an extra glass for Master Ronnie, Violet?

VIOLET. (*Mistaking his bewilderment.*) Well—I thought you might allow him just a sip, sir. Just to drink the toast. He's that grown up these days.

She turns to go. The others, with the exception of DESMOND, *who is staring gloomily into his glass, are frozen with apprehension.*

ARTHUR. Master Ronnie isn't due back from Osborne until Tuesday, Violet.

VIOLET. (*Turning.*) Oh, no, sir. He's back already. Came back unexpected this morning, all by himself.

ARTHUR. No, Violet. That isn't true. Someone has been playing
a joke——

VIOLET. Well, I saw him with my own two eyes, sir, as large as
life, just before you come in from church—and then I heard
Mrs. Winslow talking to him in his room——

ARTHUR. Grace—what does this mean?

CATHERINE. (*Instinctively taking charge.*) All right, Violet. You
can go——

VIOLET. Yes, miss.

She goes out.

ARTHUR. (*To* CATHERINE.) Did *you* know Ronnie was back?

CATHERINE. Yes——

ARTHUR. And you, Dickie?

DICKIE. Yes, Father.

ARTHUR. Grace?

GRACE. (*Helplessly.*) We thought it best you shouldn't know—
for the time being. Only for the time being, Arthur.

ARTHUR. (*Slowly.*) Is the boy very ill?

No one answers. ARTHUR *looks from one face to another in bewilderment.*

Answer me, someone! Is the boy very ill? Why must I be
kept in the dark like this? Surely I have the right to know.
If he's ill I must be with him——

CATHERINE. (*Steadily.*) No, Father. He's not ill.

ARTHUR *suddenly realizes the truth from her tone of voice.*

ARTHUR. Will someone tell me what has happened, please?

GRACE *looks at* CATHERINE *with helpless inquiry.*

CATHERINE *nods.* GRACE *takes a letter from her dress.*

GRACE. (*Timidly.*) He brought this letter for you—Arthur.

ARTHUR. Read it to me, please——

GRACE. Arthur—not in front of——

ARTHUR. Read it to me, please.

GRACE *again looks at* CATHERINE *for advice, and again receives a
nod.* GRACE *begins to read.*

GRACE. (*Reading.*) 'Confidential. I am commanded by My
Lords Commissioners of the Admiralty to inform you that
they have received a communication from the Commanding Officer of the Royal Naval College at Osborne, reporting

the theft of a five-shilling postal order at the College on the 7th instant, which was afterwards cashed at the Post Office. Investigation of the circumstances of the case leaves no other conclusion possible than that the postal order was taken by your son, Cadet Ronald Arthur Winslow. My Lords deeply regret that they must therefore request you to withdraw your son from the College.' It's signed by someone—I can't quite read his name——

She turns away quickly to hide her tears. CATHERINE *puts a comforting arm on her shoulder.* ARTHUR *has not changed his attitude. There is a pause, during which we can hear the sound of a gong in the hall outside.*

ARTHUR. (*At length.*) Desmond—be so good as to call Violet.

DESMOND *does so. There is another pause, until* VIOLET *comes in.*

VIOLET. Yes, sir.

ARTHUR. Violet, will you ask Master Ronnie to come down and see me, please?

GRACE. Arthur—he's in bed.

ARTHUR. You told me he wasn't ill.

GRACE. He's not at all well.

ARTHUR. Do as I say, please, Violet.

VIOLET. Very good, sir.

She goes out.

ARTHUR. Perhaps the rest of you would go in to luncheon? Grace, would you take them in?

GRACE. (*Hovering.*) Arthur—don't you think——

ARTHUR. (*Ignoring her.*) Dickie, will you decant that bottle of claret I brought up from the cellar? I put it on the sideboard in the dining-room.

DICKIE. Yes, Father.

He goes out.

ARTHUR. Will you go in, Desmond? And John?

The two men go out into the dining-room, in silence. GRACE *still hovers.*

GRACE. Arthur?

ARTHUR. Yes, Grace?

GRACE. Please don't—please don't—— (*She stops, uncertainly.*)

ARTHUR. What mustn't I do?

GRACE. Please don't forget he's only a child——

    ARTHUR *does not answer her.*

    CATHERINE *takes her mother's arm.*

CATHERINE. Come on, Mother.

She leads her mother to the dining-room door. At the door GRACE *looks back at* ARTHUR. *He has still not altered his position and is ignoring her. She goes into the dining-room, followed by* CATHERINE. ARTHUR *does not move after they are gone. After an appreciable pause there comes a timid knock on the door.*

ARTHUR. Come in.

    RONNIE *appears in the doorway. He is in a dressing-gown. He stands on the threshold.*

Come in and shut the door.

    RONNIE *closes the door behind him.*

Come over here.

    RONNIE *walks slowly up to his father.* ARTHUR *gazes at him steadily for some time, without speaking.*

(*At length.*) Why aren't you in your uniform?

RONNIE. (*Murmuring.*) It got wet.

ARTHUR. How did it get wet?

RONNIE. I was out in the garden in the rain.

ARTHUR. Why?

RONNIE. (*Reluctantly.*) I was hiding.

ARTHUR. From me?

    RONNIE *nods.*

Do you remember once, you promised me that if ever you were in trouble of any sort you would come to me first?

RONNIE. Yes, Father.

ARTHUR. Why didn't you come to me now? Why did you have to go and hide in the garden?

RONNIE. I don't know, Father.

ARTHUR. Are you so frightened of me?

    RONNIE *does not reply.* ARTHUR *gazes at him for a moment, then picks up the letter.*

In this letter it says you stole a postal order.

    RONNIE *opens his mouth to speak.*

    ARTHUR *stops him.*

Now, I don't want you to say a word until you've heard

what *I've* got to say. If you did it, you must tell me. I shan't
be angry with you, Ronnie—provided you tell me the truth.
But if you tell me a lie, I shall know it, because a lie between you and me can't be hidden. I shall know it, Ronnie
—so remember that before you speak. (*Pause.*) Did you steal
this postal order?

RONNIE. (*Without hesitation.*) No, Father. I didn't.

ARTHUR. (*Staring into his eyes.*) Did you steal this postal order?

RONNIE. No, Father. I didn't.

ARTHUR *continues to stare into his eyes for a second, then relaxes
and pushes him gently away.*

ARTHUR. Go on back to bed.

RONNIE *goes gratefully to the door.*

And in future I trust that a son of mine will at least show
enough sense to come in out of the rain.

RONNIE. Yes, Father.

He disappears. ARTHUR *gets up quite briskly and goes to the telephone
in the corner of the room.*

ARTHUR. (*At telephone.*) Hullo. Are you there? (*Speaking very
distinctly.*) I want to put a trunk call through, please. A
trunk call . . . Yes . . . The Royal Naval College, Osborne
. . . That's right . . . Replace receiver? Certainly.

*He replaces receiver and then, after a moment's meditation, turns and
walks briskly into the dining-room.*

CURTAIN

ACT II

SCENE: *The same, nine months later. It is about six o'clock, of a spring evening.*

DICKIE *is winding up his gramophone which, somehow or other, appears to have found its way back into the drawing-room. A pile of books and an opened notebook on the table provide evidence of interrupted labours.*

The gramophone, once started, emits a scratchy and muffled rendering of an early ragtime. DICKIE *listens for a few seconds with evident appreciation, then essays a little* pas seul.

CATHERINE *comes in. She is in evening dress.* DICKIE *switches off gramophone.*

DICKIE. Hullo. Do you think the old man can hear this upstairs?

CATHERINE. I shouldn't think so. I couldn't.

DICKIE. Soft needle and an old sweater down the horn. Is the doctor still with him?

CATHERINE *nods.*

What's the verdict, do you know?

CATHERINE. I heard him say Father needed a complete rest.

DICKIE. Don't we all.

CATHERINE. (*Indicating books.*) It doesn't look as if *you* did. He said he ought to go to the country and forget all his worries——

DICKIE. Fat chance there is of that, I'd say.

CATHERINE. I know.

DICKIE. I say, you look a treat. New dress?

CATHERINE. Is it likely? No, it's an old one I've had done up.

DICKIE. Where are you going to?

CATHERINE. Daly's. Dinner first—at the Cri.

DICKIE. Nice. You wouldn't care to take me along with you, I suppose?

CATHERINE. You suppose quite correctly.

DICKIE. John wouldn't mind.

109

CATHERINE. I dare say not. I would.

DICKIE. I wish I had someone to take me out. In your new feminist world do you suppose women will be allowed to do some of the paying?

CATHERINE. Certainly.

DICKIE. Really? Then the next time you're looking for someone to chain themselves to Mr. Asquith you can jolly well call on me——

CATHERINE. (*Laughing.*) Edwina might take you out if you gave her the hint. She's very rich——

DICKIE. If I gave Edwina a hint of that sort I wouldn't see her this side of doomsday.

CATHERINE. You sound a little bitter, Dickie dear.

DICKIE. Oh, no. Not bitter. Just realistic.

VIOLET *comes in with an evening paper on a salver.*

DICKIE. Good egg! The *Star*!

CATHERINE *makes a grab for it and gets it before* DICKIE.

VIOLET. You won't throw it away, will you, miss? If there's anything in it again, cook and I would like to read it, after you.

CATHERINE *is hastily turning over the pages, with* DICKIE *craning his head over her shoulder.*

CATHERINE. No. That's all right, Violet.

VIOLET *goes out.*

Here it is. (*Reading.*) 'The Osborne cadet.' There are two more letters. (*Reading.*) 'Sir. I am entirely in agreement with your correspondent, Democrat, concerning the scandalously high-handed treatment by the Admiralty of the case of the Osborne Cadet. The efforts of Mr. Arthur Winslow to secure a fair trial for his son have evidently been thwarted at every turn by a soulless oligarchy——'

DICKIE. Soulless oligarchy. That's rather good——

CATHERINE. —'it is high time private and peaceful citizens of this country awoke to the increasing encroachment of their ancient freedom by the new despotism of Whitehall. The Englishman's home was once said to be his castle. It seems it is rapidly becoming his prison. Your obedient servant, *Libertatis Amator*.'

DICKIE. Good for old Amator!

CATHERINE. The other's from Perplexed. (*Reading.*) 'Dear Sir. I cannot understand what all the fuss is about in the case of the Osborne Cadet. Surely we have more important matters to get ourselves worked up about than a fourteen-year-old boy and a five-shilling postal order.' Silly old fool!

DICKIE. How do you know he's old?

CATHERINE. Isn't it obvious? (*Reading.*) 'With the present troubles in the Balkans and a certain major European Power rapidly outbuilding our navy, the Admiralty might be forgiven if it stated that it had rather more urgent affairs to deal with than Master Ronnie Winslow's little troubles. A further inquiry before the Judge Advocate of the Fleet has now fully confirmed the original findings that the boy was guilty. I sincerely trust that this will finally end this ridiculous and sordid little storm in a teacup. I am, sir, etc., Perplexed.'

Pause.

DICKIE. (*Reading over her shoulder.*) 'This correspondence must now cease.—Editor.' Damn!

CATHERINE. Oh, dear! How hopeless it seems, sometimes.

DICKIE. Yes, it does, doesn't it? (*Thoughtfully, after a pause.*) You know, Kate—don't give me away to the old man, will you—but the awful thing is, if it hadn't been my own brother, I think I might quite likely have seen Perplexed's point.

CATHERINE. Might you?

DICKIE. Well, I mean—looking at it from every angle and all that—it does seem rather a much ado about damn all. I mean to say—a mere matter of pinching. (*Bitterly.*) And it's all so beastly expensive. Let's cheer ourselves up with some music. (*He sets machine going.*)

CATHERINE. (*Listening to the record.*) Is that what it's called?

DICKIE. Come and practise a few steps.

CATHERINE *joins him and they dance, in the manner of the period, with arms fully outstretched and working up and down, pump-handle style.*

(*Surprised.*) I say! Jolly good!

CATHERINE. Thank you, Dickie.

DICKIE. Who taught you? John, I suppose.

CATHERINE. No. I taught John, as it happens——

DICKIE. Feminism—even in love?

CATHERINE *nods, smiling. Pause, while they continue to dance.*
When's the happy date now?

CATHERINE. Postponed again.

DICKIE. Oh, no. Why?

CATHERINE. His father's gone abroad for six months.

DICKIE. Why pay any attention to that old—(*He substitutes the word.*)—gentleman?

CATHERINE. I wouldn't—but John does—so I have to.

Something in her tone makes DICKIE *stop dancing and gaze at her seriously.*

DICKIE. I say—nothing wrong, is there?

CATHERINE *shakes her head, smiling, but not too emphatically.*
I mean—you're not going to be left on the altar rails or anything, are you?

CATHERINE. Oh, no. I'll get him past the altar rails, if I have to drag him there.

DICKIE. (*As they resume their dance.*) Do you think you might have to?

CATHERINE. Quite frankly, yes.

DICKIE. Competition?

CATHERINE. Not yet. Only—differences of opinion.

DICKIE. I see. Well, take some advice from an old hand, will you?

CATHERINE. Yes, Dickie.

DICKIE. Suppress your opinions. Men don't like 'em in their lady friends, even if they agree with 'em. And if they don't —it's fatal. Pretend to be half-witted, like Edwina, then he'll adore you.

CATHERINE. I know. I do, sometimes, and then I forget. Still, you needn't worry. If there's ever a clash between what I believe and what I feel, there's not much doubt about which will win.

DICKIE. That's the girl. Of course, I don't know why you didn't fall in love with Ramsay MacDonald——

ARTHUR *comes in. He is walking with more difficulty than when we last saw him.* DICKIE *and* CATHERINE *hastily stop dancing, and* DICKIE *turns off the gramophone.*

CATHERINE. (*Quickly.*) It was entirely my fault, Father. I enticed Dickie from his work to show me a few dance steps.

ARTHUR. Oh? I must admit I am surprised you succeeded.

DICKIE. (*Getting off the subject.*) What did the doctor say, Father?

ARTHUR. He said, if I remember his exact words, that we weren't quite as well as when we last saw each other. That information seems expensive at a guinea. (*Seeing the evening paper.*) Oh, is that the *Star*? Let me see it, please.

CATHERINE *brings it over to him.*

John will be calling for you here, I take it?

CATHERINE. Yes, Father.

ARTHUR. It might be better, perhaps, if you didn't ask him in. This room will shortly be a clutter of journalists, solicitors, barristers, and other impedimenta.

CATHERINE. Is Sir Robert Morton coming to see you here?

ARTHUR. (*Deep in the* Star.) I could hardly go and see him, could I?

DICKIE, *in deference to his father's presence, has returned to his books.* ARTHUR *reads the* Star. CATHERINE *glances at herself in the mirror, and then wanders to the door.*

CATHERINE. I must go and do something about my hair.

DICKIE. What's the matter with your hair?

CATHERINE. Nothing, except I don't like it very much.

She goes out. DICKIE *opens two more books with a busy air and chews his pencil.* ARTHUR *finishes reading the* Star *and stares moodily into space.*

ARTHUR. (*At length.*) I wonder if I could sue "Perplexed".

DICKIE. It might be a way of getting the case into court.

ARTHUR. On the other hand, he has not been libellous. Merely base.

He throws the paper away and regards DICKIE *thoughtfully.*

DICKIE, *feeling his father's eye on him, is elaborately industrious.*

ARTHUR. (*At length, politely.*) Do you mind if I disturb you for a moment?

DICKIE. (*Pushing books away.*) No, Father.

ARTHUR. I want to ask you a question. But before I do I must impress on you the urgent necessity for an absolutely truthful answer.

DICKIE. Naturally.

ARTHUR. Naturally means by nature, and I'm afraid I have not yet noticed that it has invariably been your nature to answer my questions truthfully.

DICKIE. Oh. Well, I will, this one, Father, I promise.

ARTHUR. Very well. (*He stares at him for a moment.*) What do you suppose one of your bookmaker friends would lay in the way of odds against your getting a degree?

Pause.

DICKIE. Oh. Well, let's think. Say—about evens.

ARTHUR. Hm. I rather doubt if at that price your friend would find many takers.

DICKIE. Well—perhaps seven to four against.

ARTHUR. I see. And what about the odds against your eventually becoming a Civil Servant?

DICKIE. Well—a bit steeper, I suppose.

ARTHUR. Exactly. Quite a bit steeper.

Pause.

DICKIE. You don't want to have a bet, do you?

ARTHUR. No, Dickie. I'm not a gambler. And that's exactly the trouble. Unhappily I'm no longer in a position to gamble two hundred pounds a year on what you yourself admit is an outside chance.

DICKIE. Not an outside chance, Father. A good chance.

ARTHUR. Not good enough, Dickie, I'm afraid—with things as they are at the moment. Definitely not good enough. I fear my mind is finally made up.

There is a long pause.

DICKIE. You want me to leave Oxford—is that it?

ARTHUR. I'm very much afraid so, Dickie.

DICKIE. Oh. Straight away?

ARTHUR. No. You can finish your second year

DICKIE. And what then?

ARTHUR. I can get you a job in the bank.

DICKIE. (*Quietly.*) Oh, Lord!

Pause.

ARTHUR. (*Rather apologetically.*) It'll be quite a good job, you know. Luckily my influence in the bank still counts for something.

DICKIE *gets up and wanders about, slightly in a daze.*

DICKIE. Father—if I promised you—I mean, *really* promised you—that from now on I'll work like a black——

ARTHUR *shakes his head slowly.*

It's the case, I suppose?

ARTHUR. It's costing me a lot of money.

DICKIE. I know. It must be. Still, couldn't you—I mean, isn't there any way——

ARTHUR *again shakes his head.*

Oh, Lord!

ARTHUR. I'm afraid this is rather a shock for you. I'm sorry.

DICKIE. What? No. No, it isn't, really. I've been rather expecting it, as a matter of fact—especially since I've heard you are hoping to brief Sir Robert Morton. Still, I can't say but what it isn't a bit of a slap in the face.

There is a ring at the front door.

ARTHUR. There is a journalist coming to see me. Do you mind if we talk about this some other time?

DICKIE. No. Of course not, Father.

DICKIE *begins forlornly to gather his books.*

ARTHUR. (*With a half-smile.*) I should leave those there, if I were you.

DICKIE. Yes. I will. Good idea.

He goes to the door.

ARTHUR. (*Politely.*) Tell me—how is your nice friend, Miss Edwina Gunn, these days?

DICKIE. Very well, thanks awfully.

ARTHUR. You don't suppose she'd mind if you took her to the theatre—or gave her a little present perhaps?

DICKIE. Oh, I'm sure she wouldn't.

ARTHUR. I'm afraid I can only make it a couple of sovereigns.

ARTHUR *has taken out his sovereign case and now extracts two sovereigns.* DICKIE *comes and takes them.*

DICKIE. Thanks awfully, Father.

ARTHUR. With what's left over you can always buy something for yourself.

DICKIE. Oh. Well, as a matter of fact, I don't suppose there will be an awful lot left over. Still, it's jolly decent of you—I say, Father—I think I could do with a little spot of something. Would you mind?

ARTHUR. Of course not. You'll find the decanter in the dining-room.

DICKIE. Thanks awfully.

He goes to dining-room door.

ARTHUR. I must thank you, Dickie, for bearing what must have been a very unpleasant blow with some fortitude.

DICKIE. (*Uncomfortably.*) Oh. Rot, Father.

He goes out. ARTHUR *sighs deeply.*

VIOLET *comes in at the hall door.*

VIOLET. (*Announcing proudly.*) The *Daily News*!

MISS BARNES *comes in. She is a rather untidily dressed woman of about forty with a gushing manner.*

MISS BARNES. Mr. Winslow? So good of you to see me.

ARTHUR. How do you do?

MISS BARNES. (*Simpering.*) You're surprised to see a lady reporter? I know. Everyone is. And yet why not? What could be more natural?

ARTHUR. What indeed? Pray sit down——

MISS BARNES. My paper usually sends me out on stories which have a special appeal to women—stories with a little heart, you know, like this one—a father's fight for his little boy's honour——

ARTHUR *visibly winces.*

ARTHUR. I venture to think this case has rather wider implications than that——

MISS BARNES. Oh, yes. The political angle. I know. Very interesting but not *quite* my line of country. Now, what I'd really like to do—is to get a nice picture of you and your little boy together. I've brought my assistant and camera. They're in the hall. Where is your little boy?

ARTHUR. My son is arriving from school in a few minutes. His mother has gone to the station to meet him.

MISS BARNES. (*Making a note.*) From school? How interesting. So you got a school to take him? I mean, they didn't mind the unpleasantness?

ARTHUR. No.

MISS BARNES. And why is he coming back this time?

ARTHUR. He hasn't been expelled again, if that is what you're implying. He is coming to London to be examined by Sir Robert Morton, whom we are hoping to brief——

MISS BARNES. Sir Robert Morton! (*She whistles appreciatively.*) Well!

ARTHUR. Exactly.

MISS BARNES. (*Doubtingly.*) But do you *really* think he'll take a little case like this?

ARTHUR. (*Explosively.*) It is *not* a little case, madam——

MISS BARNES. No, no. Of course not. But still—Sir Robert Morton!

ARTHUR. I understand that he is the best advocate in the country. He is certainly the most expensive——

MISS BARNES. Oh, yes. I suppose if one is prepared to pay his fee one can get him for almost *any* case.

ARTHUR. Once more, madam—this is *not* almost any case——

MISS BARNES. No, no. Of course not. Well, now, perhaps you wouldn't mind giving me a few details. When did it all start?

ARTHUR. Nine months ago. The first I knew of the charge was when my son arrived home with a letter from the Admiralty informing me of his expulsion. I telephoned Osborne to protest and was referred by them to the Lords of the Admiralty. My solicitors then took the matter up, and demanded from the Admiralty the fullest possible inquiry. For weeks we were ignored, then met with a blank refusal, and only finally got reluctant permission to view the evidence.

MISS BARNES. (*Indifferently.*) Really?

ARTHUR. My solicitors decided that the evidence was highly unsatisfactory, and fully justified the re-opening of proceedings. We applied to the Admiralty for a Court Martial. They ignored us. We applied for a civil trial. They ignored us again.

MISS BARNES. They ignored you?

ARTHUR. Yes. But after tremendous pressure had been brought to bear—letters to the papers, questions in the House, and other means open to private citizens of this country—the Admiralty eventually agreed to what they called an independent inquiry.

MISS BARNES. (*Vaguely.*) Oh, good!

ARTHUR. It was not good, madam. At that independent inquiry, conducted by the Judge Advocate of the Fleet—against whom I am saying nothing, mind you—my son,—a child of fourteen, was not represented by counsel, solicitors, or friends. What do you think of that?

MISS BARNES. Fancy!

ARTHUR. You may well say fancy.

MISS BARNES. And what happened at the inquiry?

ARTHUR. What do you think happened? Inevitably he was found guilty again, and thus branded for the second time before the world as a thief and a forger——

MISS BARNES. (*Her attention wandering.*) What a shame!

ARTHUR. I need hardly tell you, madam, that I am not prepared to let the matter rest there. I shall continue to fight this monstrous injustice with every weapon and every means at my disposal. Now, it happens I have a plan——

MISS BARNES. Oh, what charming curtains! What are they made of? (*She rises and goes to window.*)

ARTHUR *sits for a moment in paralysed silence.*

ARTHUR (*At last.*) Madam—I fear I have no idea.

There is the sound of voices in the hall.

MISS BARNES. Ah. Do I hear the poor little chap himself?

The hall door opens and RONNIE *comes in boisterously, followed by* GRACE. *He is evidently in the highest of spirits.*

RONNIE. Hullo, Father! (*He runs to him.*)

ARTHUR. Hullo. Ronnie.

RONNIE. I say, Father! Mr. Moore says I'm to tell you I needn't come back until Monday if you like. So that gives me three whole days.

ARTHUR. Mind my leg!

RONNIE. Sorry, Father.

ARTHUR. How are you, my boy?

RONNIE. Oh, I'm absolutely tophole, Father. Mother says I've grown an inch——

MISS BARNES. Ah! Now that's exactly the way I'd like to take my picture. Would you hold it, Mr. Winslow? (*She goes to hall door and calls.*) Fred! Come in now, will you?

RONNIE. (*In a sibilant whisper.*) Who's she?

FRED *appears. He is a listless photographer, complete with apparatus.*

FRED. (*Gloomily.*) Afternoon, all.

MISS BARNES. That's the pose I suggest.

FRED. Yes. It'll do.

He begins to set up his apparatus. ARTHUR, *holding* RONNIE *close against him in the pose suggested, turns his head to* GRACE.

ARTHUR. Grace, dear, this lady is from the *Daily News.* She is extremely interested in your curtains.

GRACE. (*Delighted.*) Oh, really! How nice!

MISS BARNES. Yes, indeed. I was wondering what they were made of.

GRACE. Well, it's an entirely new material, you know. I'm afraid I don't know what it's called, but I got them at Barkers last year. Apparently it's a sort of mixture of wild silk and——

MISS BARNES. (*Now genuinely busy with her pencil and pad.*) Just a second, Mrs. Winslow. I'm afraid my shorthand isn't very good. I must just get that down——

RONNIE. (*To* ARTHUR.) Father, are we going to be in the *Daily News?*

ARTHUR. It appears so——

RONNIE. Oh, good! They get the *Daily News* in the school library and everyone's bound to see it——

FRED. Quite still, please——

He takes his photograph.

All right, Miss Barnes. (*He goes out.*)

MISS BARNES. (*Engrossed with* GRACE.) Thank you, Fred. (*To* ARTHUR.) Goodbye, Mr. Winslow, and the very best of good fortune in your inspiring fight. (*Turning to* RONNIE.) Goodbye, little chap. Remember, the darkest hour is just before the dawn. Well, it was very good of you to tell me all that, Mrs. Winslow. I'm sure our readers will be most interested.

GRACE *shows her out.*

RONNIE. What's she talking about?

ARTHUR. The case, I imagine.

RONNIE. Oh, the case. Father, do you know the train had fourteen coaches?

ARTHUR. Did it indeed?

RONNIE. Yes. All corridor.

ARTHUR. Remarkable.

RONNIE. Of course, it was one of the very biggest expresses. I walked all the way down it from one end to the other.

ARTHUR. I had your half-term report, Ronnie.

RONNIE. (*Suddenly silenced by perturbation.*) Oh, yes?

ARTHUR. On the whole it was pretty fair.

RONNIE. Oh, good.

ARTHUR. I'm glad you seem to be settling down so well. Very glad indeed.

GRACE *comes in.*

GRACE. What a charming woman, Arthur!

ARTHUR. Charming. I trust you gave her full details about our curtains?

GRACE. Oh, yes. I told her everything.

ARTHUR. (*Wearily.*) I'm so glad.

GRACE. I do think women reporters are a good idea——

RONNIE. (*Excitedly.*) I say, Father, will it be all right for me to stay still Monday? I mean, I won't be missing any work— only Divinity—— (*He jogs his father's leg again.*)

ARTHUR. Mind my leg!

RONNIE. Oh, sorry, Father. Is it bad?

ARTHUR. Yes, it is. (*To* GRACE.) Grace, take him upstairs and get him washed. Sir Robert will be here in a few minutes.

GRACE. (*To* RONNIE.) Come on, darling.

RONNIE. All right. (*On his way to the door with his mother.*) I say, do you know how long the train took? 123 miles in two hours and fifty-two minutes. That's an average of 46.73 recurring miles an hour—I worked it out. Violet! Violet! I'm back.

He disappears, still chattering shrilly.

GRACE *stops at the door.*

GRACE. Did the doctor say anything, dear?

ARTHUR. A great deal; but very little to the purpose.

GRACE. Violet says he left an ointment for your back. Four massages a day. Is that right?

ARTHUR. Something of the kind.

GRACE. I think you had better have one now, hadn't you, Arthur?

ARTHUR. No.

GRACE. But, dear, you've got plenty of time before Sir Robert comes, and if you don't have one now, you won't be able to have another before you go to bed.

ARTHUR. Precisely.

GRACE. But really, Arthur, it does seem awfully silly to spend all this money on doctors if you're not even going to do what they say.

ARTHUR. (*Impatiently.*) All right, Grace. All right. All right.

GRACE. Thank you, dear.

CATHERINE *comes in.*

CATHERINE. Ronnie's back, judging by the noise——

GRACE. (*Examining her.*) I must say that old frock has come out very well. John'll never know it isn't brand new——

CATHERINE. He's late, curse him.

ARTHUR. Grace, go on up and attend to Ronnie, and prepare the witch's brew for me. I'll come up when you are ready.

GRACE. Very well, dear. (*To* CATHERINE.) Yes, that does look good. I must say Mme Dupont's a treasure.

She goes out.

ARTHUR. (*Wearily.*) Oh, Kate, Kate! Are we both mad, you and I?

CATHERINE. What's the matter, Father?

ARTHUR. I don't know. I suddenly feel suicidally inclined. (*Bitterly.*) A father's fight for his little boy's honour. Special appeal to all women. Photo inset of Mrs. Winslow's curtains! Is there any hope for the world?

CATHERINE. (*Smiling.*) I think so, Father.

ARTHUR. Shall we drop the whole thing, Kate?

CATHERINE. I don't consider that a serious question, Father.

ARTHUR. (*Slowly.*) You realize that, if we go on, your marriage settlement must go?

CATHERINE. (*Lightly.*) Oh, yes. I gave that up for lost weeks ago.

ARTHUR. Things are all right between you and John, aren't they?

CATHERINE. Oh, yes, Father, of course. Everything's perfect.

ARTHUR. I mean—it won't make any difference between you, will it?

CATHERINE. Good heavens, no!

ARTHUR. Very well, then. Let us pin our faith to Sir Robert Morton.

CATHERINE *is silent.* ARTHUR *looks at her as if he had expected an answer, then nods.*

I see I'm speaking only for myself in saying that.

CATHERINE. (*Lightly.*) You know what I think of Sir Robert Morton, Father. Don't let's go into it again, now. It's too late, anyway.

ARTHUR. It's not too late. He hasn't accepted the brief yet.

CATHERINE. (*Shortly.*) Then I'm rather afraid I hope he never does. And that has nothing to do with my marriage settlement either.

Pause. ARTHUR *looks angry for a second, then subsides.*

ARTHUR. (*Mildly.*) I made inquiries about that fellow you suggested—I am told he is not nearly as good an advocate as Morton——

CATHERINE. He's not nearly so fashionable.

ARTHUR. (*Doubtfully.*) I want the best——

CATHERINE. The best in this case certainly isn't Morton.

ARTHUR. Then why does everyone say he is?

CATHERINE. (*Roused.*) Because if one happens to be a large monopoly attacking a Trade Union or a Tory paper libelling a Labour Leader, he *is* the best. But it utterly defeats me how you or anyone else could expect a man of his record to have even a tenth of his heart in a case where the boot is entirely on the other foot——

ARTHUR. Well, I imagine, if his heart isn't in it, he won't accept the brief.

CATHERINE. He might still. It depends what there is in it for him. Luckily there isn't much——

ARTHUR. (*Bitterly.*) There is a fairly substantial cheque——

CATHERINE. He doesn't want money. He must be a very rich man.

ARTHUR. What does he want, then?

CATHERINE. Anything that advances his interests.

ARTHUR *shrugs his shoulders. Pause.*

ARTHUR. I believe you are prejudiced because he spoke against woman's suffrage.

CATHERINE. I am. I'm prejudiced because he is always speaking against what is right and just. Did you read his speech in the House on the Trades Disputes Bill?

GRACE. (*Calling off.*) Arthur! Arthur!

ARTHUR. (*Smiling.*) Oh, well—in the words of the Prime Minister—let us wait and see.

He turns at the door. You're my only ally, Kate. Without you I believe I should have given up long ago.

CATHERINE. Rubbish.

ARTHUR. It's true. Still, you must sometimes allow me to make my own decisions. I have an instinct about Morton. CATHERINE *does not reply.*

(*Doubtfully.*) We'll see which is right—my instinct or your reason, eh?

He goes out.

CATHERINE. (*Half to herself.*) I'm afraid we will.

DICKIE *comes out of the dining-room door.*

DICKIE. (*Bitterly.*) Hullo, Kate.

CATHERINE. Hullo, Dickie.

DICKIE *crosses mournfully to the other door.*

What's the matter? Edwina jilted you or something?

DICKIE. Haven't you heard?

CATHERINE *shakes her head.*

I'm being scratched from the Oxford Stakes at the end of the year——

CATHERINE. Oh, Dickie! I'm awfully sorry——

DICKIE. Did you know it was in the wind?

CATHERINE. I knew there was a risk——

DICKIE. You might have warned a fellow. I fell plumb into the old man's trap. My gosh, I could just about murder that little brother of mine. (*Bitterly.*) What's he have to go about pinching postal orders for? And why the hell does he have to get himself nabbed doing it? Silly little blighter!

He goes out gloomily. There is a ring at the front-door. CATHERINE, *obviously believing it is* JOHN, *picks up her cloak and goes to the hall door.*

CATHERINE. (*Calling.*) All right, Violet. It's only Mr. Watherstone. I'll answer it.

She goes out. There is the sound of voices in the hall, and then CATHERINE *reappears, leading in* DESMOND *and* SIR ROBERT MORTON. SIR ROBERT *is a man in the early forties, cadaverous and immensely elegant. He wears a long overcoat, and carries his hat and stick. He looks rather a fop, and his supercilious expression bears out this view.*

(*As she re-enters.*) I'm so sorry. I was expecting a friend. Won't you sit down, Sir Robert! My father won't be long.

SIR ROBERT *bows slightly, and sits down on a hard chair, still in his overcoat.*

Won't you sit here? It's far more comfortable.

SIR ROBERT. No, thank you.

DESMOND. (*Fussing.*) Sir Robert has a most important dinner engagement, so we came a little early.

CATHERINE. I see.

DESMOND. I'm afraid he can only spare us a very few minutes of his most valuable time this evening. Of course, it's a long way for him to come—so far from his chambers—and very good of him to do it, too, if I may say so——

He bows to SIR ROBERT, *who bows slightly back.*

CATHERINE. I know. I can assure you we're very conscious of it.

SIR ROBERT *gives her a quick look, and a faint smile.*

DESMOND. Perhaps I had better advise your father of our presence——

CATHERINE. Yes, do, Desmond. You'll find him in his bedroom —having his back rubbed.

DESMOND. Oh. I see.

He goes out. There is a pause.

CATHERINE. Is there anything I can get you, Sir Robert? A whisky and soda or a brandy?

SIR ROBERT. No, thank you.

CATHERINE. Will you smoke?

SIR RQBERT. No, thank you.

CATHERINE. (*Holding her cigarette.*) I hope you don't mind me smoking?

SIR ROBERT. Why should I?

CATHERINE. Some people find it shocking.

SIR ROBERT. (*Indifferently.*) A lady in her own home is surely entitled to behave as she wishes.

Pause.

CATHERINE. Won't you take your coat off, Sir Robert?

SIR ROBERT. No, thank you.

CATHERINE. You find it cold in here? I'm sorry.

SIR ROBERT. It's perfectly all right.

Conversation languishes again. SIR ROBERT *looks at his watch.*

CATHERINE. What time are you dining?

SIR ROBERT. Eight o'clock.

CATHERINE. Far from here?

SIR ROBERT. Devonshire House.

CATHERINE. Oh. Then of course you mustn't on any account be late.

SIR ROBERT. No.

There is another pause.

CATHERINE. I suppose you know the history of this case, do you, Sir Robert?

SIR ROBERT. (*Examining his nails.*) I believe I have seen most of the relevant documents.

CATHERINE. Do you think we can bring the case into Court by a collusive action?

SIR ROBERT. I really have no idea——

CATHERINE. Curry and Curry seem to think that might hold——

SIR ROBERT. Do they? They are a very reliable firm.

Pause. CATHERINE *is on the verge of losing her temper.*

CATHERINE. I'm rather surprised that a case of this sort should interest you, Sir Robert.

SIR ROBERT. Are you?

CATHERINE. It seems such a very trivial affair, compared to most of your great forensic triumphs.

SIR ROBERT, *staring languidly at the ceiling, does not reply.*

I was in Court during your cross-examination of Len Rogers, in the Trades Union embezzlement case.

SIR ROBERT. Really?

CATHERINE. It was masterly.

SIR ROBERT. Thank you.

CATHERINE. I suppose you heard that he committed suicide a few months ago?

SIR ROBERT. Yes. I had heard.

CATHERINE. Many people believed him innocent, you know.

SIR ROBERT. So I understand. (*After a faint pause.*) As it happens, however, he was guilty.

GRACE *comes in hastily.*

GRACE. Sir Robert? My husband's so sorry to have kept you, but he's just coming.

SIR ROBERT. It's perfectly all right. How do you do?

CATHERINE. Sir Robert is dining at Devonshire House, Mother.

GRACE. Oh, really? Oh, then you have to be punctual, of course, I do see that. It's the politeness of princes, isn't it?

SIR ROBERT. So they say.

GRACE. In this case the other way round, of course. Ah, I think I hear my husband on the stairs. I hope Catherine entertained you all right?

SIR ROBERT. (*With a faint bow to* CATHERINE.) Very well, thank you.

ARTHUR *comes in, followed by* DESMOND.

ARTHUR. Sir Robert? I am Arthur Winslow.

SIR ROBERT. How do you do?

ARTHUR. I understand you are rather pressed for time.

GRACE. Yes. He's dining at Devonshire House——

ARTHUR. Are you indeed? My son should be down in a minute. I expect you will wish to examine him.

SIR ROBERT. (*Indifferently.*) Just a few questions. I fear that is all I will have time for this evening——

ARTHUR. I am rather sorry to hear that. He has made the journey especially from school for this interview and I was hoping that by the end of it I should know definitely yes or no if you would accept the brief.

DESMOND. (*Pacifically.*) Well, perhaps Sir Robert would consent to finish his examination some other time?

SIR ROBERT. It might be arranged.

ARTHUR. Tomorrow?

SIR ROBERT. Tomorrow is impossible. I am in Court all the morning and in the House of Commons for the rest of the day. (*Carelessly.*) If a further examination should prove necessary it will have to be some time next week.

ARTHUR. I see. Will you forgive me if I sit down. (*He sits in his usual chair.*) Curry has been telling me you think it might be possible to proceed by Petition of Right.

CATHERINE. What's a Petition of Right?

DESMOND. Well—granting the assumption that the Admiralty, as the Crown, can do no wrong——

CATHERINE. (*Murmuring.*) I thought that was exactly the assumption we refused to grant.

DESMOND. In law, I mean. Now, a subject can sue the Crown, nevertheless, by Petition of Right, redress being granted as a matter of grace—and the custom is for the Attorney-General—on behalf of the King—to endorse the Petition, and allow the case to come to Court.

SIR ROBERT. It is interesting to note that the exact words he uses on such occasions are: Let Right be done.

ARTHUR. Let Right be done? I like that phrase, sir.

SIR ROBERT. It has a certain ring about it—has it not? (*Languidly.*) Let Right be done.

RONNIE *comes in. He is in an Eton suit, looking very spick and span.*

ARTHUR. This is my son Ronald. Ronnie, this is Sir Robert Morton.

RONNIE. How do you do, sir?

ARTHUR. He is going to ask you a few questions. You must answer them all truthfully—as you always have. (*He begins to struggle out of his chair.*) I expect you would like us to leave——

SIR ROBERT. No. Provided, of course, that you don't interrupt.

(*To* CATHERINE.) Miss Winslow, will you sit down, please?
CATHERINE *takes a seat abruptly.*

SIR ROBERT. (*To* RONNIE.) Will you stand at the table, facing
me? (RONNIE *does so.*) That's right.

SIR ROBERT *and* RONNIE *now face each other across the table.* SIR
ROBERT *begins his examination very quietly.*

Now, Ronald, how old are you?

RONNIE. Fourteen and seven months.

SIR ROBERT. You were, then, thirteen and ten months old
when you left Osborne: is that right?

RONNIE. Yes, sir.

SIR ROBERT. Now I would like you to cast your mind back to
July 7th of last year. Will you tell me in your own words
exactly what happened to you on that day?

RONNIE. All right. Well, it was a half-holiday, so we didn't
have any work after dinner——

SIR ROBERT. Dinner? At one o'clock?

RONNIE. Yes. At least, until prep at seven.

SIR ROBERT. Prep at seven?

RONNIE. Just before dinner I went to the Chief Petty Officer
and asked him to let me have fifteen and six out of what I
had in the school bank——

SIR ROBERT. Why did you do that?

RONNIE. I wanted to buy an air pistol.

SIR ROBERT. Which cost fifteen and six?

RONNIE. Yes, sir.

SIR ROBERT. And how much money did you have in the school
bank at the time?

RONNIE. Two pounds three shillings.

ARTHUR. So you see, sir, what incentive could there possibly
be for him to steal five shillings?

SIR ROBERT. (*Coldly.*) I must ask you to be good enough not to
interrupt me, sir. (*To* RONNIE.) After you had withdrawn
the fifteen and six what did you do?

RONNIE. I had dinner.

SIR ROBERT. Then what?

RONNIE. I went to the locker-room and put the fifteen and six
in my locker.

SIR ROBERT. Yes. Then?

RONNIE. I went to get permission to go down to the Post Office. Then I went to the locker-room again, got out my money, and went down to the Post Office.

SIR ROBERT. I see. Go on.

RONNIE. I bought my postal order——

SIR ROBERT. For fifteen and six?

RONNIE. Yes. Then I went back to college. Then I met Elliot minor, and he said: 'I say, isn't it rot? Someone's broken into my locker and pinched a postal order. I've reported it to the P.O.'

SIR ROBERT. Those were Elliot minor's exact words?

RONNIE. He might have used another word for rot——

SIR ROBERT. I see. Continue——

RONNIE. Well, then just before prep I was told to go along and see Commander Flower. The woman from the Post Office was there, and the Commander said: 'Is this the boy?' and she said: 'It might be. I can't be sure. They all look so much alike.'

ARTHUR. You see? She couldn't identify him.

SIR ROBERT *glares at him.*

SIR ROBERT. (*To* RONNIE.) Go on.

RONNIE. Then she said: 'I only know that the boy who bought a postal order for fifteen and six was the same boy that cashed one for five shillings.' So the Commander said: 'Did you buy a postal order for fifteen and six?' And I said: 'Yes', and then they made me write Elliot minor's name on an envelope, and compared it to the signature on the postal order—then they sent me to the sanatorium and ten days later I was sacked—I mean—expelled.

SIR ROBERT. I see. (*Quietly.*) Did you cash a postal order belonging to Elliot minor for five shillings?

RONNIE. No, sir.

SIR ROBERT. Did you break into his locker and steal it?

RONNIE. No, sir.

SIR ROBERT. And that is the truth, the whole truth, and nothing but the truth?

RONNIE. Yes, sir.

DICKIE *has come in during this, and is standing furtively in the doorway, not knowing whether to come in or go out.* ARTHUR *waves him impatiently to a seat.*

SIR ROBERT. Right. When the Commander asked you to write Elliot's name on an envelope, how did you write it? With Christian name or initials?

RONNIE. I wrote Charles K. Elliot.

SIR ROBERT. Charles K. Elliot. Did you by any chance happen to see the forged postal order in the Commander's office?

RONNIE. Oh, yes. The Commander showed it to me.

SIR ROBERT. Before or after you had written Elliot's name on the envelope?

RONNIE. After.

SIR ROBERT. After. And did you happen to see how Elliot's name was written on the postal order?

RONNIE. Yes, sir. The same.

SIR ROBERT. The same? Charles K. Elliot?

RONNIE. Yes, sir.

SIR ROBERT. When you wrote on the envelope, what made you choose that particular form?

RONNIE. That was the way he usually signed his name——

SIR ROBERT. How did you know?

RONNIE. Well—he was a great friend of mine——

SIR ROBERT. That is no answer. How did you know?

RONNIE. I'd seen him sign things.

SIR ROBERT. What things?

RONNIE. Oh—ordinary things.

SIR ROBERT. I repeat: what things?

RONNIE. (*Reluctantly.*) Bits of paper.

SIR ROBERT. Bits of paper? And why did he sign his name on bits of paper?

RONNIE. I don't know.

SIR ROBERT. You do know. Why did he sign his name on bits of paper?

RONNIE. He was practising his signature.

SIR ROBERT. And you saw him?

RONNIE. Yes.

SIR ROBERT. Did he know you saw him?

RONNIE. Well—yes——

SIR ROBERT. In other words he showed you exactly how he wrote his signature?

RONNIE. Yes. I suppose he did.

SIR ROBERT. Did you practise writing it yourself?

RONNIE. I might have done.

SIR ROBERT. What do you mean you might have done? Did you or did you not?

RONNIE. Yes——

ARTHUR. (*Sharply.*) Ronnie! You never told me that.

RONNIE. It was only for a joke——

SIR ROBERT. Never mind whether it was for a joke or not. The fact is you practised forging Elliot's signature——

RONNIE. It wasn't forging——

SIR ROBERT. What do you call it then?

RONNIE. Writing.

SIR ROBERT. Very well. Writing. Whoever stole the postal order and cashed it also *wrote* Elliot's signature, didn't he?

RONNIE. Yes.

SIR ROBERT. And, oddly enough, in the exact form in which you had earlier been practising *writing* his signature——

RONNIE. (*Indignantly.*) I say. Which side are you on?

SIR ROBERT. (*Snarling.*) Don't be impertinent! Are you aware that the Admiralty sent up the forged postal order to Mr. Ridgely-Pearce—the greatest handwriting expert in England?

RONNIE. Yes.

SIR ROBERT. And you know that Mr. Ridgeley-Pearce affirmed that there was no doubt that the signature on the postal order and the signature you wrote on the envelope were by one and the same hand?

RONNIE. Yes.

SIR ROBERT. And you still say that you didn't forge that signature?

RONNIE. Yes, I do.

SIR ROBERT. In other words, Mr. Ridgeley-Pearce doesn't know his job?

RONNIE. Well, he's wrong anyway.

SIR ROBERT. When you went into the locker-room after dinner, were you alone?

RONNIE. I don't remember.

SIR ROBERT. I think you do. Were you alone in the locker-room?

RONNIE. Yes.

SIR ROBERT. And you knew which was Elliot's locker?

RONNIE. Yes. Of course.

SIR ROBERT. Why did you go in there at all?

RONNIE. I've told you. To put my fifteen and six away.

SIR ROBERT. Why?

RONNIE. I thought it would be safer.

SIR ROBERT. Why safer than your pocket?

RONNIE. I don't know.

SIR ROBERT. You had it in your pocket at dinner-time. Why this sudden fear for its safety?

RONNIE. (*Plainly rattled.*) I tell you, I don't know——

SIR ROBERT. It was rather an odd thing to do, wasn't it? The money was perfectly safe in your pocket. Why did you suddenly feel yourself impelled to put it away in your locker?

RONNIE. (*Almost shouting.*) I don't know.

SIR ROBERT. Was it because you knew you would be alone in the locker-room at that time?

RONNIE. No.

SIR ROBERT. Where was Elliot's locker in relation to yours?

RONNIE. Next to it, but one.

SIR ROBERT. Next, but one. What time did Elliot put his postal order in his locker?

RONNIE. I don't know. I didn't even know he had a postal order in his locker. I didn't know he had a postal order at all—

SIR ROBERT. Yet you say he was a great friend of yours——

RONNIE. He didn't tell me he had one.

SIR ROBERT. How very secretive of him! What time did you go to the locker-room?

RONNIE. I don't remember.

SIR ROBERT. Was it directly after dinner?

RONNIE. Yes. I think so.

SIR ROBERT. What did you do after leaving the locker-room?

RONNIE. I've told you. I went for permission to go to the Post Office.

SIR ROBERT. What time was that?

RONNIE. About a quarter past two.

SIR ROBERT. Dinner is over at a quarter to two. Which means that you were in the locker-room for half an hour?

RONNIE. I wasn't there all that time——

SIR ROBERT. How long were you there?

RONNIE. About five minutes.

SIR ROBERT. What were you doing for the other twenty-five?

RONNIE. I don't remember.

SIR ROBERT. It's odd that your memory is so good about some things and so bad about others——

RONNIE. Perhaps I waited outside the C.O.'s office.

SIR ROBERT. (*With searing sarcasm.*) Perhaps you waited outside the C.O.'s office! And perhaps no one saw you there either?

RONNIE. No. I don't think they did.

SIR ROBERT. What were you thinking about outside the C.O.'s office for twenty-five minutes?

RONNIE. (*Wildly.*) I don't even know if I was there. I can't remember. Perhaps I wasn't there at all.

SIR ROBERT. No. Perhaps you were still in the locker-room rifling Elliot's locker——

ARTHUR. (*Indignantly.*) Sir Robert, I must ask you——

SIR ROBERT. Quiet!

RONNIE. I remember now. I remember. Someone did see me outside the C.O.'s office. A chap called Casey. I remember I spoke to him.

SIR ROBERT. What did you say?

RONNIE. I said: 'Come down to the Post Office with me. I'm going to cash a postal order.'

SIR ROBERT. (*Triumphantly.*) *Cash* a postal order.

RONNIE. I mean get.

SIR ROBERT. You said cash. Why did you say cash if you meant get.

RONNIE. I don't know.

SIR ROBERT. I suggest cash was the truth.

RONNIE. No, no. It wasn't. It wasn't really. You're muddling me.

SIR ROBERT. You seem easily muddled. How many other lies have you told?

RONNIE. None. Really I haven't——

SIR ROBERT. (*Bending forward malevolently.*) I suggest your whole testimony is a lie——

RONNIE. No! It's the truth——

SIR ROBERT. I suggest there is barely one single word of truth in anything you have said either to me, or to the Judge Advocate, or to the Commander, I suggest that you broke into Elliot's locker, that you stole the postal order for five shillings belonging to Elliot, that you cashed it by means of forging his name——

RONNIE. (*Wailing.*) I didn't. I didn't.

SIR ROBERT. I suggest that you did it for a joke, meaning to give Elliot the five shillings back, but that when you met him and he said he had reported the matter you got frightened and decided to keep quiet——

RONNIE. No, no, no. It isn't true——

SIR ROBERT. I suggest that by continuing to deny your guilt you are causing great hardship to your own family, and considerable annoyance to high and important persons in this country——

CATHERINE. (*On her feet.*) That's a disgraceful thing to say!

ARTHUR. I agree.

SIR ROBERT. (*Leaning forward and glaring at* RONNIE *with the utmost venom.*) I suggest, that the time has at last come for you to undo some of the misery you have caused by confessing to us all now that you are a forger, a liar, and a thief!

RONNIE. (*In tears.*) I'm not! I'm not! I'm not! I didn't do it——

GRACE *has flown to his side and now envelops him.*

ARTHUR. This is outrageous, sir——

JOHN *appears at the door, dressed in evening clothes.*

JOHN. Kate, dear, I'm late. I'm most terribly sorry——

He stops short as he takes in the scene, with RONNIE *sobbing hysterically on his mother's breast, and* ARTHUR *and* CATHERINE *glaring indignantly at* SIR ROBERT, *who is engaged in putting his papers together.*

SIR ROBERT. (*To* DESMOND.) Can I drop you anywhere? My car is at the door.

DESMOND. Er—no—I thank you——

SIR ROBERT. (*Carelessly.*) Well, send all this stuff round to my chambers tomorrow morning, will you?

DESMOND. But—but will you need it now?

SIR ROBERT. Oh, yes. The boy is plainly innocent. I accept the brief.

He bows to ARTHUR *and* CATHERINE *and walks languidly to the door, past the bewildered* JOHN, *to whom he gives a polite nod as he goes out.* RONNIE *continues to sob hysterically.*

CURTAIN

ACT III

SCENE: *The same, nine months later. The time is about ten-thirty p.m.*

ARTHUR *is sitting in his favourite armchair, reading aloud from an evening paper, whose wide headline:* 'WINSLOW DEBATE: FIRST LORD REPLIES' *we can read on the front page. Listening to him are* RONNIE *and* GRACE, *though neither of them seems to be doing so with much concentration.* RONNIE *is finding it hard to keep his eyes open, and* GRACE, *darning socks in the other armchair, has evidently other and, to her, more important matters on her mind.*

ARTHUR. (*Reading.*) —'The Admiralty, during the whole of this long-drawn-out dispute, have at no time acted hastily or ill-advisedly, and it is a matter of mere histrionic hyperbole for the right honourable and learned gentleman opposite to characterize the conduct of my department as that of callousness so inhuman as to amount to deliberate malice towards the boy Winslow. Such unfounded accusations I can well choose to ignore. (An honourable Member: "You can't.") Honourable Members opposite may interrupt as much as they please, but I repeat—there is nothing whatever that the Admiralty has done, or failed to do, in the case of this cadet for which I, as First Lord, need to apologize. (Further Opposition interruptions.)' (*He stops reading and looks up.*) I must say it looks as if the First Lord's having rather a rough passage—— (*He breaks off, noticing* RONNIE'S *head has fallen back on the cushions and he is asleep.*) I trust my reading isn't keeping you awake. (*There is no answer.*) I say I trust my reading isn't keeping you awake! (*Again there is no answer. Helplessly.*) Grace!

GRACE. My poor sleepy little lamb! It's long past his bedtime, Arthur.

ARTHUR. Grace, dear—at this very moment your poor sleepy little lamb is the subject of a very violent and heated debate

136

in the House of Commons. I should have thought, in the circumstances, it might have been possible for him to contrive to stay awake for a few minutes past his bedtime——

GRACE. I expect he's over-excited.

ARTHUR *and* GRACE *both look at the tranquilly oblivious form on the sofa.*

ARTHUR. A picture of over-excitement. (*Sharply.*) Ronnie! (*No answer.*) Ronnie!

RONNIE. (*Opening his eyes.*) Yes, Father?

ARTHUR. I am reading the account of the debate. Would you like to listen, or would you rather go to bed?

RONNIE. Oh, I'd like to listen, of course, Father. I was listening, too, only I had my eyes shut——

ARTHUR. Very well. (*Reading.*) 'The First Lord continued amid further interruptions: The chief point of criticism against the Admiralty appears to centre in the purely legal question of the Petition of Right brought by Mr. Arthur Winslow and the Admiralty's demurrer thereto. Sir Robert Morton has made great play with his eloquent reference to the liberty of the individual menaced, as he puts it, by the new despotism of bureaucracy—and I was as moved as any honourable Member opposite by his resonant use of the words: Let Right be done—the time-honoured phrase with which in his opinion the Attorney-General should without question have endorsed Mr. Winslow's Petition of Right. Nevertheless, the matter is not nearly as simple as he appears to imagine. Cadet Ronald Winslow is a servant of the Crown, and has therefore no more right than any other member of His Majesty's forces to sue the Crown in open court. To allow him to do so would undoubtedly raise the most dangerous precedents. There is no doubt whatever in my mind that in certain cases private rights may have to be sacrificed for the public good——' (*He looks up.*) And what other excuse, pray, did Charles the First make for ship money and——'

RONNIE, *after a manful attempt to keep his eyes open by self-pinchings and other devices, has once more succumbed to oblivion.* (*Sharply.*) Ronnie! Ronnie!

RONNIE *stirs, turns over, and slides more comfortably into the cushions.*
Would you believe it!

GRACE. He's dead tired. I'd better take him up to his bed——

ARTHUR. No. If he must sleep, let him sleep there.

GRACE. Oh, but he'd be much more comfy in his little bed——

ARTHUR. I dare say: but the debate continues and until it's
ended the cause of it all will certainly not make himself
comfy in his little bed.

VIOLET *comes in.*

VIOLET. There are three more reporters in the hall, sir. Want
to see you very urgently. Shall I let them in?

ARTHUR. No. Certainly not. I issued a statement yesterday.
Until the debate is over I have nothing more to say. •

VIOLET. Yes, sir. That's what I told them, but they wouldn't go.

ARTHUR. Well, make them. Use force, if necessary.

VIOLET. Yes, sir. And shall I cut some sandwiches for Miss
Catherine, as she missed her dinner?

GRACE. Yes, Violet. Good idea.

VIOLET *goes out.*

VIOLET. (*Off.*) It's no good. No more statements.

Voices answer her, fading at length into silence. GRACE *puts a rug
over* RONNIE, *now sleeping very soundly.*

ARTHUR. Grace, dear——

GRACE. Yes?

ARTHUR. I fancy this might be a good opportunity of talking
to Violet.

GRACE. (*Quite firmly.*) No, dear.

ARTHUR. Meaning that it isn't a good opportunity? Or
meaning that you have no intention at all of ever talking to
Violet?

GRACE. I'll do it one day, Arthur. Tomorrow, perhaps. Not
now.

ARTHUR. I believe you'd do better to grasp the nettle. Delay
only adds to your worries——

GRACE. (*Bitterly.*) My worries? What do you know about my
worries?

ARTHUR. A good deal, Grace. But I feel they would be a lot
lessened if you faced the situation squarely.

GRACE. It's easy for you to talk, Arthur. You don't have to do it.

ARTHUR. I will, if you like.

GRACE. No, dear.

ARTHUR. If you explain the dilemma to her carefully—if you even show her the figures I jotted down for you yesterday —I venture to think you won't find her unreasonable.

GRACE. It won't be easy for her to find another place.

ARTHUR. We'll give her an excellent reference.

GRACE. That won't alter the fact that she's never been properly trained as a parlourmaid and—well—you know yourself how we're always having to explain her to people. No, Arthur, I don't mind how many figures she's shown, it's a brutal thing to do.

ARTHUR. Facts are brutal things.

GRACE. (*A shade hysterically.*) Facts? I don't think I know what facts are any more——

ARTHUR. The facts, at this moment, are that we have a half of the income we had a year ago and we're living at nearly the same rate. However you look at it that's bad economics——

GRACE. I'm not talking about economics, Arthur. I'm talking about ordinary, common or garden facts—things we took for granted a year ago and which now don't seem to matter any more.

ARTHUR. Such as?

GRACE. (*With rising voice.*) Such as a happy home and peace and quiet and an ordinary respectable life, and some sort of future for us and our children. In the last year you've thrown all that overboard, Arthur. There's your return for it, I suppose. (*She indicates the headline in the paper.*) And it's all very exciting and important, I'm sure, but it doesn't bring back any of the things that we've lost. I can only pray to God that you know what you're doing.

RONNIE *stirs in his sleep.* GRACE *lowers her voice at the end of her speech. There is a pause.*

ARTHUR. I know exactly what I'm doing, Grace. I'm going to publish my son's innocence before the world, and for that end I am not prepared to weigh the cost.

GRACE. But the cost may be out of all proportion——

ARTHUR. It may be. That doesn't concern me. I hate heroics, Grace, but you force me to say this. An injustice has been done. I am going to set it right, and there is no sacrifice in the world I am not prepared to make in order to do so.

GRACE. (*With sudden violence.*) Oh, I wish I could see the sense of it all! (*Pointing to* RONNIE.) He's perfectly happy, at a good school, doing very well. No one need ever have known about Osborne, if you hadn't gone and shouted it out to the whole world. As it is, whatever happens now, he'll go through the rest of his life as the boy in that Winslow case —the boy who stole that postal order——

ARTHUR. (*Grimly.*) The boy who didn't steal that postal order.

GRACE. (*Wearily.*) What's the difference? When millions are talking and gossiping about him, a did or a didn't hardly matters. The Winslow boy is enough. You talk about sacrificing everything for him: but when he's grown up he won't thank you for it, Arthur—even though you've given your life to—publish his innocence as you call it.

ARTHUR *makes an impatient gesture.*

Yes, Arthur—your life. You talk gaily about arthritis and a touch of gout and old age and the rest of it, but you know as well as any of the doctors what really is the matter with you. (*Nearly in tears.*) You're destroying yourself, Arthur, and me and your family besides. For what, I'd like to know? I've asked you and Kate to tell me a hundred times but you never will. For what, Arthur?

ARTHUR *has struggled painfully out of his seat and now approaches her.*

ARTHUR. (*Quietly.*) For Justice, Grace.

GRACE. That sounds very noble. Are you sure it's true? Are you sure it isn't just plain pride and self-importance and sheer brute stubbornness?

ARTHUR. (*Putting a hand out.*) No, Grace. I don't think it is. I really don't think it is——

GRACE. (*Shaking off his hand.*) No. This time I'm not going to cry and say I'm sorry, and make it all up again. I can stand anything if there is a reason for it. But for no reason at all, it's unfair to ask so much of me. It's unfair——

She breaks down. As ARTHUR *puts a comforting arm around her she pushes him off and goes out of the door.* RONNIE *has, meanwhile, opened his eyes.*

RONNIE. What's the matter, Father?

ARTHUR. (*Turning from the door.*) Your mother is a little upset——

RONNIE. (*Drowsily.*) Why? Aren't things going well?

ARTHUR. Oh, yes. (*Murmuring.*) Very well. (*He sits with more than his usual difficulty, as if he were utterly exhausted.*) Very well indeed.

RONNIE *contentedly closes his eyes again.*

(*Gently.*) You'd better go to bed now, Ronnie. You'll be more comfortable——

He sees RONNIE *is asleep again. He makes as if to wake him, then shrugs his shoulders and turns away.* VIOLET *comes in with sandwiches on a plate and a letter on a salver.*

Thank you, Violet.

VIOLET *puts the sandwiches on the table and hands* ARTHUR *the letter.* ARTHUR *puts it down on the table beside him without opening it.* VIOLET *turns to go out.*

ARTHUR. Oh, Violet——

VIOLET. (*Turning placidly.*) Yes, sir?

ARTHUR. How long have you been with us?

VIOLET. Twenty-four years come April, sir.

ARTHUR. As long as that?

VIOLET. Yes, sir. Miss Kate was that high when I first came. (*She indicates a small child.*) and Mr. Dickie hadn't even been thought of——

ARTHUR. I remember you coming to us now. I remember it well. What do you think of this case, Violet?

VIOLET. A fine old rumpus that is, and no mistake.

ARTHUR. It is, isn't it? A fine old rumpus.

VIOLET. There was a bit in the *Evening News*. Did you read it, sir.

ARTHUR. No. What did it say?

VIOLET. Oh, about how it was a fuss about nothing and a shocking waste of the Government's time, but how it was a good thing all the same because it could only happen in England——

ARTHUR. There seems to be a certain lack of logic in that argument——

VIOLET. Well, perhaps they put it a bit different, sir. Still, that's what it said all right. And when you think it's all because of our Master Ronnie—I have to laugh about it sometimes. I really do. Wasting the Government's time at his age! I never did. Well, wonders will never cease.

ARTHUR. I know. Wonders will never cease.

VIOLET. Well—would that be all, sir?

ARTHUR. Yes, Violet. That'll be all.

CATHERINE *comes in.*

CATHERINE. Good evening, Violet.

VIOLET. Good evening, miss.

She goes out.

CATHERINE. Hullo, Father. (*She kisses him. Indicating* RONNIE.) An honourable Member described that this evening as a piteous little figure, crying aloud to humanity for justice and redress. I wish he could see him now.

ARTHUR. (*Testily.*) It's long past his bedtime. What's happened? Is the debate over?

CATHERINE. As good as. The First Lord gave an assurance that in future there would be no inquiry at Osborne or Dartmouth without informing the parents first. That seemed to satisfy most Members——

ARTHUR. But what about *our* case? Is he going to allow us a fair trial?

CATHERINE. Apparently not.

ARTHUR. But that's iniquitous. I thought he would be forced to——

CATHERINE. I thought so, too. The House evidently thought otherwise.

ARTHUR. Will there be a division?

CATHERINE. There may be. If there is the Government will win.

ARTHUR. What is the motion?

CATHERINE. To reduce the First Lord's salary by a hundred pounds. (*With a faint smile.*) Naturally no one really wants to do that. (*Indicating sandwiches.*) Are these for me?

ARTHUR. Yes.

CATHERINE *starts to eat the sandwiches.*

So we're back where we started, then?

CATHERINE. It looks like it.

ARTHUR. The debate has done us no good at all?

CATHERINE. It's aired the case a little, perhaps. A few more thousand people will say to each other at breakfast to-morrow: 'That boy ought to be allowed a fair trial.'

ARTHUR. What's the good of that, if they can't make themselves heard?

CATHERINE. I think they can—given time.

ARTHUR. Given time?

Pause.

But didn't Sir Robert make any protest when the First Lord refused a trial?

CATHERINE. Not a verbal protest. Something far more spectacular and dramatic. He'd had his feet on the Treasury table and his hat over his eyes during most of the First Lord's speech—and he suddenly got up very deliberately, glared at the First Lord, threw a whole bundle of notes on the floor, and stalked out of the House. It made a magnificent effect. If I hadn't known I could have sworn he was genuinely indignant——

ARTHUR. Of course he was genuinely indignant. So would any man of feeling be——

CATHERINE. Sir Robert, Father dear, is not a man of feeling. I don't think any emotion at all can stir that fishy heart——

ARTHUR. Except perhaps a single-minded love of justice.

CATHERINE. Nonsense. A single-minded love of Sir Robert Morton.

ARTHUR. You're very ungrateful to him considering all he's done for us these last months——

CATHERINE. I'm not ungrateful, Father. He's been wonderful —I admit it freely. No one could have fought a harder fight.

ARTHUR. Well, then——

CATHERINE. It's only his motives I question. At least I *don't* question them at all. I know them.

ARTHUR. What are they?

CATHERINE. First—publicity—you know—look at me, the

staunch defender of the little man—and then second—a nice popular stick to beat the Government with. Both very useful to an ambitious man. Luckily for him we've provided them.

ARTHUR. Luckily for us too, Kate.

CATHERINE. Oh, I agree. But don't fool yourself about him, Father, for all that. The man is a fish, a hard, cold-blooded, supercilious, sneering fish.

VIOLET *enters*.

VIOLET. (*Announcing*.) Sir Robert Morton.

CATHERINE *chokes over her sandwich*.

SIR ROBERT *comes in*.

SIR ROBERT. Good evening.

CATHERINE. (*Still choking*.) Good evening.

SIR ROBERT. Something gone down the wrong way?

CATHERINE. Yes.

SIR ROBERT. May I assist? (*He pats her on the back.*)

CATHERINE. Thank you.

SIR ROBERT. (*To* ARTHUR.) Good evening sir. I thought I would call and give you an account of the day's proceedings, but I see your daughter has forestalled me.

CATHERINE. Did you know I was in the gallery?

SIR ROBERT. (*Gallantly*.) With such a charming hat, how could I have missed you?

ARTHUR. It was very good of you to call, sir, nevertheless——

SIR ROBERT. (*Seeing* RONNIE.) Ah. The *casus belli*—dormant——

ARTHUR *goes to wake him*.

SIR ROBERT. No, no. I beg of you. Please do not disturb his innocent slumbers.

CATHERINE. *Innocent* slumbers?

SIR ROBERT. Exactly. Besides, I fear since our first encounter he is, rather pardonably, a trifle nervous of me.

CATHERINE. Will you betray a technical secret, Sir Robert? What happened in that first examination to make you so sure of his innocence?

SIR ROBERT. Three things. First of all, he made far too many damaging admissions. A guilty person would have been much more careful and on his guard. Secondly, I laid him a trap; and thirdly, left him a loophole. Anyone who was guilty would have fallen into the one and darted through the other. He did neither.

CATHERINE. The trap was to ask him suddenly what time Elliot put the postal order in his locker, wasn't it?

SIR ROBERT. Yes.

ARTHUR. And the loophole?

SIR ROBERT. I then suggested to him that he had stolen the postal order for a joke—which, had he been guilty, he would surely have admitted to as being the lesser of two evils.

CATHERINE. I see. It was very cleverly thought out.

SIR ROBERT. (*With a little bow.*) Thank you.

ARTHUR. May we offer you some refreshment, Sir Robert? A whisky and soda?

SIR ROBERT. No thank you. Nothing at all.

ARTHUR. My daughter has told me of your demonstration during the First Lord's speech. She described it as— magnificent.

SIR ROBERT. (*With a glance at* CATHERINE.) Did she? That was good of her. It's a very old trick, you know. I've done it many times in the Courts. It's nearly always surprisingly effective——

CATHERINE *catches her father's eye and nods triumphantly.*

(*To* CATHERINE.) Was the First Lord at all put out by it—did you notice?

CATHERINE. How could he have failed to be? (*To* ARTHUR, *approaching his chair.*) I wish you could have seen it, Father— it was—— (*She notices the letter on the table beside* ARTHUR *and snatches it up with a sudden gesture. She examines the envelope.*) When did this come?

ARTHUR. A few minutes ago. Do you know the writing?

CATHERINE. Yes. (*She puts the letter back on the table.*)

ARTHUR. Whose is it?

CATHERINE. I shouldn't bother to read it, if I were you.

ARTHUR *looks at her, puzzled, then takes up the letter.*

ARTHUR. (*To* SIR ROBERT.) Will you forgive me?

SIR ROBERT. Of course.

ARTHUR *opens the letter and begins to read.* CATHERINE *watches him for a moment, and then turns with a certain forced liveliness to* SIR ROBERT.

CATHERINE. Well, what do you think the next step should be?

SIR ROBERT. I have already been considering that, Miss Winslow. I believe that perhaps the best plan would be to renew our efforts to get the Director of Public Prosecutions to act.

CATHERINE. (*With one eye on her father.*) But do you think there's any chance of that?

SIR ROBERT. Oh, yes. In the main it will chiefly be a question of making ourselves a confounded nuisance——

CATHERINE. We've certainly done that quite successfully so far—thanks to you——

SIR ROBERT. (*Suavely.*) Ah. That is perhaps the only quality I was born with—the ability to make myself a confounded nuisance.

He, too, has his eye on ARTHUR, *sensing something amiss.*

ARTHUR *finishes reading the letter.*

CATHERINE. (*With false vivacity.*) Father—Sir Robert thinks we might get the Director of Public Prosecutions to act——

ARTHUR. What?

SIR ROBERT. We were discussing how to proceed with the case——

ARTHUR. The case? (*He stares, a little blankly, from one to the other.*) Yes. We must think of that, mustn't we? (*Pause.*) How to proceed with the case? (*To* SIR ROBERT, *abruptly.*) I'm afraid I don't think, all things considered, that much purpose would be served by going on——

SIR ROBERT *and* CATHERINE *stare at him blankly.*

CATHERINE *goes quickly to him and snatches the letter from his lap. She begins to read.*

SIR ROBERT. (*With a sudden change of tone.*) Of course we must go on.

ARTHUR. (*In a low voice.*) It is not for you to choose, sir. The choice is mine.

SIR ROBERT. (*Harshly.*) Then you must reconsider it. To give up now would be insane.

ARTHUR. Insane? My sanity has already been called in question tonight—for carrying the case as far as I have.

SIR ROBERT. Whatever the contents of that letter, or whatever
has happened to make you lose heart, I insist that we
continue the fight——

ARTHUR. Insist? We? It is my fight—my fight alone—and it
is for me alone to judge when the time has come to give
up.

SIR ROBERT. (*Violently.*) But why give up? Why? In heaven's
name, man, why?

ARTHUR. (*Slowly.*) I have made many sacrifices for this case.
Some of them I had no right to make, but I made them
none the less. But there is a limit and I have reached it. I
am sorry, Sir Robert. More sorry, perhaps, than you are,
but the Winslow case is now closed.

SIR ROBERT. Balderdash!

ARTHUR *looks surprised at this unparliamentary expression.*
CATHERINE *has read and re-read the letter, and now breaks the*
silence in a calm, methodical voice.

CATHERINE. My father doesn't mean what he says, Sir Robert.

SIR ROBERT. I am glad to hear it.

CATHERINE. Perhaps I should explain this letter——

ARTHUR. No, Kate.

CATHERINE. Sir Robert knows so much about our family
affairs, Father, I don't see it will matter much if he learns a
little more. (*To* SIR ROBERT.) This letter is from a certain
Colonel Watherstone who is the father of the man I'm
engaged to. We've always known he was opposed to the
case, so it really comes as no surprise. In it he says that our
efforts to discredit the Admiralty in the House of Commons
today have resulted merely in our making the name of
Winslow a nation-wide laughing-stock. I think that's his
phrase. (*She consults the letter.*) Yes. That's right. A nation-
wide laughing-stock.

SIR ROBERT. I don't care for his English.

CATHERINE. It's not very good, is it? He goes on to say that
unless my father will give him a firm undertaking to drop
this whining and reckless agitation—I suppose he means

the case—he will exert every bit of influence he has over his son to prevent him marrying me.

SIR ROBERT. I see. An ultimatum.

CATHERINE. Yes—but a pointless one.

SIR ROBERT. He has no influence over his son?

CATHERINE. Oh, yes. A little, naturally. But his son is of age, and his own master——

SIR ROBERT. Is he dependent on his father for money?

CATHERINE. He gets an allowance. But he can live perfectly well—we both can live perfectly well without it.

Pause. SIR ROBERT *stares hard at her, then turns abruptly to* ARTHUR.

SIR ROBERT. Well, sir?

ARTHUR. I'm afraid I can't go back on what I have already said. I will give you a decision in a few days——

SIR ROBERT. Your daughter seems prepared to take the risk——

ARTHUR. I am not. Not, at least, until I know how great a risk it is——

SIR ROBERT. How do you estimate the risk, Miss Winslow?

Pause. CATHERINE, *for all her bravado, is plainly scared. She is engaged in lighting a cigarette as* SIR ROBERT *asks his question.*

CATHERINE. (*At length.*) Negligible.

SIR ROBERT *stares at her again. Feeling his eyes on her, she returns his glance defiantly. Pause.*

SIR ROBERT. (*Returning abruptly to his languid manner.*) I see. May I take a cigarette, too?

CATHERINE. Yes, of course. I thought you didn't smoke.

SIR ROBERT. Only occasionally. (*To* ARTHUR.) I really must apologize to you, sir, for speaking to you as I did just now. It was unforgivable.

ARTHUR. Not at all, sir. You were upset at giving up the case —and, to be frank, I liked you for it——

SIR ROBERT. (*With a deprecating gesture.*) It has been rather a tiring day. The House of Commons is a peculiarly exhausting place, you know. Too little ventilation, and far too much hot air—I really am most truly sorry.

ARTHUR. Please.

SIR ROBERT. (*Carelessly.*) Of course, you must decide about the

case as you wish. That really is a most charming hat, Miss
Winslow——

CATHERINE. I'm glad you like it.

SIR ROBERT. It seems decidedly wrong to me that a lady of
your political persuasion should be allowed to adorn herself
with such a very feminine allurement. It really looks so
awfully like trying to have the best of both worlds——

CATHERINE. I'm not a militant, you know, Sir Robert. I don't
go about breaking shop windows with a hammer or pouring
acid down pillar boxes.

SIR ROBERT. (*Languidly.*) I am truly glad to hear it. Both those
activities would be highly unsuitable in that hat——

CATHERINE *glares at him but suppresses an angry retort.*

I have never yet fully grasped what active steps you take
to propagate your cause, Miss Winslow.

CATHERINE. (*Shortly.*) I'm an organizing secretary at the West
London Branch of the Woman's Suffrage Association.

SIR ROBERT. Indeed? Is the work hard?

CATHERINE. Very.

SIR ROBERT. But not, I should imagine, particularly lucrative.

CATHERINE. The work is voluntary and unpaid.

SIR ROBERT. (*Murmuring.*) Dear me! What sacrifices you young
ladies seem prepared to make for your convictions——

VIOLET *enters.*

VIOLET. (*To Catherine.*) Mr. Watherstone is in the hall, miss.
Says he would like to have a word with you in private—
most particular——

Pause.

CATHERINE. Oh. I'll come out to him——

ARTHUR. No. See him in here.

He begins to struggle out of his chair. SIR ROBERT *assists him.*

You wouldn't mind coming to the dining-room, would you,
Sir Robert, for a moment?

SIR ROBERT. Not in the least.

CATHERINE. All right, Violet.

VIOLET. Will you come in, sir.

JOHN *comes in. He is looking depressed and anxious.* CATHERINE
greets him with a smile, which he returns only half-heartedly. This

exchange is lost on ARTHUR, *who has his back to them, but not on*
SIR ROBERT.

CATHERINE. Hello, John.

JOHN. Hullo. (*To* ARTHUR.) Good evening, sir.

ARTHUR. Good evening, John. (*He goes on towards dining-room.*)

CATHERINE. I don't think you've met Sir Robert Morton.

JOHN. No, I haven't. How do you do, sir?

SIR ROBERT. I think you promised me a whisky and soda.
(*Turning to* JOHN.) May I offer my very belated congratulations?

JOHN. Congratulations? Oh, yes. Thank you.

ARTHUR *and* SIR ROBERT *go into dining-room. There is a pause.*
CATHERINE *is watching* JOHN *with an anxious expression.*

JOHN. (*Indicating* RONNIE.) Is he asleep?

CATHERINE. Yes.

JOHN. Sure he's not shamming?

CATHERINE. Yes.

JOHN. (*After a pause.*) My father's written your father a letter.

CATHERINE. I know. I've read it.

JOHN. Oh.

CATHERINE. Did you?

JOHN. Yes. He showed it to me.

Pause. JOHN *is carefully not looking at her.*

(*At length.*) Well, what's his answer?

CATHERINE. My father? I don't suppose he'll send one.

JOHN. You think he'll ignore it?

CATHERINE. Isn't that the best answer to blackmail?

JOHN. (*Muttering.*) It was damned high-handed of the old
man, I admit.

CATHERINE. High-handed?

JOHN. I tried to get him not to send it——

CATHERINE. I'm glad.

JOHN. The trouble is—he's perfectly serious.

CATHERINE. I never thought he wasn't.

JOHN. If your father does decide to go on with the case, I'm
very much afraid he'll do everything he threatens.

CATHERINE. Forbid the match?

JOHN. Yes.

CATHERINE. (*Almost pleadingly.*) Isn't that rather an empty threat, John?

JOHN. (*Slowly.*) Well, there's always the allowance——

CATHERINE. (*Dully.*) Yes, I see. There's always the allowance.

JOHN. I tell you, Kate darling, this is going to need damned careful handling; otherwise we'll find ourselves in the soup.

CATHERINE. Without your allowance would we be in the soup?

JOHN. And without your settlement. My dear girl, of course we would. Dash it all, I can't even live on my pay as it is, but with two of us——

CATHERINE. I've heard it said that two can live as cheaply as one.

JOHN. Don't you believe it. Two can live as cheaply as two, and that's all there is to it.

CATHERINE. Yes, I see. I didn't know.

JOHN. Unlike you I have a practical mind, Kate. I'm sorry, but it's no good dashing blindly ahead without thinking of these things first. The problem has got to be faced.

CATHERINE. I'm ready to face it, John. What do you suggest?

JOHN. (*Cautiously.*) Well—I think you should consider very carefully before you take the next step——

CATHERINE. I can assure you we will, John. The question is— what *is* the next step?

JOHN. Well—this is the way I see it. I'm going to be honest now. I hope you don't mind——

CATHERINE. No. I should welcome it.

JOHN. Your young brother over there pinches or doesn't pinch a five-bob postal order. For over a year you and your father fight a magnificent fight on his behalf, and I'm sure everyone admires you for it——

CATHERINE. Your father hardly seems to——

JOHN. Well, he's a diehard. Like these old Admirals you've been up against. I meant ordinary reasonable people, like myself. But now look—you've had two inquiries, the Petition of Right case which the Admiralty had thrown out of Court, and the Appeal. And now, good heavens, you've had the whole damned House of Commons getting themselves worked up into a frenzy about it. Surely, darling, that's enough for you? My God! Surely the case can end there?

CATHERINE. (*Slowly.*) Yes. I suppose the case can end there.

JOHN. (*Pointing to* RONNIE.) *He* won't mind.

CATHERINE. No. I know he won't.

JOHN. Look at him! Perfectly happy and content. Not a care in the world. How do you know what's going on in his mind? How can you be so sure he didn't do it?

CATHERINE. (*Also gazing down at* RONNIE.) I'm not so sure he didn't.

JOHN. (*Appalled.*) Good Lord! Then why in heaven's name have you and your father spent all this time and money trying to prove his innocence?

CATHERINE. (*Quietly.*) His innocence or guilt aren't important to me. They are to my father. Not to me. I believe he didn't do it; but I may be wrong. To prove that he didn't do it is of hardly more interest to me than the identity of the college servant, or whoever it was, who did it. All that I care about is that people should know that a Government Department has ignored a fundamental human right and that it should be forced to acknowledge it. That's all that's important to me.

JOHN. But, darling, after all those long noble words, it does really resolve itself to a question of a fourteen-year-old kid and a five-bob postal order, doesn't it?

CATHERINE. Yes, it does.

JOHN. (*Reasonably.*) Well now, look. There's a European war blowing up, there's a coal strike on, there's a fair chance of civil war in Ireland, and there's a hundred and one other things on the horizon at the moment that I think you genuinely could call *important*. And yet, with all that on its mind, the House of Commons takes a whole day to discuss him (*pointing to* RONNIE) and his bally postal order. Surely you must see that's a little out of proportion——

Pause. CATHERINE *raises her head slowly.*

CATHERINE. (*With some spirit.*) All I know is, John, that if ever the time comes that the House of Commons has so much on its mind that it can't find time to discuss a Ronnie Winslow and his bally postal order, this country will be a far poorer place than it is now. (*Wearily.*) But you needn't go on, John dear. You've said quite enough. I entirely see your point of view.

JOHN. I don't know whether you realize that all this publicity you're getting is making the name of Winslow a bit of a—well——

CATHERINE. (*Steadily.*) A nation-wide laughing-stock, your father said.

JOHN. Well, that's putting it a bit steep. But people do find the case a bit ridiculous, you know. I mean, I get chaps coming up to me in the mess all the time and saying: 'I say, is it true you're going to marry the Winslow girl? You'd better be careful. You'll find yourself up in front of the House of Lords for pinching the Adjutant's bath.' Things like that. They're not awfully funny—

CATHERINE. That's nothing. They're singing a verse about us at the Alhambra—

> Winslow one day went to heaven
> And found a poor fellow in quod.
> The fellow said I didn't do it,
> So naturally Winslow sued God.

JOHN. Well, darling—you see——

CATHERINE. Yes. I see. (*Quietly.*) Do you want to marry me, John?

JOHN. What?

CATHERINE. I said: Do you want to marry me?

JOHN. Well, of course I do. You know I do. We've been engaged for over a year now. Have I ever wavered before?

CATHERINE. No. Never before.

JOHN. (*Correcting himself.*) I'm not wavering now. Not a bit— I'm only telling you what I think is the best course for us to take.

CATHERINE. But isn't it already too late? Even if we gave up the case, would you still want to marry—the Winslow girl?

JOHN. All that would blow over in no time.

CATHERINE. (*Slowly.*) And we'd have the allowance——

JOHN. Yes. We would.

CATHERINE. And that's so important——

JOHN. (*Quietly.*) It is, darling. I'm sorry, but you can't shame me into saying it isn't.

CATHERINE. I didn't mean to shame you——

JOHN. Oh, yes you did. I know that tone of voice.

CATHERINE. (*Humbly.*) I'm sorry.

JOHN. (*Confidently.*) Well, now—what's the answer?

CATHERINE. (*Slowly.*) I love you, John, and I want to be your wife.

JOHN. Well, then, that's all I want to know. Darling! I was sure nothing so stupid and trivial could possibly come between us.

He kisses her. She responds wearily. The telephone rings. After a pause she releases herself and picks up the receiver.

CATHERINE. Hullo . . . Yes . . . Will you wait a minute? (*She goes to the dining-room door and calls.*) Sir Robert! Someone wants you on the telephone——

SIR ROBERT *comes out of the dining-room.*

SIR ROBERT. Thank you. I'm so sorry to interrupt.

CATHERINE. You didn't. We'd finished our talk.

SIR ROBERT *looks at her inquiringly. She gives him no sign. He walks to the telephone.*

SIR ROBERT. (*Noticing sandwiches.*) How delicious. May I help myself?

CATHERINE. Do.

SIR ROBERT. (*Into receiver.*) Hello . . . Yes, Michael . . . F.E.? I didn't know he was going to speak . . . I see . . . Go on . . .

SIR ROBERT *listens, with closed eyelids, munching a sandwich, meanwhile.*

(*At length.*) Thank you, Michael.

He rings off. ARTHUR *has appeared in the dining-room doorway.*

SIR ROBERT. (*To* ARTHUR.) There has been a most interesting development in the House, sir.

ARTHUR. What?

SIR ROBERT. My secretary tells me that a barrister friend of mine who, quite unknown to me, was interested in the case, got on his feet shortly after nine-thirty and delivered one of the most scathing denunciations of a Government Department ever heard in the House. (*To* CATHERINE.) What a shame we missed it—his style is quite superb——

ARTHUR. What happened?

SIR ROBERT. The debate revived, of course, and the First Lord, who must have felt himself fairly safe, suddenly found himself under attack from all parts of the House. It appears that rather than risk a division he has this moment given an undertaking that he will instruct the Attorney-General to endorse our Petition of Right. The case of Winslow versus Rex can now therefore come to Court.

There is a pause. ARTHUR *and* CATHERINE *stare at him unbelievingly.* (*At length.*) Well, sir. What are my instructions?

ARTHUR. (*Slowly.*) The decision is no longer mine, sir. You must ask my daughter.

SIR ROBERT. What are my instructions, Miss Winslow?

CATHERINE *looks down at the sleeping* RONNIE. ARTHUR *is watching her intently.* SIR ROBERT, *munching sandwiches, is also looking at her.*

CATHERINE. (*In a flat voice.*) Do you need my instructions, Sir Robert? Aren't they already on the Petition? Doesn't it say: Let Right be done?

JOHN *makes a move of protest towards her. She does not look at him. He turns abruptly to the door.*

JOHN. (*Furiously.*) Kate! Good night.

He goes out. SIR ROBERT, *with languid speculation, watches him go.*

SIR ROBERT. (*His mouth full.*) Well, then—we must endeavour to see that it is.

CURTAIN

ACT IV

SCENE: *The same, about five months later. It is a stiflingly hot June day—nearly two years less one month since* RONNIE'S *dismissal from Osborne. The glass door to the garden stands open, and a bath chair, unoccupied, has been placed near by.* ON THE RISE OF THE CURTAIN *the stage is empty and the telephone is ringing insistently.*

DICKIE *comes in from the hall carrying a suitcase, evidently very hot, his straw hat pushed on to the back of his head and panting from his exertions. He is wearing a neat, dark blue suit, a sober tie, and a stiff collar. He puts the suitcase down and mops his face with his handkerchief. Then he goes to the hall door and calls:*

DICKIE. Mother! (*There is no reply.*) Violet! (*Again no reply.*) Anyone about?

He goes to the telephone—taking off the receiver.

Hullo . . . No, not senior—junior . . . I don't know where he is . . . *Daily Mail*? . . . No, I'm the brother . . . Elder brother —that's right . . . Well—I'm in the banking business . . . That's right. Following in father's footsteps . . . My views on the case? Well—I—er—I don't know I have any, except, I mean, I hope we win and all that . . . No, I haven't been in Court. I've only just arrived from Reading . . . Reading . . . Yes. That's where I work . . . Yes, I've come up for the last two days of the trial. Verdict's expected tomorrow, isn't it? . . . Twenty-two, last March . . . *Seven* years older . . . No. He was thirteen when it happened, but now he's fifteen . . . Well, I suppose, if I'm anything I'm a sort of Liberal-Conservative . . . Single . . . No. No immediate prospects. I say, is this at all interesting to you? . . . Well, a perfectly ordinary kid, just like any other—makes a noise, does fretwork, doesn't wash and all that . . . Doesn't wash . . . (*Alarmed.*) I say, don't take that too literally. I mean he does, sometimes . . . Yes. All right. Goodbye . . .

He rings off and exits through centre door. Telephone rings again. He

156

comes back to answer it, when GRACE *dressed for going out, comes out of the dining-room.*

GRACE. Oh, hullo, darling. When did you get here?

She picks up the telephone receiver.

(Into receiver.) Everyone out.

She rings off and embraces DICKIE.

You're thinner. I like your new suit.

DICKIE. Straight from Reading's Savile Row. Off the peg at three and a half guineas. *(Pointing to telephone.)* I say—does that go on all the time?

GRACE. All blessed day. The last four days it simply hasn't stopped.

DICKIE. I had to fight my way in through an army of reporters and people——

GRACE. Yes, I know. You didn't say anything, I hope, Dickie dear. It's better not to say a word——

DICKIE. I don't think I said anything much . . . *(Carelessly.)* Oh, yes. I did say that I personally thought he did it——

GRACE. *(Horrified.)* Dickie! You didn't! *(He is smiling at her.)* Oh, I see. It's a joke. You mustn't say things like that, even in fun, Dickie dear——

DICKIE. How's it all going?

GRACE. I don't know. I've been there all four days now and I've hardly understood a word that's going on. Kate says the judge is against us, but he seems a charming old gentleman to me. *(Faintly shocked.)* Sir Robert's so rude to him——

Telephone rings. GRACE *answers it automatically.*

Nobody in.

She rings off and turns to garden door.

(Calling.) Arthur! Lunch! I'll come straight down. Dickie's here. *(To* DICKIE.*)* Kate takes the morning session, then she comes home and relieves me with Arthur, and I go to the Court in the afternoons, so you can come with me as soon as she's in.

DICKIE. Will there be room for me?

GRACE. Oh, yes. They reserve places for the family. You never saw such crowds in all your life. And such excitement! Cheers and applause and people being turned out. It's thrilling—you'll love it, Dickie.

DICKIE. Well—if I don't understand a word——

GRACE. Oh, that doesn't matter. They all get so terribly worked up you find yourself getting worked up, too. Sir Robert and the Attorney-General go at each other hammer and tongs —you wait and hear them—all about Petitions and demurrers and prerogatives and things. Nothing to do with Ronnie at all—seems to me——

DICKIE. How did Ronnie get on in the witness box?

GRACE. Two days he was cross-examined. Two whole days. Imagine it, the poor little pet! I must say he didn't seem to mind much. He said two days with the Attorney-General wasn't nearly as bad as two minutes with Sir Robert. Kate says he made a very good impression with the jury——

DICKIE. How is Kate, Mother?

GRACE. Oh, all right. You heard about John, I suppose——

DICKIE. Yes. That's what I meant. How has she taken it?

GRACE. You can never tell with Kate. She never lets you know what she's feeling. We all think he's behaved very badly——

ARTHUR *appears at the garden door, walking very groggily.*

Arthur! You shouldn't have come up the stairs by yourself.

ARTHUR. I had little alternative.

GRACE. I'm sorry, dear. I was talking to Dickie.

GRACE *helps* ARTHUR *into the bath chair.*

ARTHUR. How are you, Dickie?

DICKIE. (*Shaking hands.*) Very well, thank you, Father.

ARTHUR. I've been forced to adopt this ludicrous form of propulsion. I apologize.

He wheels himself into the room and examines DICKIE.

You look very well. A trifle thinner, perhaps——

DICKIE. Hard work, Father.

ARTHUR. Or late hours?

DICKIE. You can't keep late hours in Reading.

ARTHUR. You could keep late hours anywhere. I've had quite a good report about you from Mr. Lamb.

DICKIE. Good egg! He's a decent old stick, the old baa-lamb. I took him racing last Saturday. Had the time of his life and lost his shirt.

ARTHUR. Did he? I have no doubt that, given the chance,

you'll succeed in converting the entire Reading branch of
the Westminster Bank into a bookmaking establishment.
Mr. Lamb says you've joined the Territorials.

DICKIE. Yes, Father.

ARTHUR. Why have you done that?

DICKIE. Well, from all accounts there's a fair chance of a bit
of a scrap quite soon. If there is I don't want it to be all
over before I can get in on it——

ARTHUR. If there is what you call a scrap you'll do far better
to stay in the bank——

DICKIE. Oh, no, Father. I mean, the bank's all right—but still
—a chap can't help looking forward to a bit of a change—I
can always go back to the bank afterwards——

The telephone rings. ARTHUR *takes receiver off and puts it down on
table.*

GRACE. Oh, no, dear. You can't do that.

ARTHUR. Why not?

GRACE. It annoys the exchange.

ARTHUR. I prefer to annoy the exchange rather than have the
exchange annoy me. (*To* GRACE.) Catherine's late. She was
in at half-past yesterday.

GRACE. Perhaps they're taking the lunch interval later today.

ARTHUR. Lunch interval? This isn't a cricket match. (*Looking
at her.*) Nor, may I say, is it a matinée at the Gáiety. Why
are you wearing that highly unsuitable get-up?

GRACE. Don't you like it, dear? I think it's Mme Dupont's
best.

ARTHUR. Grace—your son is facing a charge of theft and
forgery——

GRACE. Oh, dear! It's so difficult! I simply can't be seen in
the same old dress, day after day. (*A thought strikes her.*) I
tell you what, Arthur. I'll wear my black coat and skirt
tomorrow—for the verdict.

ARTHUR *glares at her, helplessly, then turns his chair to the
dining-room.*

ARTHUR. Did you say my lunch was ready?

GRACE. Yes, dear. It's only cold. I did the salad myself. Violet
and cook are at the trial.

DICKIE. Is Violet still with you? She was under sentence last time I saw you——

GRACE. She's been under sentence for the last six months, poor thing—only she doesn't know it. Neither your father nor I have the courage to tell her——

ARTHUR. (*Stopping at door.*) I have the courage to tell her.

GRACE. It's funny that you don't, then, dear.

ARTHUR. I will.

GRACE. (*Hastily.*) No, no, you mustn't. When it's to be done, I'll do it.

ARTHUR. You see, Dickie? These taunts of cowardice are daily flung at my head; but should I take them up I'm forbidden to move in the matter. Such is the logic of women.

He goes into the dining-room. DICKIE, *who has been holding the door open, closes it after him.*

DICKIE. (*Seriously.*) How *is* he?

GRACE *shakes her head quietly.*

Will you take him away after the trial?

GRACE. He's promised to go into a nursing home.

DICKIE. Do you think he will?

GRACE. How do I know? He'll probably find some new excuse——

DICKIE. But surely, if he loses this time, he's lost for good, hasn't he?

GRACE. (*Slowly.*) So they say, Dickie dear—I can only hope it's true.

DICKIE. How did you keep him away from the trial?

GRACE. Kate and Sir Robert together. He wouldn't listen to me or the doctor.

DICKIE. Poor old Mother! You must have been having a pretty rotten time of it, one way and another——

GRACE. I've said my say, Dickie. He knows what I think. Not that he cares. He never has—all his life. Anyway, I've given up worrying. He's always said he knew what he was doing. It's my job to try and pick up the pieces, I suppose.

CATHERINE *comes in.*

CATHERINE. Lord! The heat! Mother, can't you get rid of those reporters—Hullo, Dickie.

DICKIE. (*Embracing her.*) Hullo, Kate.

CATHERINE. Come to be in at the death.

DICKIE. Is that what it's going to be?

CATHERINE. Looks like it. I could cheerfully strangle that old brute of a judge, Mother. He's dead against us.

GRACE. (*Fixing her hat in the mirror.*) Oh, dear!

CATHERINE. Sir Robert's very worried. He said the Attorney-General's speech made a great impression on the jury. I must say it was very clever. To listen to him yesterday you would have thought that a verdict for Ronnie would simultaneously cause a mutiny in the Royal Navy and triumphant jubilation in Berlin.

ARTHUR *appears in his chair, at the dining-room door.*

ARTHUR. You're late, Catherine.

CATHERINE. I know, Father. I'm sorry. There was such a huge crowd outside as well as inside the Court that I couldn't get a cab. And I stayed to talk to Sir Robert.

GRACE. (*Pleased.*) Is there a bigger crowd even than yesterday, Kate?

CATHERINE. Yes, Mother. Far bigger.

ARTHUR. How did it go this morning?

CATHERINE. Sir Robert finished his cross-examination of the postmistress. I thought he'd demolished her completely. She admitted she couldn't identify Ronnie in the Commander's office. She admitted she couldn't be sure of the time he came in. She admitted that she was called away to the telephone while he was buying his fifteen-and-six postal order, and that all Osborne cadets looked alike to her in their uniforms, so that it might quite easily have been another cadet who cashed the five shillings. It was a brilliant cross-examination. So gentle and quiet. He didn't bully her, or frighten her—he just coaxed her into tying herself into knots. Then, when he'd finished the Attorney-General asked her again whether she was absolutely positive that the same boy that bought the fifteen-and-six postal order also cashed the five-shilling one. She said yes. She was quite, quite sure because Ronnie was such a good-looking little boy that she had specially noticed him. She hadn't said that in her examination-in-chief. I could see those twelve good men and true nodding away to each other. I believe it undid the whole of that magnificent cross-examination.

ARTHUR. If she thought him so especially good-looking, why couldn't she identify him the same evening?

CATHERINE. Don't ask me, Father. Ask the Attorney-General. I'm sure he has a beautifully reasonable answer.

DICKIE. Ronnie good-looking! What utter rot! She must be lying, that woman.

GRACE. Nonsense, Dickie! I thought he looked very well in the box yesterday, didn't you, Kate?

CATHERINE. Yes, Mother.

ARTHUR. Who else gave evidence for the other side?

CATHERINE. The Commander, the Chief Petty Officer, and one of the boys at the College.

ARTHUR. Anything very damaging?

CATHERINE. Nothing that we didn't expect. The boy showed obviously he hated Ronnie and was torn to shreds by Sir Robert. The Commander scored, though. He's an honest man and genuinely believes Ronnie did it.

GRACE. Did you see anybody interesting in Court, dear?

CATHERINE. Yes, Mother. John Watherstone.

GRACE. John? I hope you didn't speak to him, Kate.

CATHERINE. Of course I did.

GRACE. Kate, how could you! What did he say?

CATHERINE. He wished us luck.

GRACE. What impertinence! The idea of John Watherstone coming calmly up in Court to wish you luck—I think it's the most disgraceful, cold-blooded——

ARTHUR. Grace—you will be late for the resumption.

GRACE. Oh, will I? Are you ready, Dickie?

DICKIE. Yes, Mother.

GRACE. You don't think that nice, grey suit of yours you paid so much money for——

ARTHUR. What time are they resuming, Kate?

CATHERINE. Two o'clock.

ARTHUR. It's twenty past two now.

GRACE. Oh, dear! We'll be terribly late. Kate—that's your fault. Arthur, you must finish your lunch——

ARTHUR. Yes, Grace.

GRACE. Promise now.

ARTHUR. I promise.

GRACE. (*To herself.*) I wonder if Violet will remember to pick up those onions. Perhaps I'd better do it on the way back from the Court. (*As she passes* CATHERINE.) Kate, dear, I'm so sorry——

CATHERINE. What for, Mother?

GRACE. John proving such a bad hat. I never did like him very much, you know.

CATHERINE. No, I know.

GRACE. Now, Dickie, when you get to the front-door put your head down, like me, and just charge through them all.

ARTHUR. Why don't you go out by the garden?

GRACE. I wouldn't like to risk this dress getting through that hedge. Come on, Dickie. I always shout: 'I'm the maid and don't know nothing', so don't be surprised.

DICKIE. Right-oh, Mother.

GRACE *goes out.* DICKIE *follows her.*

There is a pause.

ARTHUR. Are we going to lose this case, Kate?

CATHERINE *quietly shrugs her shoulders.*

It's our last chance.

CATHERINE. I know.

ARTHUR. (*With sudden violence.*) We've got to win it.

CATHERINE *does not reply.*

What does Sir Robert think?

CATHERINE. He seems very worried.

ARTHUR. (*Thoughtfully.*) I wonder if you were right, Kate. I wonder if we could have had a better man.

CATHERINE. No, Father. We couldn't have had a better man.

ARTHUR. You admit that now, do you?

CATHERINE. Only that he's the best advocate in England and for some reason—prestige, I suppose—he seems genuinely anxious to win this case. I don't go back on anything else I've ever said about him.

ARTHUR. The papers said that he began today by telling the judge he felt ill and might have to ask for an adjournment. I trust he won't collapse——

CATHERINE. He won't. It was just another of those brilliant tricks of his that he's always boasting about. It got him the sympathy of the Court and possibly—no, I won't say that——

ARTHUR. Say it.

CATHERINE. (*Slowly.*) Possibly provided him with an excuse if he's beaten.

ARTHUR. You don't like him, do you?

CATHERINE. (*Indifferently.*) There's nothing in him to like or dislike, Father. I admire him.

DESMOND *appears at the garden door. Standing inside the room, he knocks diffidently.* CATHERINE *and* ARTHUR *turn and see him.*

DESMOND. I trust you do not object to me employing this rather furtive entry. The crowds at the front-door are most alarming——

ARTHUR. Come in, Desmond. Why have you left the Court?

DESMOND. My partner will be holding the fort. He is perfectly competent, I promise you.

ARTHUR. I'm glad to hear it.

DESMOND. I wonder if I might see Catherine alone. I have a matter of some urgency to communicate to her——

ARTHUR. Oh. Do you wish to hear this urgent matter, Kate?

CATHERINE. Yes, Father.

ARTHUR. Very well. I shall go and finish my lunch.

He wheels his chair to the dining-room door. DESMOND *flies to help.*

DESMOND. Allow me.

ARTHUR. Thank you. I can manage this vehicle without assistance.

He goes out.

DESMOND. I fear I should have warned you of my visit. Perhaps I have interrupted——

CATHERINE. No, Desmond. Please sit down.

DESMOND. Thank you. I'm afraid I have only a very short time. I must get back to Court for the cross-examination of the judge-advocate.

CATHERINE. Yes, Desmond. Well?

DESMOND. I have a taxicab waiting at the end of the street.

CATHERINE. (*Smiling.*) How very extravagant of you, Desmond.

DESMOND. (*Also smiling.*) Yes. But it shows you how rushed this visit must necessarily be. The fact of the matter is—it suddenly occurred to me during the lunch recess that I had far better see you today.

CATHERINE. (*Her thoughts far distant.*) Why?

DESMOND. I have a question to put to you, Kate, which, if I had postponed putting until after the verdict, you might— who knows—have thought had been prompted by pity—if we had lost. Or—if we had won, your reply might—again who knows—have been influenced by gratitude. Do you follow me, Kate?

CATHERINE. Yes, Desmond. I think I do.

DESMOND. Ah. Then possibly you have some inkling of what the question is I have to put to you?

CATHERINE. Yes. I think I have.

DESMOND. (*A trifle disconcerted.*) Oh.

CATHERINE. I'm sorry, Desmond. I ought, I know, to have followed the usual practice in such cases, and told you I had no inkling whatever.

DESMOND. No, no. Your directness and honesty are two of the qualities I so much admire in you. I am glad you have guessed. It makes my task the easier——

CATHERINE. (*In a matter-of-fact voice.*) Will you give me a few days to think it over?

DESMOND. Of course. Of course.

CATHERINE. I need hardly tell you how grateful I am, Desmond.

DESMOND. (*A trifle bewildered.*) There is no need, Kate. No need at all——

CATHERINE *has risen brusquely.*

CATHERINE. You mustn't keep your taxi waiting——

DESMOND. Oh, bother my taxi! (*Recovering himself.*) Forgive me, Kate, but you see I know very well what your feelings for me really are.

CATHERINE. (*Gently.*) You do, Desmond?

DESMOND. Yes, Kate. I know quite well they have never

amounted to much more than a sort of—well—shall we say, friendliness? As warm friendliness, I hope. Yes, I think perhaps we can definitely say, warm. But no more than that. That's true, isn't it?

CATHERINE. (*Quietly.*) Yes, Desmond.

DESMOND. I know, I know. Of course, the thing is that even if I proved the most devoted and adoring husband that ever lived—which, I may say—if you give me the chance, I intend to be—your feelings for me would never—could never—amount to more than that. When I was young it might, perhaps, have been a different story. When I played cricket for England——

He notices the faintest expression of pity that has crossed CATHERINE'S *face.*

(*Apologetically.*) And, of course, perhaps even that would not have made so much difference. Perhaps you feel I cling too much to my past athletic prowess. I feel it myself, sometimes—but the truth is I have not much else to cling to save that and my love for you. The athletic prowess is fading, I'm afraid, with the years and the stiffening of the muscles—but my love for you will never fade.

CATHERINE. (*Smiling.*) That's very charmingly said, Desmond.

DESMOND. Don't make fun of me, Kate, please. I meant it, every word. (*Clearing his throat.*) However, let's take a more mundane approach and examine the facts. Fact one: You don't love me, and never can. Fact two: I love you, always have, and always will. That is the situation—and it is a situation which, after most careful consideration, I am fully prepared to accept. I reached this decision some months ago, but thought at first it would be better to wait until this case, which is so much on all our minds, should be over. Then at lunch today I determined to anticipate the verdict tomorrow, and let you know what was in my mind at once. No matter what you feel or don't feel for me, no matter what you feel for anyone else, I want you to be my wife.

Pause.

CATHERINE. (*At length.*) I see. Thank you, Desmond. That makes everything much clearer.

DESMOND. There is much more that I had meant to say, but I shall put it in a letter.

CATHERINE. Yes, Desmond. Do.

DESMOND. Then I may expect your answer in a few days?

CATHERINE. Yes, Desmond.

DESMOND. (*Looking at his watch.*) I must get back to Court. (*He collects his hat, stick, and gloves.*) How did you think it went this morning?

CATHERINE. I thought the postmistress restored the Admiralty's case with that point about Ronnie's looks——

DESMOND. Oh, no, no. Not at all. There is still the overwhelming fact that she couldn't identify him. What a brilliant cross-examination, was it not?

CATHERINE. Brilliant.

DESMOND. He is a strange man, Sir Robert. At times, so cold and distant and—and——

CATHERINE. Fishlike.

DESMOND. Fishlike, exactly. And yet he has a real passion about this case. A real passion. I happen to know—of course this must on no account go any further—but I happen to know that he has made a very, very great personal sacrifice in order to bring it to court.

CATHERINE. Sacrifice? What? Of another brief?

DESMOND. No, no. That is no sacrifice to him. No—he was offered—you really promise to keep this to yourself?

CATHERINE. My dear Desmond, whatever the Government offered him can't be as startling as all that; he's in the Opposition.

DESMOND. As it happens it was quite startling, and a most graceful compliment, if I may say so, to his performance as Attorney-General under the last Government.

CATHERINE. What was he offered, Desmond?

DESMOND. The appointment of Lord Chief Justice. He turned it down simply in order to be able to carry on with the case of Winslow versus Rex. Strange are the ways of men are they not? Goodbye, my dear.

CATHERINE. Goodbye, Desmond.

Exit DESMOND.

CATHERINE *turns from the window deep in thought. She has a puzzled, strained expression. It does not look as though it were Desmond she was thinking of.* ARTHUR *opens dining-room door and peers round.*

ARTHUR. May I come in now?

CATHERINE. Yes, Father. He's gone.

ARTHUR. I'm rather tired of being gazed at from the street while eating my mutton, as though I were an animal at the Zoo.

CATHERINE. (*Slowly.*) I've been a fool, Father.

ARTHUR. Have you, my dear?

CATHERINE. An utter fool.

ARTHUR *waits for* CATHERINE *to make herself plain. She does not do so.*

ARTHUR. In default of further information, I can only repeat, have you, my dear?

CATHERINE. There can be no further information. I'm under a pledge of secrecy.

ARTHUR. Oh. What did Desmond want?

CATHERINE. To marry me.

ARTHUR. I trust the folly you were referring to wasn't your acceptance of him?

CATHERINE. (*Smiling.*) No, Father. (*She comes and sits on the arm of his chair.*) Would it be such folly, though?

ARTHUR. Lunacy.

CATHERINE. Oh, I don't know. He's nice, and he's doing very well as a solicitor.

ARTHUR. Neither very compelling reasons for marrying him.

CATHERINE. Seriously—I shall have to think it over.

ARTHUR. Think it over, by all means. But decide against it.

CATHERINE. I'm nearly thirty, you know.

ARTHUR. Thirty isn't the end of life.

CATHERINE. It might be—for an unmarried woman, with not much looks.

ARTHUR. Rubbish.

CATHERINE *shakes her head.*

Better far to live and die an old maid than to marry Desmond.

CATHERINE. Even an old maid must eat. (*Pause.*)

ARTHUR. I am leaving you and your mother everything, you know.

CATHERINE. (*Quietly.*) Everything?

ARTHUR. There is still a little left. (*Pause.*) Did you take my suggestion as regards your Suffrage Association?

CATHERINE. Yes, Father.

ARTHUR. You demanded a salary?

CATHERINE. I asked for one.

ARTHUR. And they're going to give it to you, I trust?

CATHERINE. Yes, Father. Two pounds a week.

ARTHUR. (*Angrily.*) That's insulting.

CATHERINE. No. It's generous. It's all they can afford. We're not a very rich organization—you know.

ARTHUR. You'll have to think of something else.

CATHERINE. What else? Darning socks? That's about my only other accomplishment.

ARTHUR. There must be something useful you can do.

CATHERINE. You don't think the work I am doing at the W.S.A. is useful?

ARTHUR *is silent.*

You may be right. But it's the only work I'm fitted for, all the same. (*Pause.*) No, Father. The choice is quite simple. Either I marry Desmond and settle down into quite a comfortable and not really useless existence—or I go on for the rest of my life earning two pounds a week in the service of a hopeless cause.

ARTHUR. A hopeless cause? I've never heard you say that before.

CATHERINE. I've never felt it before.

ARTHUR *is silent.* CATHERINE *leans her head against his chair.*

CATHERINE. John's going to get married next month.

ARTHUR. Did he tell you?

CATHERINE. Yes. He was very apologetic.

ARTHUR. Apologetic!

CATHERINE. He didn't need to be. It's a girl I know slightly. She'll make him a good wife.

ARTHUR. Is he in love with her?

CATHERINE. No more than he was with me. Perhaps, even, a little less.

ARTHUR. Why is he marrying her so soon after—after——

CATHERINE. After jilting me? Because he thinks there's going to be a war. If there is, his regiment will be among the first to go overseas. Besides, his father approves strongly. She's a general's daughter. Very, very suitable.

ARTHUR. Poor Kate!

Pause. He takes her hand slowly.

How I've messed up your life, haven't I?

CATHERINE. No, Father. Any messing-up that's been done has been done by me.

ARTHUR. I'm so sorry, Kate. I'm so sorry.

CATHERINE. Don't be, Father. We both knew what we were doing.

ARTHUR. Did we?

CATHERINE. I think we did.

ARTHUR. Yet our motives seem to have been different all along —yours and mine, Kate? Can we both have been right?

CATHERINE. I believe we can. I believe we have been.

ARTHUR. And yet they've always been so infernally logical, our opponents, haven't they?

CATHERINE. I'm afraid logic has never been on our side.

ARTHUR. Brute stubbornness—a selfish refusal to admit defeat. That's what your mother thinks have been our motives——

CATHERINE. Perhaps she's right. Perhaps that's all they've been.

ARTHUR. But perhaps brute stubbornness isn't such a bad quality in the face of injustice?

CATHERINE. Or in the face of tyranny. (*Pause.*) If you could go back, Father, and choose again—would your choice be different?

ARTHUR. Perhaps.

CATHERINE. I don't think so.

ARTHUR. I don't think so, either.

CATHERINE. I still say we both knew what we were doing. And we were right to do it.

ARTHUR *kisses the top of her head.*

ARTHUR. Dear Kate. Thank you.

There is a silence. A newsboy can be heard dimly, shouting from the street outside.

You aren't going to marry Desmond, are you?

CATHERINE. (*With a smile.*) In the words of the Prime Minister, Father—wait and see.

He squeezes her hand. The newsboy can still be heard—now a little louder.

ARTHUR. What's that boy shouting, Kate?

CATHERINE. Only—Winslow case—Latest.

ARTHUR. It didn't sound to me like 'Latest'.

CATHERINE *gets up to listen at the window. Suddenly we hear it quite plainly: 'Winslow Case Result! Winslow Case Result!'* Result?

CATHERINE. There must be some mistake.

There is another sudden outburst of noise from the hall as the front-door is opened. It subsides again. VIOLET *comes in quickly with a broad smile.*

VIOLET. Oh, sir! Oh, sir!

ARTHUR. What's happened?

VIOLET. Oh, Miss Kate, what a shame you missed it! Just after they come back from lunch, and Mrs. Winslow she wasn't there neither, nor Master Ronnie. The cheering and the shouting and the carrying-on—you never heard anything like it in all your life—and Sir Robert standing there at the table with his wig on crooked and the tears running down his face—running down his face they were, and not able to speak because of the noise. Cook and me we did a bit of crying too, we just couldn't help it—you couldn't, you know. Oh, it was lovely! We did enjoy ourselves. And then cook had her hat knocked over her eyes by the man behind who was cheering and waving his arms about something chronic, and shouting about liberty—you would have laughed, miss, to see her, she was that cross—but she didn't mind really, she was only pretending, and we kept on cheering and the judge kept on shouting, but it wasn't any good, because even the jury joined in, and some of them climbed out of the box to shake hands with Sir Robert. And then

outside in the street it was just the same—you couldn't move
for the crowd, and you'd think they'd all gone mad the way
they were carrying on. Some of them were shouting 'Good
old Winslow!' and singing 'For he's a jolly good fellow',
and cook had her hat knocked off again. Oh, it was lovely!
(*To* ARTHUR.) Well, sir, you must be feeling nice and
pleased, now it's all over?

ARTHUR. Yes, Violet. I am.

VIOLET. That's right. I always said it would come all right in
the end, didn't I?

ARTHUR. Yes. You did.

VIOLET. Two years all but one month it's been, now, since
Master Ronnie come back that day. Fancy.

ARTHUR. Yes.

VIOLET. I don't mind telling you, sir, I wondered sometimes
whether you and Miss Kate weren't just wasting your time
carrying on the way you have all the time. Still—you
couldn't have felt that if you'd been in Court today——

She turns to go and stops.

Oh, sir, Mrs. Winslow asked me to remember most particular to pick up some onions from the greengrocer, but——

CATHERINE. That's all right, Violet. I think Mrs. Winslow is
picking them up herself, on her way back——

VIOLET. I see, miss. Poor Madam! What a sell for her when she
gets to the Court and finds it's all over. Well, sir—congratulations, I'm sure.

ARTHUR. Thank you, Violet.

Exit VIOLET.

ARTHUR. It would appear, then, that we've won.

CATHERINE. Yes, Father, it would appear that we've won.

She breaks down and cries, her head on her father's lap.

ARTHUR. (*Slowly.*) I would have liked to have been there.

Pause.

Enter VIOLET.

VIOLET. (*Announcing.*) Sir Robert Morton!

SIR ROBERT *walks calmly and methodically into the room. He looks
as spruce and neat as ever, and* VIOLET's *description of him in
Court does not seem to tally with his composed features.*

CATHERINE *jumps up hastily and dabs her eyes.*

Exit VIOLET.

SIR ROBERT. I thought you might like to hear the actual terms of the Attorney-General's statement—— (*He pulls out a scrap of paper.*) So I jotted it down for you. (*Reading.*) 'I say now, on behalf of the Admiralty, that I accept the declaration of Ronald Arthur Winslow that he did not write the name on the postal order, that he did not take it and that he did not cash it, and that consequently he was innocent of the charge which was brought against him two years ago. I make that statement without any reservation of any description, intending it to be a complete acceptance of the boy's statements.'

He folds the paper up and hands it to ARTHUR.

ARTHUR. Thank you, sir. It is rather hard for me to find the words I should speak to you.

SIR ROBERT. Pray do not trouble yourself to search for them, sir. Let us take these rather tiresome and conventional expressions of gratitude for granted, shall we? Now, on the question of damages and costs. I fear we shall find the Admiralty rather niggardly. You are likely still to be left considerably out of pocket. However, doubtless we can apply a slight spur to the First Lord's posterior in the House of Commons——

ARTHUR. Please, sir—no more trouble—I beg. Let the matter rest here. (*He shows the piece of paper.*) This is all I have ever asked for.

SIR ROBERT. (*Turning to* CATHERINE.) A pity you were not in Court, Miss Winslow. The verdict appeared to cause quite a stir.

CATHERINE. So I heard. Why did the Admiralty throw up the case?

SIR ROBERT. It was a foregone conclusion. Once the hand-writing expert had been discredited—not for the first time in legal history—I knew we had a sporting chance, and no jury in the world would have convicted on the postmistress's evidence.

CATHERINE. But this morning you seemed so depressed.

SIR ROBERT. Did I? The heat in the courtroom was very trying, you know. Perhaps I was a little fatigued——

Enter VIOLET.

VIOLET. (*To* ARTHUR.) Oh, sir, the gentlemen at the front door
say please will you make a statement. They say they won't
go away until you do.

ARTHUR. Very well, Violet. Thank you.

VIOLET. Yes, sir.

Exit VIOLET.

ARTHUR. What shall I say?

SIR ROBERT. (*Indifferently.*) I hardly think it matters. Whatever
you say will have little bearing on what they write.

ARTHUR. What shall I say, Kate?

CATHERINE. You'll think of something, Father.

She begins to wheel his chair towards the door.

ARTHUR. (*Sharply.*) No! I refuse to meet the Press in this ridiculous chariot. (*To* CATHERINE.) Get me my stick!

CATHERINE. (*Protestingly.*) Father—you know what the doctor——

ARTHUR. Get me my stick!

   CATHERINE, *without more ado, gets his stick for him. She and* SIR
   ROBERT *help him out of his chair.*

   How is this? I am happy to have lived long enough to have
   seen justice done to my son——

CATHERINE. It's a little gloomy, Father. You're going to live
for ages yet——

ARTHUR. Am I? Wait and see. I could say: This victory is not
mine. It is the people who have triumphed—as they always
will triumph—over despotism. How does that strike you,
sir? A trifle pretentious, perhaps.

SIR ROBERT. Perhaps, sir. I should say it, none the less. It will
be very popular.

ARTHUR. Hm! Perhaps I had better say what I really feel,
which is merely: Thank God we beat 'em.

He goes out. SIR ROBERT *turns abruptly to* CATHERINE.

SIR ROBERT. Miss Winslow—might I be rude enough to ask
you for a little of your excellent whisky?

CATHERINE. Of course.

She goes into the dining-room. SIR ROBERT, *left alone, droops his shoulders wearily. He subsides into a chair. When* CATHERINE *comes back with the whisky he straightens his shoulders instinctively, but does not rise.*

SIR ROBERT. That is very kind. Perhaps you would forgive me not getting up? The heat in that courtroom was really so infernal.

He takes the glass from her and drains it quickly. She notices his hand is trembling slightly.

CATHERINE. Are you feeling all right, Sir Robert?

SIR ROBERT. Just a slight nervous reaction—that's all. Besides, I have not been feeling myself all day. I told the Judge so, this morning, if you remember, but I doubt if he believed me. He thought it was a trick. What suspicious minds people have, have they not?

CATHERINE. Yes.

SIR ROBERT. (*Handing her back the glass.*) Thank you.

CATHERINE *puts the glass down, then turns slowly back to face him as if nerving herself for an ordeal.*

CATHERINE. Sir Robert—I'm afraid I have a confession and an apology to make to you.

SIR ROBERT. (*Sensing what is coming.*) Dear lady—I am sure the one is rash and the other superfluous. I would far rather hear neither——

CATHERINE. (*With a smile.*) I am afraid you must. This is probably the last time I shall see you and it is a better penance for me to say this than to write it. I have entirely misjudged your attitude to this case, and if in doing so I have ever seemed to you either rude or ungrateful, I am sincerely and humbly sorry.

SIR ROBERT. (*Indifferently.*) My dear Miss Winslow, you have never seemed to me either rude or ungrateful. And my attitude to this case has been the same as yours—a determination to win at all costs. Only—when you talk of gratitude— you must remember that those costs were not mine, but yours.

CATHERINE. Weren't they also yours, Sir Robert?

SIR ROBERT. I beg your pardon?

CATHERINE. Haven't you too made a certain sacrifice for the case?

Pause.

SIR ROBERT. The robes of that office would not have suited me.

CATHERINE. Wouldn't they?

SIR ROBERT. (*With venom.*) And what is more, I fully intend to have Curry expelled from the Law Society.

CATHERINE. Please don't. He did me a great service by telling me——

SIR ROBERT. I must ask you never to divulge it to another living soul, and even to forget it yourself.

CATHERINE. I shall never divulge it. I'm afraid I can't promise to forget it myself.

SIR ROBERT. Very well. If you choose to endow an unimportant incident with a romantic significance, you are perfectly at liberty to do so. I must go. (*He gets up.*)

CATHERINE. Why are you always at such pains to prevent people knowing the truth about you, Sir Robert?

SIR ROBERT. Am I, indeed?

CATHERINE. You know you are. Why?

SIR ROBERT. Perhaps because *I* do not know the truth about myself.

CATHERINE. That is no answer.

SIR ROBERT. My dear Miss Winslow, are you cross-examining me?

CATHERINE. On this point, yes. Why are you so ashamed of your emotions?

SIR ROBERT. Because, as a lawyer, I must necessarily distrust them.

CATHERINE. Why?

SIR ROBERT. To fight a case on emotional grounds, Miss Winslow, is the surest way of losing it. Emotions muddy the issue. Cold, clear logic—and buckets of it—should be the lawyer's only equipment.

CATHERINE. Was it cold, clear logic that made you weep today at the verdict?

Pause.

SIR ROBERT. Your maid, of course, told you that? It doesn't

matter. It will be in the papers tomorrow, anyway. (*Fiercely.*) Very well, then, if you must have it, here it is. I wept today because right had been done.

CATHERINE. Not justice?

SIR ROBERT. No. Not justice. Right. It is easy to do justice— very hard to do right. Unfortunately, while the appeal of justice is intellectual, the appeal of right appears for some odd reason to induce tears in court. That is my answer and my excuse. And now, may I leave the witness box?

CATHERINE. No. One last question. How can you reconcile your support of Winslow against the Crown with your political beliefs?

SIR ROBERT. Very easily. No one party has a monopoly of concern for individual liberty. On that issue all parties are united.

CATHERINE. I don't think so.

SIR ROBERT. You don't?

CATHERINE. No. Not all parties. Only some people from all parties.

SIR ROBERT. That is a wise remark. We can only hope, then, that those same people will always prove enough people. You would make a good advocate.

CATHERINE. Would I?

SIR ROBERT. Yes. (*Playfully.*) Why do you not canalize your feministic impulses towards the law courts, Miss Winslow, and abandon the lost cause of women's suffrage?

CATHERINE. Because I don't believe it *is* a lost cause.

SIR ROBERT. No? Are you going to continue to pursue it?

CATHERINE. Certainly.

SIR ROBERT. You will be wasting your time.

CATHERINE. I don't think so.

SIR ROBERT. A pity. In the House of Commons in days to come I shall make a point of looking up at the Gallery in the hope of catching a glimpse of you in that provocative hat.

RONNIE *comes in. He is fifteen now, and there are distinct signs of an incipient man-about-town. He is very smartly dressed in lounge suit and homburg hat.*

RONNIE. I say, Sir Robert, I'm most awfully sorry. I didn't know anything was going to happen.

SIR ROBERT. Where were you?

RONNIE. At the pictures.

SIR ROBERT. Pictures? What is that?

CATHERINE. Cinematograph show.

RONNIE. I'm most awfully sorry. I say—we won, didn't we?

SIR ROBERT. Yes. We won. Goodbye, Miss Winslow. Shall I see you in the House then, one day?

CATHERINE. (*With a smile.*) Yes, Sir Robert. One day. But not in the Gallery. Across the floor.

SIR ROBERT. (*With a faint smile.*) Perhaps. Goodbye. (*He turns to go.*)

CURTAIN

THE BROWNING VERSION

The Browning Version was first produced at the Phoenix Theatre, London, on September 8th, 1948, with the following cast:

JOHN TAPLOW	...	...	...	*Peter Scott*
FRANK HUNTER	...	...	...	*Hector Ross*
MILLIE CROCKER-HARRIS	...			*Mary Ellis*
ANDREW CROCKER-HARRIS	...			*Eric Portman*
DR. FROBISHER	...	...	...	*Campbell Cotts*
PETER GILBERT	...	...	...	*Anthony Oliver*
MRS. GILBERT	...	...	...	*Henryetta Edwards*

The play directed by PETER GLENVILLE

SCENE: The sitting-room of the Crocker-Harrises' rooms in a public school in the South of England.

THE BROWNING VERSION

SCENE: *The sitting-room of the Crocker-Harrises' rooms in a public school in the South of England. It is between six and seven o'clock on a July evening. The building in which the rooms are situated is large and Victorian, and at some fairly recent date has been converted into flats of varying size for masters, married and unmarried. The Crocker-Harrises have the ground floor and their sitting-room is probably the biggest—and gloomiest—room in the house. It boasts, however, access (through a stained-glass door, L.) to a small garden, and is furnished with chintzy and genteel cheerfulness. Another door, back R., leads into the hall and the rest of the flat. This door is concealed by a screen.*

The room is empty at the rise of the curtain, but we hear the front-door opening and closing and, immediately after, a timorous knock on the door, repeated after a pause.

Finally the door opens and JOHN TAPLOW *makes his appearance. He is a plain, moon-faced boy of about sixteen, with glasses. He stands in doubt at the door for a moment, then goes back into the hall, where we hear him calling.*

TAPLOW. (*Calling off.*) Sir! Sir!

After a pause, he re-enters. He is dressed in grey flannels, a dark blue coat, and white scarf. He goes to the garden door and opens it.

(*Calling.*) Sir!

There is no reply. TAPLOW, *standing in the bright sunshine at the door, emits a plaintive sigh, then closes it firmly and goes to a table on which he places a book, a notebook, and a pen.*

On the table is a small box of chocolates, probably the Crocker-Harrises' ration for the month. TAPLOW *opens the box, counts the number inside, and removes two. One of these he eats and the other, after a second's struggle, either with his conscience or his judgment of what he might be able to get away with, he virtuously replaces in the box. Finally he picks up a walking-stick with a crooked handle and makes a couple of golf swings, with an air of great concentration.*

181

FRANK HUNTER *appears from behind the screen covering the door. He is a rugged young man—not perhaps quite as rugged as his deliberately-cultivated manner of ruthless honesty makes him appear, but wrapped in all the self-confidence of the popular master. He watches* TAPLOW, *whose back is to the door, making his swing.*

FRANK. Roll the wrists away from the ball. Don't break them like that.

He walks over quickly and puts his large hands over the abashed TAPLOW'S.

Now swing.

TAPLOW, *guided by* FRANK'S *evidently expert hands, succeeds in hitting the carpet with more effect than before.*

Too quick. Slow back and stiff left arm. It's no good just whacking the ball as if you were the headmaster and the ball was you. It'll never go more than fifty yards if you do. Get a rhythm. A good golf swing is a matter of aesthetics, not of brute strength.

TAPLOW, *only half-listening, is gazing at the carpet.*

FRANK. What's the matter?

TAPLOW. I think we've made a tear in the carpet, sir.

FRANK *examines the carpet perfunctorily.*

FRANK. Nonsense. That was there already. (*He puts the stick in a corner of the room.*) Do I know you?

TAPLOW. No, sir.

FRANK. What's your name?

TAPLOW. Taplow.

FRANK. Taplow! No, I don't. You're not a scientist I gather?

TAPLOW. No, sir. I'm still in the lower fifth. I can't specialize until next term—that's to say if I've got my remove all right.

FRANK. Don't you know yet if you've got your remove?

TAPLOW. No, sir. Mr. Crocker-Harris doesn't tell us the results like the other masters.

FRANK. Why not?

TAPLOW. Well, you know what he's like, sir.

FRANK. I believe there *is* a rule that form results should only be announced by the headmaster on the last day of term.

TAPLOW. Yes—but who else pays any attention to it—except Mr. Crocker-Harris?

FRANK. I don't, I admit—but that's no criterion. So you've got to wait until tomorrow to know your fate, have you?

TAPLOW. Yes, sir.

FRANK. Supposing the answer is favourable—what then?

TAPLOW. Oh—science, sir, of course.

FRANK. (*Sadly.*) Yes. We get all the slackers.

TAPLOW. (*Protestingly.*) I'm extremely interested in science, sir.

FRANK. Are you? I'm not. Not at least in the science I have to teach.

TAPLOW. Well, anyway, sir, it's a good deal more exciting than this muck. (*Indicating his book.*)

FRANK. What is this muck?

TAPLOW. Aeschylus, sir. The *Agamemnon*.

FRANK. And your considered view is that the *Agamemnon* of Aeschylus is muck, is it?

TAPLOW. Well, no, sir. I don't think the play is muck—exactly. I suppose, in a way, it's rather a good plot, really, a wife murdering her husband and having a lover and all that. I only meant the way it's taught to us—just a lot of Greek words strung together and fifty lines if you get them wrong.

FRANK. You sound a little bitter, Taplow.

TAPLOW. I am rather, sir.

FRANK. Kept in, eh?

TAPLOW. No, sir. Extra work.

FRANK. Extra work—on the last day of school?

TAPLOW. Yes, sir—and I might be playing golf. You'd think *he'd* have enough to do anyway himself, considering he's leaving tomorrow for good—but oh no. I missed a day last week when I had 'flu—so here I am—and look at the weather, sir.

FRANK. Bad luck. Still, there's one consolation. You're pretty well bound to get your remove tomorrow for being a good boy in taking extra work.

TAPLOW. Well, I'm not so sure, sir. That would be true of the ordinary masters, all right. They just wouldn't dare not give a chap a remove after his taking extra work—it would be such a bad advertisement for them. But those sort of rules don't apply to the Crock—Mr. Crocker-Harris. I asked him

yesterday outright if he'd given me a remove and do you
know what he said, sir?

FRANK. No. What?

TAPLOW. (*Mimicking a very gentle, rather throaty voice.*) 'My dear
Taplow, I have given you exactly what you deserve. No
less; and certainly no more.' Do you know, sir, I think he
may have marked me down, rather than up, for taking
extra work. I mean, the man's barely human. (*He breaks off
quickly.*) Sorry, sir. Have I gone too far?

FRANK. Yes. Much too far.

TAPLOW. Sorry, sir. I got sort of carried away.

FRANK. Evidently. (*He picks up* The Times *and opens it.*) Er—
Taplow.

TAPLOW. Yes, sir?

FRANK. What was that Mr. Crocker-Harris said to you? Just
—er—repeat it, would you?

TAPLOW. (*Mimicking again.*) 'My dear Taplow, I have given you
exactly what you deserve. No less; and certainly no more.'

FRANK *snorts, then looks stern.*

FRANK. Not in the least like him. Read your nice Aeschylus
and be quiet.

TAPLOW. (*With weary disgust.*) Aeschylus.

FRANK. Look, what time did Mr. Crocker-Harris tell you to be
here?

TAPLOW. Six-thirty, sir.

FRANK. Well, he's ten minutes late. Why don't you cut? You
could still get nine holes in before lock-up.

TAPLOW. (*Genuinely shocked.*) Oh, no, I couldn't cut. Cut the
Crock—Mr. Crocker-Harris? I shouldn't think it's ever
been done in the whole time he's been here. God knows
what would happen if I did. He'd probably follow me
home, or something——

FRANK. I must admit I envy him the effect he seems to have on
you boys in his form. You all seem scared to death of him.
What does he do—beat you all, or something?

TAPLOW. Good lord, no. He's not a sadist, like one or two of
the others.

FRANK. I beg your pardon?

TAPLOW. A sadist, sir, is someone who gets pleasure out of giving pain.

FRANK. Indeed? But I think you went on to say that some other masters——

TAPLOW. Well, of course they are, sir. I won't mention names, but you know them as well as I do. Of course I know most masters think we boys don't understand a thing—but dash it, sir, you're different. You're young—well comparatively anyway—and you're science and you canvassed for Labour in the last election. You must know what sadism is.

FRANK. (*After a pause.*) Good lord! What are public schools coming to?

TAPLOW. Anyway the Crock isn't a sadist. That's what I'm saying. He wouldn't be so frightening if he were—because at least it would show he had some feelings. But he hasn't. He's all shrivelled up inside like a nut and he seems to hate people to like him. It's funny, that. I don't know any other master who doesn't like being liked——

FRANK. And I don't know any boy who doesn't trade on that very foible.

TAPLOW. Well, it's natural, sir. But not with the Crock——

FRANK. (*Making a feeble attempt at re-establishing the correct relationship.*) Mr. Crocker-Harris.

TAPLOW. Mr. Crocker-Harris. The funny thing is that in spite of everything, I do rather like him. I can't help it. And sometimes I think he sees it and that seems to shrivel him up even more——

FRANK. I'm sure you're exaggerating.

TAPLOW. No, sir. I'm not. In form the other day he made one of his little classical jokes. Of course nobody laughed because nobody understood it, myself included. Still, I knew he'd meant it as funny, so I laughed. Not out of sucking-up, sir, I swear, but ordinary common politeness, and feeling a bit sorry for him having made a dud joke. (*He goes to the table and sits down.*) Now I can't remember what the joke was— but let's say it was (*adopting his imitative voice again.*) benedictus, benedicatur, benedictine . . . Now, you laugh, sir——

FRANK *laughs.* TAPLOW *looks at him over an imaginary pair of spectacles, and then, very gently, crooks his forefinger to him in indication to approach the table.* FRANK *does so—simply, not clowning. He is genuinely interested in the incident.*

(*In a gentle, throaty voice*). 'Taplow—you laughed at my little pun, I noticed. I must confess I am flattered at the evident advance your Latinity has made that you should so readily have understood what the rest of the form did not. Perhaps, now, you would be good enough to explain it to them, so that they too can share your pleasure.'

The door behind the screen is pushed open and MILLIE CROCKER-HARRIS *appears. She is a thin woman in the late thirties, rather more smartly dressed than the general run of schoolmasters' wives. She stands by the screen pulling off her gloves and watching* TAPLOW *and* FRANK. *It is a few seconds before they notice her.*

'Come along, Taplow. Do not be so selfish as to keep a good joke to yourself. Tell the others——' (*He breaks off suddenly, seeing* MILLIE.) Oh lord!

FRANK *turns quickly, and seems infinitely relieved at seeing* MILLIE.

FRANK. Oh, hullo.

MILLIE. (*Without expression.*) Hullo.

She puts down a couple of parcels she has been carrying, and goes back into the hall to take off her hat.

TAPLOW. (*Frantically whispering to* FRANK.) Do you think she heard?

FRANK *shakes his head comfortably.*

I think she did. She was standing there quite a time. If she did and she tells him, there goes my remove——

FRANK. Nonsense——

MILLIE *comes back into the room.*

MILLIE. (*To* TAPLOW.) Waiting for my husband?

TAPLOW. Er—yes.

MILLIE. He's at the Bursar's and might be there quite a time. If I were you I'd go.

TAPLOW. (*Doubtfully.*) He said most particularly I was to come——

MILLIE. Well, why don't you run away for a quarter of an hour and come back?

TAPLOW. Supposing he gets here before me?

MILLIE. (*Smiling.*) I'll take the blame. I tell you what—you can do a job for him. Take this prescription to the chemist and get it made up.

TAPLOW. All right, Mrs. Crocker-Harris.

MILLIE. And while you're there you might as well slip into Stewarts and have an ice. Here. Catch. (*She takes a shilling from her bag and throws it to him.*)

TAPLOW. Thanks awfully. (*He passes* FRANK *on his way to the door. In a whisper.*) See she doesn't tell him.

FRANK. O.K.

MILLIE. (*Turning as* TAPLOW *is going.*) Oh, Taplow——

TAPLOW. Yes, Mrs. Crocker-Harris.

MILLIE. I had a letter from my father today in which he says he once had the pleasure of meeting your mother——

TAPLOW. (*Uninterested, but polite.*) Oh, really?

MILLIE. Yes. It was at some fête or other in Bradford. My uncle —that's Sir William Bartop, you know—made a speech and so did your mother. My father met her afterwards at tea——

TAPLOW. Oh, really?

MILLIE. He said he found her quite charming.

TAPLOW. Yes, she's jolly good at those sort of functions. (*Aware of his lack of tact.*) I mean—I'm sure she found him charming, too. Well, I'd better get going. So long.

TAPLOW *goes out.*

MILLIE. Thank you for coming round.

FRANK. That's all right.

MILLIE. You're staying for dinner?

FRANK. If I may.

MILLIE. If you may! Give me a cigarette.

He extends his case. She takes a cigarette.

(*Indicating case.*) You haven't given it away yet, I see.

FRANK. Do you think I would?

MILLIE. Frankly, yes. Luckily it's a man's case. I don't suppose any of your girl friends would want it——

FRANK. Don't be silly.

MILLIE. Where have you been all this week?

FRANK. Correcting exam papers—making reports. You know what end of term is like——

MILLIE. I do know what end of term is like. But even Andrew has managed this last week to take a few hours off to say goodbye to people——

FRANK. I really have been appallingly busy. Besides I'm coming to stay with you in Bradford——

MILLIE. Not for over a month. Andrew doesn't start his new job until September first. That's one of the things I had to tell you.

FRANK. Oh, I had meant to be in Devonshire in September.

MILLIE. (*Quickly.*) Who with?

FRANK. My family.

MILLIE. Surely you can go earlier, can't you? Go in August.

FRANK. It'll be difficult.

MILLIE. Then you'd better come to me in August.

FRANK. But Andrew will still be there.

MILLIE. Yes.

Pause.

FRANK. I think I can manage September.

MILLIE. That'd be better—from every point of view. Except that it means I shan't see you for six weeks.

FRANK. (*Lightly.*) You'll survive that, all right.

MILLIE. Yes, I'll survive it—but not as easily as you will.

FRANK *says nothing.*

I haven't much pride, have I? (*She approaches him.*) Frank, darling, I love you so much——

He kisses her, on the mouth, but a trifle perfunctorily, and then breaks quickly away, as if afraid someone had come into the room.

(*Laughing.*) You're very nervous.

FRANK. I'm afraid of that screen arrangement. You can't see people coming in——

MILLIE. Oh, yes. That reminds me. What were you and Taplow up to when I came in just now? Making fun of my husband?

FRANK. Afraid so. Yes.

MILLIE. It sounded rather a good imitation. I must get him to do it for me some time. It was very naughty of you to encourage him.

FRANK. I know. It was.

MILLIE. (*Ironically.*) Bad for discipline.

FRANK. Exactly. Currying favour with the boys, too. My God, how easy it is to be popular. I've only been a master three years but I've already slipped into an act and a vernacular that I just can't get out of. Why can't anyone ever be natural with the little blighters?

MILLIE. They probably wouldn't like it if you were.

FRANK. I don't see why not. No one seems to have tried it yet, anyway. I suppose the trouble is—we're all too scared of them. Either one gets forced into an attitude of false and hearty and jocular bonhomie like myself, or into the sort of petty, soulless tyranny which your husband uses to protect himself against the lower fifth.

MILLIE. (*Rather bored with this.*) He'd never be popular whatever he did——

FRANK. Possibly not. He ought never to have become a schoolmaster, really. Why did he?

MILLIE. It was his vocation, he said. He was sure he'd make a big success of it, especially when he got his job here first go off. (*Bitterly.*) Fine success he's made, hasn't he?

FRANK. You should have stopped him.

MILLIE. How was I to know? He talked about getting a house, then a headmastership.

FRANK. The Crock a headmaster! That's a pretty thought.

MILLIE. Yes, it's funny to think of it now, all right. Still he wasn't always the Crock, you know. He had a bit more gumption once. At least I thought he had. Don't let's talk any more about him—it's too depressing.

FRANK. I'm sorry for him.

MILLIE. (*Indifferently.*) He's not sorry for himself, so why should you be? It's me you should be sorry for.

FRANK. I am.

MILLIE. (*Smiling.*) Then show me.

She stretches out her arms to him. He kisses her again quickly and lightly, but she holds him hungrily. He has to free himself almost roughly.

FRANK. What have you been doing all day?

MILLIE. Calling on the other masters' wives—saying fond farewells. I've worked off twelve. I've another seven to do
tomorrow.

FRANK. You poor thing! I don't envy you.

MILLIE. It's the housemasters' wives that are the worst. They're
all so damn patronizing. You should have heard Betty
Carstairs. 'My dear—it's such terrible bad luck on you
both—that your husband should get this heart trouble just
when, if only he'd stayed on, he'd have been bound to get
a house. I mean, he's considerably senior to my Arthur as it
is, and they simply couldn't have gone on passing him over,
could they?'

FRANK. There's a word for Betty Carstairs, my dear, that I
would hesitate to employ before a lady.

MILLIE. She's got her eye on you, anyway.

FRANK. Betty Carstairs? What utter rot!

MILLIE. Oh, yes, she has. I saw you at that concert. Don't
think I didn't notice.

FRANK. Millie, darling! Really! I detest the woman.

MILLIE. Then what were you doing in her box at Lord's?

FRANK. Carstairs invited me. I went there because it was a
good place to see the match from.

MILLIE. Yes, I'm sure it was. Much better than the grandstand,
anyway.

FRANK. (As if remembering something suddenly.) Oh, my God!

MILLIE. It's all right, my dear. Don't bother to apologize.
We gave the seat away, as it happens——

FRANK. I'm most terribly sorry.

MILLIE It's all right. We couldn't afford a box, you see——

FRANK. It wasn't that. You know it wasn't that. It's just that I
—well, I clean forgot.

MILLIE. Funny you didn't forget the Carstairs's invitation——

FRANK. Millie—don't be a fool.

MILLIE. It's you who are the fool. (Appealingly.) Frank—have
you never been in love? I know you're not in love with me
—but haven't you ever been in love with anyone? Don't
you realize what torture you inflict on someone who loves
you when you do a thing like that?

FRANK. I've told you I'm sorry—I don't know what more I can say.

MILLIE. Why not the truth?

FRANK. The truth is—I clean forgot.

MILLIE. The truth is—you had something better to do—and why not say it?

FRANK. All right. Believe that if you like. It happens to be a lie, but believe it all the same. Only for God's sake stop this——

MILLIE. Then for God's sake show me some pity. Do you think it's any pleasanter for me to believe that you cut me because you forgot? Do you think that doesn't hurt either?

FRANK turns away.

Oh, damn! I was so determined to be brave and not mention Lord's. Why did I? Frank, just tell me one thing. Just tell me you're not running away from me—that's all I want to hear.

FRANK. I'm coming to Bradford.

MILLIE. I think, if you don't, I'll kill myself.

FRANK. I'm coming to Bradford.

The door is pushed open. FRANK has made a move towards MILLIE, but stops at the sound. MILLIE has recovered herself as ANDREW CROCKER-HARRIS appears by the screen. Despite the summer sun he wears a serge suit and a stiff collar. He carries a portfolio and looks, as ever, neat, complacent, and unruffled. He speaks in a very gentle voice which he rarely raises.

ANDREW. Is Taplow here?

MILLIE. I sent him to the chemist to get your prescription made up——

ANDREW. What prescription?

MILLIE. Your heart medicine. Don't you remember? You told me this morning it had run out——

ANDREW. Of course I remember, my dear, but there was no need to send Taplow for it. If you had telephoned the chemist he would have sent it round in plenty of time. He knows the prescription. Now Taplow will be late and I am so pressed for time I hardly know how to fit him in.

This colloquy has taken place near the door, the screen and MILLIE

blocking ANDREW's *view of the room. As he now comes in he sees*
FRANK.

Ah, Hunter! How are you?

FRANK. Very well, thanks.

They shake hands.

ANDREW. Most kind of you to drop in, but, as Millie should
have warned you, I am expecting a pupil for extra work
and——

MILLIE. He's staying to dinner, Andrew.

ANDREW. Good. Then I shall see something of you. However,
when Taplow returns I'm sure you won't mind——

FRANK. (*Making a move.*) No, of course not. I'll make myself
scarce now, if you'd rather—I mean, if you're busy——

ANDREW. Oh, no. There is no need for that. Sit down, do.
Will you smoke? I don't, as you know, but Millie does.
Millie, give our guest a cigarette——

MILLIE. I haven't any, I'm afraid. I've had to cadge from him.
FRANK *takes out his cigarette case and offers it to* MILLIE *who
exchanges a glance with him as she takes one.*

ANDREW. We expected you at Lord's, Hunter.

FRANK. What? Oh, yes. I'm most terribly sorry. I——

MILLIE. He clean forgot, Andrew. Imagine.

ANDREW. Forgot?

MILLIE. Not everyone is blessed with your superhuman
memory, you see.

FRANK. I really can't apologize enough——

ANDREW. Please don't bother to mention it. On the second
day we managed to sell the seat to a certain Dr. Lambert,
who wore, I regret to say, the colours of the opposing fac-
tion, but who otherwise seemed a passably agreeable person.
You liked him, didn't you, Millie?

MILLIE. (*Looking at* FRANK.) Very much, indeed. I thought him
quite charming.

ANDREW. A charming old gentleman. (*To* FRANK.) You have
had tea?

FRANK. Yes—thank you——

ANDREW. Is there any other refreshment I can offer you?

FRANK. No, thank you.

ANDREW. Would it interest you to see the new timetable I have drafted for next term?

FRANK. Yes, very much.

ANDREW *has taken out a long roll of paper, made by pasting pieces of foolscap together and which is entirely covered by his meticulous writing.*

I never knew you drafted our timetables——

ANDREW. Didn't you? I have done so for the last fifteen years. Of course they are always issued in mimeograph under the headmaster's signature—Now what form do you take? upper fifth Science—there you are—that's the general picture, but on the back you will see each form specified under separate headings—there—that's a new idea of mine—Millie, this might interest you——

MILLIE. (*Suddenly harsh.*) You know it bores me to death——

FRANK *looks up, surprised and uncomfortable.* ANDREW *does not remove his eyes from the timetable.*

ANDREW. Millie has no head for this sort of work. There you see. Now here you can follow the upper fifth Science throughout every day of the week.

FRANK. (*Indicating timetable.*) I must say, I think this is a really wonderful job.

ANDREW. Thank you. It has the merit of clarity, I think.

FRANK. I don't know what they'll do without you.

ANDREW. (*Without expression.*) They'll find somebody else, I expect.

Pause.

FRANK. What sort of job is this you're going to?

ANDREW. (*Looking at his wife for the first time.*) Hasn't Millie told you?

FRANK. She said it was a cr—— a private school.

ANDREW. A crammer's—for backward boys. It is run by an old Oxford contemporary of mine who lives in Dorset. The work will not be so arduous as here and my doctor seems to think I will be able to undertake it without—er—danger——

FRANK. (*With genuine sympathy.*) It's the most rotten bad luck for you. I'm awfully sorry.

ANDREW. (*Raising his voice a little.*) My dear Hunter, there is nothing whatever to be sorry for. I am looking forward to the change——

There is a knock at the door.

ANDREW. Come in.

TAPLOW *appears, a trifle breathless and guilty-looking. He carries a medicine bottle wrapped and sealed.*

Ah, Taplow. Good. You have been running, I see.

TAPLOW. Yes, sir. (*He hands the bottle to* MILLIE.)

ANDREW. There was a queue at the chemist's, I suppose?

TAPLOW. Yes, sir.

ANDREW. And doubtless an even longer one at Stewarts?

TAPLOW. Yes, sir—I mean—no, sir—I mean—(*He looks at* MILLIE.)—yes, sir.

MILLIE. You were late, yourself, Andrew.

ANDREW. Exactly. And for that I apologize, Taplow.

TAPLOW. That's all right, sir.

ANDREW. Luckily we have still a good hour before lock-up, so nothing has been lost——

FRANK. (*To* MILLIE.) May I use the short cut? I'm going back to my digs.

MILLIE. Yes. Go ahead. Come back soon. If Andrew hasn't finished we can sit in the garden. (*Moving to door.*) I'd better go and see about dinner.

She goes out at back.

ANDREW. (*To* FRANK.) Taplow is desirous of obtaining a remove from my form, Hunter, so that he can spend the rest of his career here playing happily with the crucibles, retorts, and bunsen burners of your Science fifth.

FRANK. (*At door.*) Oh. Has he?

ANDREW. Has he what?

FRANK. Obtained his remove?

ANDREW. (*After a pause.*) He has obtained exactly what he deserves. No less; and certainly no more.

TAPLOW *utters an explosion of mirth.*

FRANK *nods, thoughtfully, and goes out through the garden door.* ANDREW *has caught sight of* TAPLOW's *contorted face, but passes no remark on it. He sits at the table and makes a sign for* TAPLOW

to sit beside him. He picks up a text of the Agamemnon *and*
TAPLOW *does the same.*

Line thirteen hundred and ninety-nine. Begin.

TAPLOW. Chorus. We—are surprised at——

ANDREW. (*Automatically.*) We marvel at.

TAPLOW. We marvel at—thy tongue—how bold thou art—
that you——

ANDREW. Thou. (ANDREW'S *interruptions are automatic. His
thoughts are evidently far distant.*)

TAPLOW. Thou—can——

ANDREW. Canst——

TAPLOW. Canst—boastfully speak——

ANDREW. Utter such a boastful speech——

TAPLOW. Utter such a boastful speech—over—(*In a sudden
rush of inspiration.*)—the bloody corpse of the husband you
have slain——

ANDREW *looks down at his text for the first time.* TAPLOW *looks
apprehensive.*

ANDREW. Taplow—I presume you are using a different text
from mine——

TAPLOW. No, sir.

ANDREW. That is strange for the line as I have it reads: ἥτις
τοιόνδ᾽ ἐπ᾽ ἀνδρὶ κομπάζεις λόγον. However diligently I
search I can discover no 'bloody'—no 'corpse'—no 'you
have slain'. Simply 'husband'——

TAPLOW. Yes, sir. That's right.

ANDREW. Then why do you invent words that simply are not
there?

TAPLOW. I thought they sounded better, sir. More exciting.
After all she did kill her husband, sir. (*With relish.*) She's
just been revealed with his dead body and Cassandra's
weltering in gore——

ANDREW. I am delighted at this evidence, Taplow, of your
interest in the rather more lurid aspects of dramaturgy, but
I feel I must remind you that you are supposed to be con-
struing Greek, not collaborating with Aeschylus.

TAPLOW. (*Greatly daring.*) Yes, but still, sir, translator's licence,

sir—I didn't get anything wrong—and after all it *is* a play
and not just a bit of Greek construe.

ANDREW. (*Momentarily at a loss.*) I seem to detect a note of end
of term in your remarks. I am not denying that the *Agamemnon* is a play. It is perhaps the greatest play ever written——

TAPLOW. (*Quickly.*) I wonder how many people in the form
think that?

Pause. TAPLOW *is instantly frightened of what he has said.*

Sorry, sir. Shall I go on?

ANDREW *does not answer. He sits motionless staring at his book.*

Shall I go on, sir?

There is another pause. ANDREW *raises his head slowly from his book.*

ANDREW. (*Murmuring gently, not looking at* TAPLOW.) When I
was a very young man, only two years older than you are
now, Taplow, I wrote, for my own pleasure, a translation of
the *Agamemnon*—a very free translation—I remember—in
rhyming couplets.

TAPLOW. The whole *Agamemnon*—in verse? That must have
been hard work, sir.

ANDREW. It was hard work; but I derived great joy from it.
The play had so excited and moved me that I wished to
communicate, however imperfectly, some of that emotion
to others. When I had finished it, I remember, I thought it
very beautiful—almost more beautiful than the original.

TAPLOW. Was it ever published, sir?

ANDREW. No. Yesterday I looked for the manuscript while I
was packing my papers. I was unable to find it. I fear it is
lost—like so many other things. Lost for good.

TAPLOW. Hard luck, sir.

ANDREW *is silent again.* TAPLOW *steals a timid glance at him.*

Shall I go on, sir?

ANDREW, *with a slight effort, lowers his eyes again to his text.*

ANDREW. (*Raising his voice slightly.*) No. Go back and get that
last line right.

TAPLOW, *out of* ANDREW'S *vision, as he thinks, makes a disgusted
grimace in his direction.*

TAPLOW. That—thou canst utter such a boastful speech over
thy husband——

ANDREW. Yes. And, now, if you would be so kind, you will do the line again, without the facial contortion which you just found necessary to accompany it——

TAPLOW *is just beginning the line again, when* MILLIE *appears hurriedly. She has on an apron.*

MILLIE. The headmaster's just coming up the drive. Don't tell him I'm in. The fish pie isn't in the oven yet.

She disappears.

TAPLOW, *who has jumped up on* MILLIE's *entrance, turns hopefully to* ANDREW.

TAPLOW. I'd better go, hadn't I, sir? I mean—I don't want to be in the way——

ANDREW. We do not yet know that it is I the headmaster wishes to see. Other people live in this building.

There is a knock at the door.

ANDREW. Come in.

DR. FROBISHER *comes in. He looks more like a distinguished diplomat than a doctor of literature and classical scholar. He is in the middle fifties and goes to a very good tailor.*

FROBISHER. Ah, Crocker-Harris, I've caught you in. I'm so glad. I hope I'm not disturbing you?

ANDREW. I have been taking a pupil in extra work——

FROBISHER. On the penultimate day of term? That argues either great conscientiousness on your part or considerable backwardness on his.

ANDREW. Perhaps a combination of both——

FROBISHER. Quite so, but as this is my only chance of speaking to you before tomorrow, I think that perhaps your pupil will be good enough to excuse us—— (*He turns politely to* TAPLOW.)

TAPLOW. Oh, yes, sir. That's really quite all right. (*He collects his books and dashes to the door.*)

ANDREW. I'm extremely sorry, Taplow. You will please explain to your father exactly what occurred over this lost hour and tell him that I shall in due course be writing to him to return the money involved——

TAPLOW. (*Hurriedly.*) Yes, sir. But please don't bother, sir. I know it's all right, sir. Thank you, sir.

He darts out.

FROBISHER. Have the Gilberts called on you, yet?

ANDREW. The Gilberts, sir? Who are they?

FROBISHER. Gilbert is your successor with the lower fifth. He is down here today with his wife, and as they will be taking over this flat I thought perhaps you wouldn't mind if they came in to look it over.

ANDREW. Of course not.

FROBISHER. I've told you about him, I think. He is a very brilliant young man and won exceptionally high honours at Oxford.

ANDREW. So I understand, sir.

FROBISHER. Not, of course, as high as the honours you yourself won there. He didn't, for instance, win the Chancellor's prize for Latin verse or the Gaisford.

ANDREW. He won the Hertford Latin, then?

FROBISHER. No. (*Mildly surprised.*) Did you win that, too?

ANDREW *nods.*

It's sometimes rather hard to remember that you are perhaps the most brilliant classical scholar we have ever had at the school——

ANDREW. You are very kind.

FROBISHER. (*Urbanely corrects his gaffe.*) Hard to remember, I mean—because of your other activities—your brilliant work on the school timetable, for instance, and also for your heroic battle for so long and against such odds with the soul-destroying lower fifth.

ANDREW. I have not found that my soul has been destroyed by the lower fifth, headmaster.

FROBISHER. I was joking, of course.

ANDREW. Oh. I see.

FROBISHER. Is your wife in?

ANDREW. Er—no. Not at the moment.

FROBISHER. I shall have a chance of saying goodbye to her tomorrow. I am rather glad I have got you to myself. I have a delicate matter—two rather delicate matters—to broach.

ANDREW. Please sit down.

FROBISHER. Thank you. (*He sits.*) Now you have been with us, in all, eighteen years, haven't you?

ANDREW *nods*.

It is extremely unlucky that you should have had to retire at so comparatively early an age and so short a time before you would have been eligible for a pension.

The HEADMASTER *is regarding his nails, as he speaks, studiously avoiding* ANDREW'S *gaze.*

ANDREW. Pension? (*After a pause.*) You have decided then, not to award me a pension?

FROBISHER. Not I, my dear fellow. It has nothing at all to do with me. It's the governors who, I'm afraid, have been forced to turn down your application. I put your case to them as well as I could, but they decided, with great regret, that they couldn't make an exception to the rule.

ANDREW. But I thought—my wife thought, that an exception was made some five years ago——

FROBISHER. Ah. In the case of Buller, you mean? True. But the circumstances with Buller were quite remarkable. It was, after all, in playing rugger against the school that he received that injury——

ANDREW. Yes. I remember.

FROBISHER. And then the governors received a petition from boys, old boys, and parents with over five hundred signatures.

ANDREW. I would have signed that petition myself, but through some oversight I was not asked——

FROBISHER. He was a splendid fellow, Buller. Splendid. Doing very well, too, now, I gather.

ANDREW. I'm delighted to hear it.

FROBISHER. Your own case, of course, is equally deserving. If not more so—for Buller was a younger man. Unfortunately —rules are rules—and are not made to be broken every few years; at any rate that is the governors' view.

ANDREW. I quite understand.

FROBISHER. I knew you would. Now might I ask you a rather impertinent question.

ANDREW. Certainly.

FROBISHER. You have, I take it, private means?

ANDREW. My wife has some.

FROBISHER. Ah, yes. Your wife has often told me of her family connections. I understand her father has a business in— Bradford—isn't it?

ANDREW. Yes. He runs a men's clothing shop in the Arcade.

FROBISHER. Indeed? Your wife's remarks had led me to imagine something a little more—extensive.

ANDREW. My father-in-law made a settlement on my wife at the time of our marriage. She has about three hundred a year of her own. I have nothing. Is that the answer to your question, headmaster?

FROBISHER. Yes. Thank you for your frankness. Now, this private school you are going to——

ANDREW. My salary at the crammer's is to be two hundred pounds a year.

FROBISHER. Quite so. With board and lodging, of course?

ANDREW. For eight months of the year.

FROBISHER. Yes, I see. (*He ponders a second.*) Of course, you know, there is the School Benevolent Fund that deals with cases of actual hardship——

ANDREW. There will be no actual hardship, headmaster.

FROBISHER. No. I am glad you take that view. I must admit, though, I had hoped that your own means had proved a little more ample. Your wife had certainly led me to suppose——

ANDREW. I am not denying that a pension would have been very welcome, headmaster, but I see no reason to quarrel with the governors' decision. What is the other delicate matter you have to discuss?

FROBISHER. Well, it concerns the arrangements at prize-giving tomorrow. You are, of course, prepared to say a few words.

ANDREW. I had assumed you would call on me to do so.

FROBISHER. Of course. It is always done, and I know the boys appreciate the custom.

ANDREW. I have already made a few notes of what I am going to say. Perhaps you would care——

FROBISHER. No, no. That isn't necessary at all. I know I can trust your discretion—not to say your wit. It will be, I know, a very moving moment for you—indeed for us all—but, as I'm sure you realize, it is far better to keep these occasions from becoming too heavy and distressing. You know how little the boys appreciate sentiment——

ANDREW. I do.

FROBISHER. That is why I've planned my own reference to you at the end of my speech to be rather more light and jocular than I would otherwise have made it.

ANDREW. I quite understand. I too have prepared a few little jokes and puns for my speech. One—a play of words on *vale*, farewell, and Wally, the Christian name of a backward boy in my class, is, I think, rather happy.

FROBISHER. Yes. (*He laughs belatedly.*) Very neat. That should go down extremely well.

ANDREW. I'm glad you like it.

FROBISHER. Well, now—there is a particular favour I have to ask of you in connection with the ceremony, and I know I shall not have to ask in vain. Fletcher, as you know, is leaving, too.

ANDREW. Yes. He is going into the City, they tell me.

FROBISHER. Yes. Now he is, of course, considerably junior to you. He has only been here—let me see—five years. But, as you know, he has done great things for our cricket—positive wonders, when you remember what doldrums we were in before he came——

ANDREW. Our win at Lord's this year was certainly most inspiriting——

FROBISHER. Exactly. Now I'm sure that tomorrow the boys will make the occasion of his farewell speech a tremendous demonstration of gratitude. The applause might go on for minutes—you know what the boys feel about Lord's—and I seriously doubt my ability to cut it short or even, I admit, the propriety of trying to do so. Now, you see the quandary in which I am placed?

ANDREW. Perfectly. You wish to refer to me and for me to make my speech before you come to Fletcher?

FROBISHER. It's extremely awkward, and I feel wretched about asking it of you—but it's more for your own sake than for mine or Fletcher's that I do. After all, a climax is what one must try to work up to on these occasions.

ANDREW. Naturally, headmaster, I wouldn't wish to provide an anti-climax.

FROBISHER. You really mustn't take it amiss, my dear fellow. The boys, in applauding Fletcher for several minutes and yourself say—for—well, for not quite so long—won't be making any personal demonstration between you. It will be quite impersonal—I assure you—quite impersonal.

ANDREW. I understand.

FROBISHER. (*Warmly.*) I knew you would, and I can hardly tell you how wisely I think you have chosen. Well now—as that is all my business, I think perhaps I had better be getting along. This has been a terribly busy day for me—for you too, I imagine.

ANDREW. Yes.

MILLIE *comes in. She has taken off her apron, and tidied herself up.*

MILLIE. (*In her social manner.*) Ah, headmaster. How good of you to drop in.

FROBISHER. (*More at home with her than with Andrew.*) Mrs. Crocker-Harris. How are you?

They shake hands.

You're looking extremely well, I must say. Has anyone ever told you, Crocker-Harris, that you have a very attractive wife?

ANDREW. Many people, sir. But then I hardly need to be told.

MILLIE. Can I persuade you to stay a few moments and have a drink, headmaster. It's so rarely we have the pleasure of seeing you——

FROBISHER. Unfortunately, dear lady, I was just on the point of leaving. I have two frantic parents waiting for me at home. You are dining with us tomorrow—both of you, aren't you?

MILLIE. Yes, indeed—and so looking forward to it.

FROBISHER. I'm so glad. We can say our sad farewells then. (*To* ANDREW.) Au revoir, Crocker-Harris, and thank you very much.

ANDREW *bows.*

MILLIE *holds the door open for* FROBISHER *and follows him out into the hall.*

MILLIE. (*To* ANDREW *as she goes out with* FROBISHER.) Don't forget to take your medicine, dear, will you?

ANDREW. No.

FROBISHER. (*In the hall.*) Lucky invalid! To have such a very charming nurse——

MILLIE. (*Also in the hall.*) I really don't know what to say to all these compliments, headmaster. I don't believe you mean a word of them.

FROBISHER. Every word. Till tomorrow, then? Goodbye.

We hear the door slam. ANDREW *is staring out of the window.* MILLIE *reappears.*

MILLIE. Well? Do we get it?

ANDREW. (*Absently.*) Get what?

MILLIE. The pension, of course. Do we get it?

ANDREW. No.

MILLIE. My God! Why not?

ANDREW. It's against the rules.

MILLIE. Buller got it, didn't he? Buller got it? What's the idea of giving it to him and not to us?

ANDREW. The governors are afraid of establishing a precedent.

MILLIE. The mean old brutes! My God, what I wouldn't like to say to them! (*Rounding on* ANDREW.) And what did you say? Just sat there and made a joke in Latin, I suppose?

ANDREW. There wasn't very much I could say, in Latin or any other language.

MILLIE. Oh, wasn't there? I'd have said it all right. I wouldn't just have sat there twiddling my thumbs and taking it from that old phoney of a headmaster. But then, of course, I'm not a man.

ANDREW *is turning the pages of the* Agamemnon, *not looking at her.*

What do they expect you to do? Live on my money, I suppose.

ANDREW. There has never been any question of that. I shall be perfectly able to support myself.

MILLIE. Yourself? Doesn't the marriage service say something about the husband supporting his wife? Doesn't it? You ought to know?

ANDREW. Yes, it does.

MILLIE. And how do you think you're going to do that on two hundred a year?

ANDREW. I shall do my utmost to save some of it. You're welcome to it, if I can.

MILLIE. Thank you for precisely nothing.

ANDREW *underlines a word in the text he is reading.*

What else did the old fool have to say?

ANDREW. The headmaster? He wants me to make my speech tomorrow before instead of after Fletcher.

MILLIE. Yes. I knew he was going to ask that.

ANDREW. (*Without surprise.*) You knew?

MILLIE. Yes. He asked my advice about it a week ago. I told him to go ahead. I knew you wouldn't mind, and as there isn't a Mrs. Fletcher to make *me* look a fool, I didn't give two hoots.

There is a knock on the door.

Come in.

MR. *and* MRS. GILBERT *come in. He is about twenty-two, and his wife a year or so younger.*

GILBERT. Mr. Crocker-Harris?

ANDREW. (*Rising.*) Yes. Is it Mr. and Mrs. Gilbert? The headmaster told me you might look in.

MRS. GILBERT. I do hope we're not disturbing you.

ANDREW. Not at all. This is my wife.

MRS. GILBERT. How do you do.

ANDREW. Mr. and Mrs. Gilbert are our successors to this flat my dear.

MILLIE. Oh, yes. How nice to meet you both.

GILBERT. How do you do? We really won't keep you more than a second—my wife thought as we were here you wouldn't mind us taking a squint at our future home.

MRS. GILBERT. (*Unnecessarily.*) This is the drawing-room, I suppose?

MILLIE. That's right. Well, it's really a living-room. Andrew uses it as a study.

MRS. GILBERT. How charmingly you've done it!

MILLIE. Oh, do you think so? I'm afraid it isn't nearly as nice as I'd like to make it—but a schoolmaster's wife has to think of so many other things besides curtains and covers. Boys with dirty boots and a husband with leaky fountain pens, for instance.

MRS. GILBERT. Yes, I suppose so. Of course I haven't been a schoolmaster's wife for very long, you know.

GILBERT. Don't swank, darling. You haven't been a schoolmaster's wife at all yet.

MRS. GILBERT. Oh yes, I have—for two months. You were a schoolmaster when I married you.

GILBERT. Prep school doesn't count.

MILLIE. Have you only been married two months?

MRS. GILBERT. Two months and sixteen days.

GILBERT. Seventeen.

MILLIE. (*Sentimentally.*) Andrew, did you hear? They've only been married two months.

ANDREW. Indeed? Is that all?

MRS. GILBERT. (*At the garden door.*) Oh, look, darling. They've got a garden. It is yours, isn't it?

MILLIE. Oh, yes. It's only a pocket handkerchief, I'm afraid, but it's very useful to Andrew. He often works out there, don't you, dear?

ANDREW. Yes, indeed. I find it very agreeable.

MILLIE. Shall I show you the rest of the flat? It's a bit untidy, I'm afraid, but you must forgive that.

MRS. GILBERT. Oh, of course.

MILLIE. (*As they move to the door.*) And the kitchen is in a terrible mess. I'm in the middle of cooking dinner——

MRS. GILBERT. (*Breathlessly.*) Oh. Do you cook?

MILLIE. Oh, yes. I have to. We haven't had a maid for five years.

MRS. GILBERT. Oh, I do think that's wonderful of you. I'm scared stiff of having to do it for Peter—I know the first dinner I have to cook for him will wreck our married life——

GILBERT. Highly probable.

MILLIE. (*Following* MRS. GILBERT *out.*) Well, these days we've all got to try and do things we weren't really brought up to do.

They disappear.

ANDREW. (*To* GILBERT.) Don't you want to see the rest of the flat?

GILBERT. No. I leave all that sort of thing to my wife. She's the boss. I thought perhaps you could tell me something about the lower fifth.

ANDREW. What would you like to know?

GILBERT. Well, sir, quite frankly, I'm petrified.

ANDREW. I don't think you need to be. May I give you some sherry?

GILBERT. Thank you.

ANDREW. They are mostly boys of about fifteen or sixteen. They are not very difficult to handle.

GILBERT. The headmaster said you ruled them with a rod of iron. He called you the Himmler of the lower fifth.

ANDREW. Did he? The Himmler of the lower fifth? I think he exaggerated. I hope he exaggerated. The Himmler of the lower fifth?

GILBERT. (*Puzzled.*) He only meant that you kept the most wonderful discipline. I must say I do admire you for that. I couldn't even manage that with eleven-year-olds, so what I'll be like with fifteens and sixteens I shudder to think.

ANDREW. It is not so difficult. They aren't bad boys. Some-times—a little wild and unfeeling, perhaps—but not bad. The Himmler of the lower fifth? Dear me!

GILBERT. Perhaps I shouldn't have said that. I've been tactless, I'm afraid.

ANDREW. Oh, no, please sit down.

GILBERT. Thank you, sir.

ANDREW. From the very beginning I realized that I didn't possess the knack of making myself liked—a knack that you will find you do possess.

GILBERT. Do you think so?

ANDREW. Oh, yes. I am quite sure of it. It is not a quality of great importance to a schoolmaster, though, for too much of it, as you may also find, is as great a danger as the total lack of it. Forgive me lecturing, won't you?

GILBERT. I want to learn.

ANDREW. I can only teach you from my own experience. For two or three years I tried very hard to communicate to the boys some of my own joy in the great literature of the past. Of course, I failed, as you will fail, nine hundred and ninety-nine times out of a thousand. But a single success can atone and more than atone for all the failures in the world. And sometimes—very rarely, it is true—but sometimes I had that success. That was in the early years.

GILBERT. (*Eagerly listening.*) Please go on, sir.

ANDREW. In early years, too, I discovered an easy substitute for popularity. I had, of course, acquired—we all do—many little mannerisms and tricks of speech, and I found that the boys were beginning to laugh at me. I was very happy at that, and encouraged the boys' laughter by playing up to it. It made our relationship so very much easier. They didn't like me as a man, but they found me funny as a character, and you can teach more things by laughter than by earnestness—for I never did have much sense of humour. So, for a time, you see, I was quite a success as a school-master—(*He stops.*)—I fear this is all very personal and embarrassing to you. Forgive me. You need have no fears about the lower fifth.

GILBERT. (*After a pause.*) I'm afraid I said something that hurt you very much. It's myself you must forgive, sir. Believe me, I'm desperately sorry.

ANDREW. There's no need. You were merely telling me what I should have known for myself. Perhaps I did in my heart, and hadn't the courage to acknowledge it. I knew, of course, that I was not only not liked, but now positively disliked. I had realized, too, that the boys—for many long years now—had ceased to laugh at me. I don't know why they no longer found me a joke. Perhaps it was my illness. No, I don't think it was that. Something deeper than that. Not a sickness of the body, but a sickness of the soul. At all events it didn't take much discernment on my part to realize I had become an utter failure as a schoolmaster. Still, stupidly enough, I hadn't realized that I was also feared. The Himmler of the lower fifth! I suppose that will become my epitaph.

GILBERT *is now deeply embarrassed and rather upset, but he remains silent.*

(*With a mild laugh.*) I cannot for the life of me imagine why I should choose to unburden myself to you—a total stranger —when I have been silent to others for so long. Perhaps it is because my very unworthy mantle is about to fall on your shoulders. If that is so I shall take a prophet's privilege and foretell that you will have a very great success with the lower fifth.

GILBERT. Thank you, sir. I shall do my best.

ANDREW. I can't offer you a cigarette, I'm afraid. I don't smoke.

GILBERT. That's all right, sir. Nor do I.

MILLIE *and* MRS. GILBERT *can be heard in the hall outside.*

MRS. GILBERT. (*Off.*) Thank you so much for showing me round.

MILLIE *and* MRS. GILBERT *come in.*

ANDREW. I trust your wife has found no major snags in your new flat.

MRS. GILBERT. No. None at all. Just imagine, Peter. Mr. and Mrs. Crocker-Harris first met each other on a holiday in the Lake District. Isn't that a coincidence!

GILBERT. (*A little distrait.*) Yes. Yes, it certainly is. On a walking tour, too?

MILLIE. Andrew was on a walking tour. No walking for me. I can't abide it. I was staying with my uncle—that's Sir William Bartop, you know—you may have heard of him?

GILBERT *and* MRS. GILBERT *try to look as though they had heard of him constantly.*

He'd taken a house near Windermere—quite a mansion it was really—rather silly for an old gentleman living alone—

and Andrew knocked on our front-door one day and asked
the footman for a glass of water. So my uncle invited him in
to tea.

MRS. GILBERT. Our meeting wasn't quite as romantic as that.

GILBERT. I knocked her flat on her face.

MRS. GILBERT. Not with love at first sight. With the swing doors
of our hotel bar. So, of course, then he apologized and——

GILBERT. (*Brusquely.*) Darling. The Crocker-Harrises, I'm sure,
have far more important things to do than to listen to your
detailed but inaccurate account of our very sordid little
encounter. Why not just say I married you for your money
and leave it at that? Come on, we must go.

MRS. GILBERT. (*To* MILLIE.) Isn't he awful to me?

MILLIE. Men have no souls, my dear. My husband is just as
bad.

MRS. GILBERT. Goodbye, Mr. Crocker-Harris.

ANDREW. (*Bowing.*) Goodbye.

MRS. GILBERT. (*As she goes out with* MILLIE.) I think your idea
about the dining-room is awfully good—if only I can get
the permit——

MILLIE *and* MRS. GILBERT *go out.* GILBERT *has dallied to say
goodbye alone to* ANDREW.

GILBERT. Goodbye, sir.

ANDREW. Er—you will, I know, respect the confidences I have
just made to you——

GILBERT. I should hate you to think I wouldn't.

ANDREW. I am sorry to have embarrassed you. I don't know
what came over me. I have not been very well, you know.
Goodbye, my dear fellow, and my best wishes.

GILBERT. Thank you. The very best of good luck to you too,
sir, in your future career.

ANDREW. My future career? Yes. Thank you.

GILBERT. Well, goodbye, sir.

GILBERT *goes out.*

We hear voices in the hall, cut short as the front-door closes. MILLIE
comes back.

MILLIE. Good-looking couple.

ANDREW. Very.

MILLIE. He looks as if he'd got what it takes. I should think he'll be a success all right.

ANDREW. That's what I thought.

MILLIE. I don't think it's much of a career, though—a schoolmaster—for a likely young chap like that.

ANDREW. I know you don't.

MILLIE. Still I bet when he leaves this place it won't be without a pension. It'll be roses, roses all the way, and tears and cheers and goodbye, Mr. Chips.

ANDREW. I expect so.

MILLIE. What's the matter with you?

ANDREW. Nothing.

MILLIE. You're not going to have another of your attacks, are you? You look dreadful.

ANDREW. I'm perfectly all right.

MILLIE. (*Indifferently.*) You know best. Your medicine's there, anyway, if you want it.

She goes out.

ANDREW, *left alone, continues for a time staring at the text he has been pretending to read. Then he puts one hand over his eyes. There is a knock on the door.*

ANDREW. Come in.

TAPLOW *appears timidly from behind the screen.*

(*Sharply.*) Yes, Taplow? What is it?

TAPLOW. Nothing, sir.

ANDREW. What do you mean, nothing?

TAPLOW. (*Timidly.*) I just came back to say goodbye, sir.

ANDREW. Oh. (*He gets up.*)

TAPLOW. I didn't have a chance with the head here. I rather dashed out, I'm afraid. I thought I'd just come back and—and wish you luck, sir.

ANDREW. Thank you, Taplow. That's good of you.

TAPLOW. I—er—thought this might interest you, sir. (*He quickly thrusts a small book into ANDREW's hand.*)

ANDREW. What is it?

TAPLOW. Verse translation of the *Agamemnon*, sir. The Browning version. It's not much good. I've been reading it in the Chapel gardens.

ANDREW *very deliberately turns over the pages of the book.*

ANDREW. Very interesting, Taplow. (*He seems to have a little difficulty in speaking. He clears his throat and then goes on in his level, gentle voice.*) I know the translation, of course. It has its faults, I agree, but I think you will enjoy it more when you get used to the metre he employs.

He hands it to TAPLOW *who brusquely thrusts it back to him.*

TAPLOW. It's for you, sir.

ANDREW. For me?

TAPLOW. Yes, sir. I've written in it.

ANDREW *opens the fly-leaf and reads whatever is written there.*

ANDREW. Did you buy this?

TAPLOW. Yes, sir. It was only second-hand.

ANDREW. You shouldn't have spent your pocket-money this way.

TAPLOW. That's all right, sir. It wasn't very much. The price isn't still inside, is it?

ANDREW *carefully wipes his glasses and puts them on again.*

ANDREW. (*At length.*) No. Just what you've written. Nothing else.

TAPLOW. Good. I'm sorry you've got it already. I thought you probably would have——

ANDREW. I haven't got it already. I may have had it once. I can't remember. But I haven't got it now.

TAPLOW. That's all right, then.

ANDREW *continues to stare at* TAPLOW'S *inscription on the fly-leaf.* (*Suspiciously.*) What's the matter, sir? Have I got the accent wrong on εὐμενῶς?

ANDREW. No. The perispomenon is perfectly correct.

He lowers the book and we notice his hands are shaking from some intense inner effort as he takes off his spectacles.

Taplow, would you be good enough to take that bottle of medicine, which you so kindly brought in, and pour me out one dose in a glass which you will find in the bathroom?

TAPLOW. (*Seeing something is wrong.*) Yes, sir.

ANDREW *sits at his seat by the table.*

ANDREW. The doses are clearly marked on the bottle. I usually put a little water with it.

TAPLOW. Yes, sir.

He takes the bottle and darts out.

    ANDREW, *the moment he is gone, breaks down and begins to sob uncontrollably. He makes a desperate attempt, after a moment, to control himself, but when* TAPLOW *comes back his emotion is still very apparent.*

ANDREW. (*Taking the glass.*) Thank you. (*He drinks it, turning his back on* TAPLOW *as he does so. At length.*) You must forgive this exhibition of weakness, Taplow. The truth is I have been going through rather a strain lately.

TAPLOW. Of course, sir. I quite understand.

There is a knock on the garden door.

ANDREW. Come in.

    FRANK *comes in.*

FRANK. Oh, sorry. I thought you'd be finished by now——

ANDREW. Come in, Hunter, do. It's perfectly all right. Our lesson was over some time ago, but Taplow most kindly came back to say goodbye.

    FRANK, *taking in* TAPLOW's *rather startled face and* ANDREW's *obvious emotion, looks a little puzzled.*

FRANK. Are you sure I'm not intruding?

ANDREW. No, no. I want you to see this book that Taplow has given me, Hunter. Look. (*He hands it to* HUNTER.) A translation of the *Agamemnon* by Robert Browning. Do you see the inscription he has put into it?

FRANK. Yes, but it's no use to me, I'm afraid. I never learnt Greek.

ANDREW. Then we'll have to translate it for him, won't we, Taplow? (*Reciting by heart.*) τὸν κρατοῦντα μαλθακῶς θεὸς πρόσωθεν εὐμενῶς προσδέρκεται. That means—in a rough translation: 'God from afar looks graciously upon a gentle master.' It comes from a speech of Agamemnon's to Clytaemnestra.

FRANK. I see. Very pleasant and very apt. (*He hands the book back to* ANDREW.)

ANDREW. Very pleasant. But perhaps not, after all, so very apt.

He turns quickly away from both of them as emotion once more seems about to overcome him. FRANK *brusquely jerks his head to the bewildered* TAPLOW *to get out.* TAPLOW *nods.*

TAPLOW. Goodbye, sir, and the best of luck.

ANDREW. Goodbye, Taplow, and thank you very much.

TAPLOW *flees quickly.*

FRANK *watches* ANDREW'S *back with a mixture of embarrassment and sympathy.*

(*Turning at length, slightly recovered.*) Dear me, what a fool I made of myself in front of that boy. And in front of you, Hunter. I can't imagine what you must think of me.

FRANK. Nonsense.

ANDREW. I am not a very emotional person, as you know, but there was something so very touching and kindly about his action, and coming as it did just after—— (*He stops, then glances at the book in his hand.*) This is a very delightful thing to have, don't you think?

FRANK. Delightful.

ANDREW. The quotation, of course, he didn't find entirely by himself. I happened to make some little joke about the line in form the other day. But he must have remembered it all the same to have found it so readily—and perhaps he means it.

FRANK. I'm sure he does, or he wouldn't have written it.

MILLIE *comes in.*

MILLIE. Hullo, Frank. I'm glad you're in time. (*She picks up the medicine bottle and the glass from the table and puts them aside. To* FRANK.) Lend me a cigarette. I've been gasping for one for an hour.

FRANK *once more extends his case and* MILLIE *takes a cigarette which he lights.*

FRANK. Your husband has just had a very nice present.

MILLIE. Oh? Who from?

FRANK. Taplow.

MILLIE. (*Smiling.*) Oh, Taplow. Let's see. (*She takes the book from* ANDREW.)

ANDREW. He bought it with his own pocket-money, Millie, and wrote a very charming inscription inside.

FRANK. God looks kindly upon a gracious master.

ANDREW. No—not gracious—gentle, I think— τὸν κρατοῦντα μαλθακῶς —yes I think gentle is the better translation. I would rather have had this present than almost anything I can think of.

Pause. MILLIE *laughs suddenly.*

MILLIE. The artful little beast——

FRANK. (*Urgently.*) Millie——

ANDREW. Artful? Why artful?

MILLIE *looks at* FRANK *who is staring meaningly at her.*

Why artful, Millie?

MILLIE *laughs again, quite lightly, and turns from* FRANK *to* ANDREW.

MILLIE. My dear, because I came into this room this afternoon to find him giving an imitation of you to Frank here. Obviously he was scared stiff I was going to tell you, and you'd ditch his remove or something. I don't blame him for trying a few bobs' worth of appeasement.

She hands the book back to ANDREW *who stands quite still looking down at it.*

ANDREW. ·(*Nodding, at length.*) I see. (*He puts the book gently on the table and walks to the door.*)

MILLIE. Where are you going, dear? Dinner's nearly ready.

ANDREW. Only to my room for a moment. I won't be long.

He takes the medicine bottle and a glass.

MILLIE. You've just had a dose of that, dear. I shouldn't have another, if I were you.

ANDREW. I am allowed two at a time.

MILLIE. Well, see it is two and no more, won't you?

ANDREW *meets her eye for a moment, at the door, then goes out quietly.*

MILLIE *turns to* FRANK *with an expression half defiant and half ashamed.*

FRANK. (*With a note of real repulsion in his voice.*) Millie! My God! How could you?

MILLIE. Well, why not? Why should he be allowed his comforting little illusions? I'm not.

FRANK. (*Advancing on her.*) Listen. You're to go to his room now and tell him that was a lie.

MILLIE. Certainly not. It wasn't a lie.

FRANK. If you don't, I will.

MILLIE. I shouldn't, if I were you. It'll only make things worse.
He won't believe you.

FRANK. (*Moving.*) We'll see about that.

MILLIE. Go ahead. See what happens. He knows I don't lie
to him. He knows what I told him was the truth, and he
won't like your sympathy. He'll think you're making fun
of him, like Taplow.

FRANK *hesitates at the door then comes slowly back into the room.*
MILLIE *watches him, a little frightened.*

FRANK. (*At length.*) We're finished, Millie—you and I.

MILLIE. (*Laughing.*) Frank, really! Don't be hysterical.

FRANK. I'm not. I mean it.

MILLIE. (*Lightly.*) Oh, yes, you mean it. Of course you mean
it. Now just sit down, dear, and relax and forget all about
artful little boys and their five-bob presents, and talk to
me.

She touches his arm. He moves away from her brusquely.

FRANK. Forget? If I live to be a hundred I shall never forget
that little glimpse you've just given me of yourself.

MILLIE. Frank—you're making a frightening mountain out of
an absurd little molehill.

FRANK. Of course, but the mountain I'm making in my
imagination is so frightening that I'd rather try to forget
both it and the repulsive little molehill that gave it birth.
But as I know I never can, I tell you, Millie—from this
moment you and I are finished.

MILLIE. (*Quietly.*) You can't scare me, Frank. I know that's
what you're trying to do, but you can't do it.

FRANK. (*Quietly.*) I'm not trying to scare you, Millie. I'm telling
you the simple truth. I'm not coming to Bradford.

MILLIE. (*After a pause, with an attempt at bravado.*) All right, my
dear, if that's the way you feel about it. Don't come to
Bradford.

FRANK. Right. Now I think you ought to go to your room and
look after Andrew. I'm leaving.

MILLIE *runs quickly to stop him.*

MILLIE. What is this? Frank, I don't understand, really I
don't. What have I done?

FRANK. I think you know what you've done, Millie. Go and look after Andrew.

MILLIE. Andrew? Why this sudden concern for Andrew?

FRANK. Because I think he's just been about as badly hurt as a human being can be; and as he's a sick man and in a rather hysterical state it might be a good plan to go and see how he is.

MILLIE. (*Scornfully.*) Hurt? Andrew hurt? You can't hurt Andrew. He's dead.

FRANK. Why do you hate him so much, Millie?

MILLIE. Because he keeps me from you.

FRANK. That isn't true.

MILLIE. Because he's not a man at all.

FRANK. He's a human being.

MILLIE. You've got a fine right to be so noble about him, after deceiving him for six months.

FRANK. Twice in six months—at your urgent invitation.

MILLIE *slaps his face, in a violent paroxysm of rage.*

Thank you for that. I deserved it. I deserve a lot worse than that, too——

MILLIE. (*Running to him.*) Frank, forgive me—I didn't mean it——

FRANK. (*Quietly.*) You'd better have the truth, Millie. It had to come some time. I've never loved you. I've never told you I loved you.

MILLIE. I know, Frank, I know—I've always accepted that.

FRANK. You asked me just now if I was running away from you. Well, I was.

MILLIE. I knew that too.

FRANK. But I was coming to Bradford. It was going to be the very last time I was ever going to see you and at Bradford I would have told you that.

MILLIE. You wouldn't. You wouldn't. You've tried to tell me that so often before—and I've always stopped you somehow —somehow. I would have stopped you again.

FRANK. (*Quietly.*) I don't think so, Millie. Not this time.

MILLIE. Frank, I don't care what humiliations you heap on me. I know you don't give two hoots for me as a person. I've

always known that. I've never minded so long as you cared
for me as a woman. And you do, Frank. You do. You do,
don't you?

FRANK *is silent.*

It'll be all right at Bradford, you see. It'll be all right,
there——

FRANK. I'm not coming to Bradford, Millie.

The door opens slowly and ANDREW *comes in, carrying the bottle of
medicine. He hands it to* MILLIE *and passes on.* MILLIE *quickly
holds the bottle up to the light.* ANDREW *turns and sees her.*

ANDREW. (*Gently.*) You should know me well enough by now,
my dear, to realize how unlikely it is that I should ever take
an overdose.

MILLIE, *without a word, puts the bottle down and goes out.*

ANDREW *goes to a cupboard at back and produces a decanter of
sherry and a glass.*

FRANK. I'm not staying to dinner, I'm afraid.

ANDREW. Indeed? I'm sorry to hear that. You'll have a glass
of sherry?

FRANK. No, thank you.

ANDREW. You will forgive me if I do.

FRANK. Of course.

ANDREW *pours himself a glass.*

Perhaps I'll change my mind.

ANDREW *pours* FRANK *a glass.*

About Taplow——

ANDREW. Oh, yes?

FRANK. It *is* perfectly true that he was imitating you. I, of
course, was mostly to blame in that, and I'm very sorry.

ANDREW. That is perfectly all right. Was it a good imitation?

FRANK. No.

ANDREW. I expect it was. Boys are often very clever mimics.

FRANK. We talked about you, of course, before that. He said
—you probably won't believe this, but I thought I ought to
tell you—he said he liked you very much.

ANDREW *smiles slightly.*

ANDREW. Indeed?

FRANK. I can remember very clearly his exact words. He said:

'He doesn't seem to like people to like him—but in spite of that, I do—very much.' (*Lightly*.) So you see it looks after all as if the book might not have been a mere question of—appeasement.

ANDREW. The book? (*He picks it up*.) Dear me! What a lot of fuss about a little book—and a not very good little book at that. (*He drops it on the table*.)

FRANK. I would like you to believe me.

ANDREW. Possibly you would, my dear Hunter; but I can assure you I am not particularly concerned about Taplow's views of my character: or about yours either, if it comes to that.

FRANK. (*Hopelessly*.) I think you should keep that book all the same. You may find it'll mean something to you after all.

ANDREW. Exactly. It will mean a perpetual reminder to myself of the story with which Taplow is at this very moment regaling his friends in the House. 'I gave the Crock a book, to buy him off, and he blubbed. The Crock blubbed. I tell you I was there. I saw it. The Crock blubbed.' My mimicry is not as good as his, I fear. Forgive me. And now let us leave this idiotic subject and talk of more pleasant things. Do you like this sherry? I got it on my last visit to London——

FRANK. If Taplow ever breathes a word of that story to any one at all, I'll murder him. But he won't. And if you think I will you greatly underestimate my character as well as his. (*He drains his glass*.) Goodbye.

ANDREW. Are you leaving so soon? Goodbye, my dear fellow.

He does not get up nor offer to shake hands. FRANK *goes to the window.*

FRANK. As this is the last time I shall probably ever see you I'm going to offer you a word of advice.

ANDREW. (*Politely*.) I shall be glad to listen to it.

FRANK. Leave your wife.

Pause. ANDREW *takes a sip of his sherry.*

ANDREW. (*At length*.) So that you may the more easily carry on your intrigue with her?

FRANK *stares at him, then comes back into the room.*

FRANK. How long have you known that?

ANDREW. Since it first began.

FRANK. How did you find out?

ANDREW. By information.

FRANK. By whose information?

ANDREW. By someone's whose word I could hardly discredit.

Pause.

FRANK. (*Slowly, with repulsion.*) No! That's too horrible to think of.

ANDREW. Nothing is ever too horrible to think of, Hunter. It is simply a question of facing facts.

FRANK. She might have told you a lie. Have you faced that fact?

ANDREW. She never tells me a lie. In twenty years she has never told me a lie. Only the truth.

FRANK. This was a lie.

ANDREW. No, my dear Hunter. Do you wish me to quote you dates?

FRANK. (*Still unable to believe it.*) And she told you six months ago?

ANDREW. Isn't it seven?

FRANK. (*Savagely.*) Then why have you allowed me inside your home? Why haven't you done something—reported me to the governors—anything—made a scene, knocked me down?

ANDREW. Knocked you down?

FRANK. You didn't have to invite me to dinner.

ANDREW. My dear Hunter, if, over the last twenty years, I had allowed such petty considerations to influence my choice of dinner guests I would have found it increasingly hard to remember which master to invite and which to refuse. You see, Hunter, you mustn't flatter yourself you are the first. My information is a good deal better than yours, you understand. It's authentic.

Pause.

FRANK. She's evil.

ANDREW. That's hardly a kindly epithet to apply to a lady whom, I gather, you have asked to marry.

FRANK. Did she tell you that?

ANDREW. She's a dutiful wife. She tells me everything.

FRANK. That, at least, was a lie.

ANDREW. She never lies.

FRANK. That was a lie. Do you want the truth? Can you bear the truth?

ANDREW. I can bear anything.

FRANK. What I did, I did cold-bloodedly out of weakness and ignorance and crass stupidity. I'm bitterly, bitterly ashamed of myself, but, in a sense, I'm glad you know, though I'd rather a thousand times that you'd heard it from me than from your wife. I won't ask you to forgive me. I can only tell you, with complete truth, that the only emotion she has ever succeeded in arousing in me she aroused in me for the first time ten minutes ago—an intense and passionate disgust.

ANDREW. What a delightfully chivalrous statement——

FRANK. Forget chivalry, Crock, for God's sake. Forget all your fine Mosaic scruples. You must leave her—it's your only chance.

ANDREW. She's my wife, Hunter. You seem to forget that. As long as she wishes to remain my wife, she may.

FRANK. She's out to kill you.

ANDREW. My hear Hunter, if that was indeed her purpose, you should know by now that she fulfilled it long ago.

FRANK. Why won't you leave her?

ANDREW. Because I wouldn't wish to add another grave wrong to one I have already done her.

FRANK. What wrong have you done her?

ANDREW. To marry her.

Pause. FRANK *stares at him in silence.*

You see, my dear Hunter, she is really quite as much to be pitied as I. We are both of us interesting subjects for your microscope. Both of us needing from the other something that would make life supportable for us, and neither of us able to give it. Two kinds of love. Hers and mine. Worlds apart, as I know now, though when I married her I didn't think they were incompatible. In those days I hadn't thought that her kind of love—the love she requires and which I was unable to give her—was so important that its absence would drive out the other kind of love—the kind of love that I require and which I thought, in my folly, was by far the greater part of love. I may have been, you see, Hunter, a brilliant classical scholar, but I was woefully ignorant of the facts of life. I know better now, of course. I know that in both of us, the love that we should have borne each other has turned to bitter hatred. That's all the problem is. Not a very unusual one, I venture to think—nor nearly as tragic as you seem to imagine. Merely the problem of an unsatisfied wife and a henpecked husband. You'll find it all over the world. It is usually, I believe, a subject for farce. And now, if you have to leave us, my dear fellow, please don't let me detain you any longer.

He turns his back deliberately on FRANK, *who makes no move to go.*

FRANK. Don't go to Bradford. Stay here, until you take up your new job.

ANDREW. I think I've already told you I'm not interested in your advice.

FRANK. Leave her. It's the only way.

ANDREW. (*Violently.*) Will you please go!

FRANK. All right. I'd just like you to say goodbye to me, properly, though. Will you? I shan't see you again.

ANDREW *rises and walks slowly over to him.*

I know you don't want my pity, but I would like to be of some help.

ANDREW. If you think, by this expression of kindness, Hunter, that you can get me to repeat the shameful exhibition of emotion I made to Taplow a moment ago, I must tell you that you have no chance. My hysteria over that book just now was no more than a sort of reflex action of the spirit. The muscular twitchings of a corpse. It can never happen again.

FRANK. A corpse can be revived.

ANDREW. I don't believe in miracles.

FRANK. Don't you? Funnily enough, as a scientist, I do.

ANDREW. Your faith would be touching, if I were capable of being touched by it.

FRANK. You are, I think. (*After a pause.*) I'd like to come and visit you at this crammer's.

ANDREW. That is an absurd suggestion.

FRANK. I suppose it is rather, but all the same I'd like to do it. May I?

ANDREW. Of course not.

FRANK. Your term begins on the first of September, doesn't it?

ANDREW. I tell you the idea is quite childish——

FRANK. I could come about the second week.

ANDREW. You would be bored to death. So, probably, would I.

FRANK. (*Glancing at pocket calendar.*) Let's say Monday the twelfth, then.

ANDREW. (*His hands beginning to tremble again.*) Say anything you like, only please go. Please go, Hunter.

FRANK. (*Writing in his book and not looking at* ANDREW.) That's fixed, then. Monday, September the twelfth. Will you remember that?

ANDREW. (*After a pause, speaking with difficulty.*) I suppose I'm at least as likely to remember it as you are.

FRANK. That's fixed, then. (*He slips the book into his pocket and puts out his hand.*) Goodbye, until then.

ANDREW, *after hesitation, shakes his hand.*

ANDREW. Goodbye.

FRANK. May I go out through your garden?

ANDREW. (*Nodding.*) Of course.

FRANK. I'm off to have a quick word with Taplow. By the way, may I take him a message from you?

ANDREW. What message?

FRANK. Has he or has he not got his remove?

ANDREW. He has.

FRANK. May I tell him?

ANDREW. It is highly irregular. Yes, you may.

FRANK. Good. (*He turns to go then turns back.*) Oh, by the way, I'd better have the address of that crammer's. (*He takes out his notebook and points his pencil, ready to write.*

MILLIE *comes in with tray, dishes, and cutlery. She starts to set the table.*)

MILLIE. Dinner's ready. You're staying, Frank, aren't you?

FRANK. (*Politely.*) No. I'm afraid not. (*To* ANDREW.) What's that address?

ANDREW. (*After great hesitation.*) The Old Deanery, Malcombe, Dorset.

FRANK. I'll write to you and you can let me know about trains. (*To* MILLIE.) Goodbye. (*To* ANDREW.) Goodbye.

He goes out.

MILLIE *is silent for a moment. Then she laughs.*

MILLIE. That's a laugh, I must say.

ANDREW. What's a laugh, my dear?

MILLIE. You inviting him to stay with you.

ANDREW. I didn't. He suggested it.

MILLIE. He's coming to Bradford.

ANDREW. Yes. I remember your telling me so.

MILLIE *comes close to* ANDREW.

MILLIE. He's coming to Bradford. He's not going to you.

ANDREW. The likeliest contingency is, that he's not going to either of us. Shall we have dinner?

MILLIE. He's coming to Bradford.

ANDREW. I expect so. Oh, by the way, I'm not. I shall be staying here until I go to Dorset.

MILLIE. (*Indifferently.*) Suit yourself—what makes you think I'll join you there?

ANDREW. I don't.

MILLIE. You needn't expect me.

ANDREW. I don't think either of us has the right to expect anything further from the other.

The telephone rings.

ANDREW. I don't. Excuse me. (*He picks up the receiver.*) Hullo . . . Yes, headmaster . . . The timetable? . . . It's perfectly simple. The middle fourth B division will take a ten-minute break on Tuesdays and a fifteen-minute break on alternate Wednesdays; while exactly the reverse procedure will apply to the lower Shell, C division. I thought I had sufficiently explained that on my chart . . . Oh, I see . . . Thank you, that is very good of you . . . yes. I think you will find it will work out quite satisfactorily . . . Oh, by the way, head-master. I have changed my mind about the prize-giving ceremony. I intend to speak after, instead of before, Fletcher, as is my privilege . . . Yes, I quite understand, but I am now seeing the matter in a different light. . . . I know, but I am of opinion that occasionally an anti-climax can be surprisingly effective. Goodbye. (*He rings off and goes and sits at table.*) Come along, my dear. We mustn't let our dinner get cold.

MILLIE *slowly sits and begins to serve dinner.*

CURTAIN

HARLEQUINADE

A FARCE

Harlequinade was first produced at the Phoenix Theatre, London, on September 8th, 1948, with the following cast:

ARTHUR GOSPORT	...	...	*Eric Portman*
EDNA SELBY ...	...	...	...	*Mary Ellis*
DAME MAUD GOSPORT ...	...	*Marie Löhr*
JACK WAKEFIELD ...	...	...	*Hector Ross*
GEORGE CHUDLEIGH	...	...	*Kenneth Edwards*
FIRST HALBERDIER	...	...	*Peter Scott*
SECOND HALBERDIER	...	...	*Basil Howes*
MISS FISHLOCK	...	...	...	*Noel Dyson*
FRED INGRAM	...	...	...	*Anthony Oliver*
JOHNNY ...	...	...	...	...	*Henry Bryce*
MURIEL PALMER	...	...	...	*Thelma Ruby*
TOM PALMER	...	...	...	*Patrick Jordan*
MR. BURTON	...	...	...	*Campbell Cotts*
JOYCE LANGLAND ...	...	...	*Henryetta Edwards*
POLICEMAN ...	...	...	...	*Manville Tarrant*

The play directed by PETER GLENVILLE

SCENE: The stage of a theatre in a Midlands town.

HARLEQUINADE

SCENE: *The stage of a theatre in a Midlands town. The lights are out on the rise of the curtain. They come on gradually to reveal the graceful figure of* ARTHUR GOSPORT *as he enters. He is dressed in doublet and tights.*

ARTHUR. (*Shouting over his shoulder.*) He jests at scars that never felt a wound.

The lights now reveal enough for us to see that he has found himself in an unmistakable, if rather severely functional, fifteenth-century Italian garden, with, at one side, the balcony of a house, from the window of which is shining a light.

But, soft! What light through yonder window breaks?
It is the east, and Juliet is the sun!
Arise, fair sun, and kill the envious moon,
Who is already sick and pale with grief,
That thou her maid art far more fair than she:
Be not her maid, since she is envious;
Her vestal livery is but sick and green,
And none but fools do wear it; cast it off.

Juliet, in the person of EDNA SELBY, *appears at the balcony above.*

It is my lady; O, it is my love!
O, that she knew she were!

EDNA *emits a melodious sigh and gives a sad shake of the head.*

She speaks, yet she says nothing; and what of that?
Her eye discourses, I will answer it.

He comes forward, then leaps back.

I am too bold, 'tis not to me she speaks:
Two of the fairest stars in all the heaven,
Having some business, do entreat her eyes
To twinkle in their spheres till they return.
What if her eyes were there, they in her head?
The brightness of her cheek would shame those stars,
As daylight doth a lamp; her eyes in heaven
Would through the airy region stream so bright

227

That birds would sing, and think it were not night.

EDNA *emits another melodious sigh, and rests her cheek thoughtfully upon her hand.*

See how she leans her cheek upon her hand!

O, that I were a glove upon that hand,

That I might touch that cheek!

EDNA. Ah me!

ARTHUR.   She speaks:

O, speak again, bright angel! for thou art

As glorious to this night, being o'er my head,

As is a winged messenger of heaven

Unto the white-upturned wondering eyes

Of mortals that fall back to gaze on him

When he bestrides the lazy-pacing clouds

And sails upon the bosom of the air.

EDNA. O Romeo, Romeo! Wherefore art thou Romeo?

Deny thy father and refuse thy name;

Or, if thou wilt not, be but sworn my love,

And I'll no longer be a Capulet.

ARTHUR. (*Aside.*) Shall I hear more, or shall I speak at this?

In the intense excitement of his passion he gives a boyish leap on to a garden stool. EDNA's *glance momentarily wavers from the upper regions of the theatre, on which her eyes have been sentimentally fixed since the beginning of the scene.*

EDNA. 'Tis but thy name that is my enemy;

Thou art thyself though, not a Montague.

What's Montague?

Darling, are you going to do that tonight?

ARTHUR. What?

EDNA. That little jump.

ARTHUR. Well—yes—I thought I would. Why? Does it bother you?

EDNA. No, darling. Just so long as I know, that's all.

ARTHUR. Sorry, darling. That's quite all right. Let's go back. (*To prompt corner.*) Yes?

JOHNNY. (*From prompt corner.*) 'Tis but thy name——

EDNA. (*Sharply.*) No. Before that. I want to give Mr. Gosport the cue for his little jump.

JOHNNY. (*Off.*) What little jump, Miss Selby?

EDNA. The little jump he does on to that stool.

Enter JOHNNY.

JOHNNY. Mr. Gosport doesn't do a little jump, Miss Selby.

EDNA. Yes, he does do a little jump. He's just done a little jump.

JOHNNY. He's never done a little jump before.

EDNA. I know he's never done a little jump before. But he's doing a little jump now. He's just put a little jump in.

ARTHUR. Look—I don't think I'll do the little jump, after all.

EDNA. Yes, you shall, my darling. You shall do the little jump. It looked very charming—very youthful. (*To prompt corner.*) When Mr. Gosport says: 'Shall I speak at this?' he does a little jump on to a stool. Now what's my line before that?

JOHNNY. (*Going off.*) And I'll no longer be a Capulet.

EDNA. (*Resuming her pose.*) Or, if thou wilt not, be but sworn my love,

And I'll no longer be a Capulet.

ARTHUR *does his leap again, only this time it is, perhaps, not quite so boyish as before.*

ARTHUR. Shall I hear more or shall I speak at this?

EDNA. 'Tis but thy name that is my enemy;

Thou art thyself though, not a Montague.

What's Montague?

While speaking she has appeared to be struggling to keep her composure. She now loses the battle and laughs outright.

Sorry, darling.

ARTHUR. Does it look awfully silly? I won't do it, then.

EDNA. Oh no—you must do it. Come on. Let's try again.

ARTHUR. No. I won't do it if it's as funny as all that. I only thought it might help the boyishness of the line, that's all.

EDNA. And it does. It looks very boyish. (*To prompt corner.*) Doesn't it look boyish, Johnny?

JOHNNY. (*Off.*) Very boyish, Miss Selby.

EDNA. I was only laughing at your suddenly putting in a thing like that, after our having done this play so many hundreds

of times together and never a little jump in fifteen years until
now—just before a first night.

ARTHUR. All right. All right. Let's forget the whole thing. I'll
say the line standing as still as the Rock of Ages, and looking just about twice as old—let's go on.

EDNA. It's silly to say that, Arthur. If you feel you're too old
for the part you'll only get a complex about it.

ARTHUR. I am much too old for the part. I'm not seventeen.

EDNA. Well, if it comes to that, darling, I'm not thirteen, but
I shan't let that worry me tonight. It's all up here—(*She
taps her forehead.*)—it's not just a question of doing little
jumps——

ARTHUR. I am *not* doing any little jump. That's dead, once
and for all. Now, for God's sake, let's go on.

EDNA. Besides, it's silly to think you don't look young. That
wig is very, very becoming. (*She shields her eyes and looks over
the footlights at the audience.*) Auntie Maud! Are you in
front, dear?

DAME MAUD GOSPORT *appears from the wings. She is an imposing
old lady dressed as the Nurse.*

DAME MAUD. I've just come from in front, dear. What is it?

EDNA. How did you think Arthur looked?

DAME MAUD. Far too old.

EDNA. Oh. Too much light on him?

DAME MAUD. Far too much.

ARTHUR. What about Edna, Auntie Maud? How did she
look?

DAME MAUD. Far too old, too.

ARTHUR. Too much light on her too?

DAME MAUD. Yes. Far too much.

EDNA. I don't think Auntie Maud sees very well. Do you,
Auntie Maud, dear? (*To* ARTHUR, *in an undertone.*) She's
getting so shortsighted, you know, Arthur——

DAME MAUD. (*Firmly.*) Yes, I do. I see very well. I had my specs
on, and I was right at the back, and you both looked far
too old.

She goes off.

ARTHUR. (*Calling.*) Jack! Jack! Where's the stage manager?

JACK WAKEFIELD, *the stage manager, comes on from the prompt corner. He is a grave-faced young man in the late twenties.*

JACK. Yes, Mr. Gosport?

ARTHUR. The lighting for this scene has gone mad. This isn't our plot. There's far too much light. What's gone wrong with it?

JACK. I think the trouble is they've crept in numbers two and three too early. (*Calling up to the flies.*) Will—check your plot, please. Number two and three spots should be down to a quarter instead of full.

VOICE. (*From above.*) O.K.

JACK. And you've got your floats too high, too. You're burning Mr. Gosport up——

EDNA. What about me? I've got an enormous searchlight on me from somewhere out there.

JACK. (*Looking.*) That's the front of house, Miss Selby. It's in the plot.

EDNA. Well, take it out——

ARTHUR. No, you can't. You've got to have some light on this scene. We can't have it played as just our two voices coming out of pitch darkness, much as we both might like to.

EDNA. Well, I don't see why you should skulk about in romantic moonlight while I'm on my balcony, being burnt to a cinder by Eddystone Lighthouse.

ARTHUR. Let me see that plot.

DAME MAUD *comes on to join* EDNA *on balcony.*

DAME MAUD. As you've stopped, dear, I thought you wouldn't mind if I gave you one or two teeny little hints about this scene. It's the first time I've seen it from the front. You don't mind an old lady's interference, do you, dear?

EDNA. (*Rather too sweetly.*) No, of course not, Auntie Maud. You know how delighted I always am to have your teeny hints.

JACK *and* ARTHUR *pay no attention to* DAME MAUD, *continuing to rearrange the lighting.*

JACK. Take it right down, Will . . . That's it.

DAME MAUD. (*To* EDNA.) Now when I played Juliet I used to rest my hand on my cheek, like this—(*She demonstrates.*)

using just the very tips of my fingers. Now as you do it you look just a little like Rodin's *Thinker*.

EDNA. Oh. Do I?

ARTHUR. (*Lighting.*) That's too low. Now bring it up a bit.

JACK. Bring it up, Will.

EDNA. Well, you know, Auntie Maud, dear, tastes have changed a little since you played Juliet with Arthur's father.

DAME MAUD. I know they have, dear, and more's the pity.

EDNA. The theatre's gone through a revolution since 1900.

DAME MAUD. It was 1914 I played Juliet, dear. I remember the date well, because the declaration of war damaged our business so terribly.

EDNA. There's been another war since then, Auntie Maud, and I don't think you quite understand the immense change that has come over the theatre in the last few years. You see, dear—I know it's difficult for you to grasp, but the theatre of today has at last acquired a social conscience, and a social purpose. Why else do you think we're opening at this rat-hole of a theatre instead of the Opera House, Manchester?

DAME MAUD. Oh, I didn't know it was social purpose that brought us here. I thought it was C.E.M.A.

EDNA. C.E.M.A. is social purpose.

DAME MAUD. Is it, dear? Fancy!

ARTHUR. (*Still lighting.*) Take it down. That's too high.

JACK. (*Calling.*) Too high, Will.

An old actor, GEORGE CHUDLEIGH, *comes on to the stage. He is dressed as a fifteenth-century Italian peasant, and carries a flute.*

GEORGE. (*Loudly and with clear articulation.*) Faith, we may put up our pipes and begone.

ARTHUR. What?

GEORGE. Oh, am I wrong? I heard my cue, so I came on.

ARTHUR. Well, kindly go off.

GEORGE. Yes. Still, you gave me my cue, you know. You can't say you didn't.

ARTHUR. What is your cue?

GEORGE. Well, it's really a pause, when everyone's stopped speaking.

ARTHUR. My dear Mr.——

GEORGE. Chudleigh. George Chudleigh.

ARTHUR. My dear Mr. Chudleigh, if every time there's a pause in the play you're going to come on to the stage and speak that line, it's going to make the plot rather difficult to follow——

GEORGE. I meant that's just my cue to come on. My real cue is 'High will'——

JACK. (*Unruffled.*) 'Move them no more by crossing their high will.' He's quite right, Mr. Gosport. (*To* GEORGE.) That *is* your cue, but your line doesn't come till the next act and you ought to have been paying more attention. Now will you please get off the stage as we're rather busy.

GEORGE. Well—that's all very well, but you said it, you know. I heard it quite distinctly. So of course I thought you'd cut a bit out and so I counted five and on I came.

ARTHUR. (*In a fury of impatience.*) Get off the stage, you silly old man——

GEORGE. (*Stolidly indignant.*) Here. Don't you talk to me like that, young chap. I acted with your father.

ARTHUR. I don't care if you acted with Garrick's father. Get off the stage!

GEORGE. You'd better be careful, young feller, talking to people like that. It's not right.

DAME MAUD *now intervenes.* EDNA, *on her balcony, is sitting down, her back to the commotion, reading a newspaper.*

DAME MAUD. You say you acted with my brother?

GEORGE. That's right. In this play I was, too. I played Peter.

DAME MAUD. Yes, I remember now. I remember you well. You were just as incompetent then as you are now.

GEORGE. (*Under his breath.*) That's enough from you, you old bag!

DAME MAUD. (*Triumphantly.*) There you are! That shows exactly why you've never got on in the theatre. If you have a line like that to say, you don't mouth it and throw it away, you say it right out. It's a glorious word to say—bag. (*Enunciating.*) Form the word with your lips, like that. BAG. B-A-G. B—A—G.

ARTHUR. All right, Auntie Maud. All right. (*To* GEORGE.)

Look, my dear chap, just go to the wings—there's a good
fellow—and wait for your scene, which doesn't come for
hours yet, while we get on with our work.

GEORGE. I certainly won't. I've been insulted and I'm leaving.

ARTHUR. Nonsense. You can't leave.

GEORGE. Oh yes, I can. I know my rights. What's more, I'm
not just leaving, I'm retiring. I'm sixty-seven and I'd have
been fifty years on the stage, come April.

DAME MAUD. My dear Mr.—er—you really mustn't take on
like this just because——

GEORGE. (*Brushing her aside.*) I've never been a good actor, and
when I look at some that are, I thank God for it. What's
more I've never liked the life—and I've never needed the
money. Why I've gone on all these years mucking about
with never more than a line or two to say, sharing dressing
rooms with chaps I detest is more than I can fathom. Well,
I'm finished with it all now, anyway. Finished with it for
good, and you don't know how happy that makes me feel.
Goodbye, all.

He goes off.

There is a silence after he has gone, broken by DAME MAUD.

DAME MAUD. (*Scornfully.*) Can't even make an exit properly.

EDNA. Must have a film job.

ARTHUR. Oh. All right. One of the supers can do the pipes
line. Break for an hour for tea, but don't strike this set. I
want to rehearse the farewell scene before the show.

JACK. Yes, Mr. Gosport. (*Calling.*) Break for an hour for tea,
everyone! Back at 5.30, please! Curtain up at 7.30.

ARTHUR. Then I'll rehearse the duel.

JACK. Yes, Mr. Gosport.

ARTHUR. And I could see those girls for *The Winter's Tale.*

JACK. Yes, Mr. Gosport.

ARTHUR. And then, if there's time, I can rehearse the jig.

JACK. Yes, Mr. Gosport. (*He goes towards wings.*)

DAME MAUD. Oh, Jack—send someone out for some sandwiches for me—and a bottle of Guinness, would you?

JACK. Yes, Dame Maud.

DAME MAUD. Better make it a couple of bottles. It's so good for my back.

JACK. Yes, Dame Maud.

JACK *goes off.*

DAME MAUD. Goodbye, my children. I'm sure from what I've seen it's all going to be splendid.

Exit.

JOHNNY *comes on with sandwiches for* ARTHUR, *and then goes out.*

ARTHUR. Sandwich, dear?

EDNA. (*To* ARTHUR.) No thank you, darling. I'll have a proper tea for us in our room, my darling.

ARTHUR. Thank you, darling.

EDNA. Don't worry, my precious. That wig is a dream. And you can do your little jump if you want to.

ARTHUR. No, thank you, darling. Edna—I'm not too old for the part, am I?

EDNA. No; of course not, my angel. Or, if you are, then I am.

ARTHUR. But you're three years younger, aren't you?

EDNA. What's three among so many?

She goes out through her bedroom window.

Enter JOHNNY.

Two young men, dressed as HALBERDIERS *and trailing spears, cross the stage at back, chatting to each other in confidential whispers.*

ARTHUR. Johnny, draw the tabs and rehearse some of the lighting cues during the break, will you. (*Over the footlights.*) Miss Fishlock? Would you come to my room for a moment? I want you to take some notes on *The Winter's Tale.* (*He turns and sees the young men.*) Would you come here, you two? (*They both obey with alacrity.*)

(*To one of them.*) Just say—Faith, we may put up our pipes and begone.

1ST HALBERDIER. (*In a flat, faintly Cockney accent.*) Faith, we may put up our pipes and begone.

ARTHUR. (*To the other.*) Now you.

2ND HALBERDIER. (*Going much too far, vocally and in gesture.*) Faith, we may put up our pipes and begone.

ARTHUR. (*Pointing to* 1ST HALBERDIER.) Right. You'll do it.

1ST HALBERDIER. (*Transported.*) You mean—I'm going to have a line to say, Mr. Gosport?

ARTHUR. Yes. (*He hands him the script.*) I'll rehearse you in a few minutes.

MISS FISHLOCK *comes on.*

Ah, Miss Fishlock. Would you get in touch with the London Office at once and inform Mr. Wilmot that the six girls he sent up specially for *The Winter's Tale* are quite out of the question.

MISS FISHLOCK. Yes, Mr. Gosport.

1ST HALBERDIER. Oh, Mr. Gosport! (*To* 2ND HALBERDIER.) Oh bad luck, Cyril. *Exit* MISS FISHLOCK *and* ARTHUR.

2ND HALBERDIER. (*They drift away, peering at the script together.*) I bet it was because you picked up his gloves at the station on Friday.

He disappears.

1ST HALBERDIER *looks round the stage cautiously, and finding himself alone, goes down to the footlights.*

1ST HALBERDIER. (*In a hoarse whisper, across the footlights.*) Mum! Mum!

JACK *appears, unseen by the* HALBERDIER.

I've got a part. It's only a line, but it's awfully important . . . Yes, isn't it wonderful?

JACK. (*Approaching him.*) Who are you talking to?

1ST HALBERDIER. (*Confused.*) Oh, Mr. Wakefield. I didn't see you. It's only my mother. She's up there. (*He waves towards the upper circle.*)

JACK. Then I'm afraid you must ask her to go. You know the rule about strangers in front at rehearsal.

1ST HALBERDIER. Oh, but can't she stay and hear me speak my line?

JACK. No, I'm afraid not. She'll have to come back at 7.30 when we start.

1ST HALBERDIER. But she has to get back to Birmingham to-night. She only came for the day——

JACK. (*Firmly.*) I'm extremely sorry, but rules are rules and Mr.

and Mrs. Gosport are very strict about this particular one.
She shouldn't be here at all.

*He turns away as a man in the costume of Tybalt (*FREDERICK
INGRAM*) comes on to the stage with a cup of tea and a sausage
roll.*

INGRAM. (*To* JACK.) What the hell does he want me for?

JACK. The duel.

INGRAM. Oh, my God! Not again!

The 1ST HALBERDIER *has meanwhile been gesticulating across the footlights to his mother, making uncomplimentary and furtive gestures
towards* JACK. *When he has conveyed his meaning he goes off.*

I'm slipping across to the Feathers for a quick one. Do you
think I've got time?

JACK. Yes, Mr. Ingram. I'll warn you.

INGRAM *goes off.*

*The assistant stage manager (*JOHNNY*) puts his head on.*

JOHNNY. 'Ere—there's a baby in a pram in the wings. Is that
a prop in the play?

JACK. Not unless they've considerably rewritten it. Is it alive?

JOHNNY. Oh, I don't know. I'll just see.

His head momentarily disappears. We hear, faintly, a baby's gurgle.
JOHNNY's *head reappears.*

Yes. It's alive. What shall I do with it?

JACK. I suppose you'd better leave it there. Presumably it
belongs to someone. My God! What with Mums in front
and babies in the wings it's not so much a dress rehearsal
as old home week.

*A nondescript, rather shabbily dressed girl of about twenty (*MURIEL*),
accompanied by a* SOLDIER, *about ten years older, have come timidly
on to the stage and are staring about them.* JOHNNY's *head has
meanwhile disappeared.*

Yes? What do you want?

MURIEL. (*In a strong Midland accent.*) Could I speak to my Dad,
please?

JACK. And who may your Dad be?

MURIEL. He's an actor.

JACK. Then I'm afraid you've come to the wrong theatre. Try
the Palace of Varieties across the street.

MR. BURTON, *the theatre manager, has come on.*

BURTON. Good evening, Mr. Wakefield.

JACK. Good evening, Mr. Burton.

BURTON. I hope you find our theatre to your satisfaction.

JACK. How are our bookings?

BURTON. Not bad. Not half bad, considering what the show is. Of course, we've never had these two up here before, you know, but it's a big help that feller Fred Ingram being in that picture at the Super.

MURIEL. (*To* JACK.) Look—I'm sure it *is* this theatre——

JACK. No, my dear. They've got a sort of circus here this week. The Palace is what you want. Through that door there, up the stairs and into the street.

He moves away again. MURIEL *and the* SOLDIER *go off slowly.*

BURTON. Funny for them to choose to open up here, I must say——

JACK. Social purpose, Mr. Burton.

BURTON. Social purpose? Now what the blazes is that when it's at home?

JACK. As far as I can see it means playing Shakespeare to audiences who'd rather go to the films; while audiences who'd rather go to Shakespeare are driven to the films because they haven't got Shakespeare to go to. It's all got something to do with the new Britain and apparently it's an absolutely splendid idea.

ARTHUR *comes on, now in a dressing-gown.*

Here's Mr. Gosport. He can tell you all about it. This is Mr. Burton, sir. The theatre manager.

ARTHUR. Oh, how do you do? My wife and I are simply thrilled to be opening in your beautiful theatre and this delightful town.

BURTON. Thank you, Mr. Gosport, and I can assure you it's a great honour for us all to have you both up here.

ARTHUR. Thank you. As a matter of fact you've always been very kind to us here in Sheffield——

BURTON. But it's next week you're playing Sheffield, Mr. Gosport.

ARTHUR. Oh! What's this town, then?

BURTON. Brackley.

ARTHUR. Oh yes, of course. They added a week, didn't they? How idiotic of them!

BURTON. That's all right, Mr. Gosport. Great men are always a bit absent-minded.

ARTHUR. Brackley. Of course it is. (*With a sudden change of expression.*) Brackley! Good lord!

JACK. What's the matter?

ARTHUR. I was just remembering something. Brackley! Good heavens!

JACK. Is anything wrong, Mr. Gosport?

ARTHUR *is lost in a reverie.* BURTON *looks at* JACK *a trifle bewildered.* JACK *touches his forehead.* BURTON *nods.*

ARTHUR. Tell me, Mr.—er—hrrhm—, is there a square place in your town with a perfectly repulsive building in glazed brick with a ridiculous dome on top?

BURTON. (*Doubtfully.*) The Civic Centre?

ARTHUR. (*Impatiently.*) Yes, yes. And then, dead opposite, is there an enormous white concrete and glass object that looks just like a public lavatory?

BURTON. (*Too hurt even to protest.*) The Civic Library, Mr. Gosport.

JACK. (*Hastily.*) Do you know this town, then, Mr. Gosport?

ARTHUR. Yes. Only too well.

JACK *manages to get in a nudge.*

Only too well. I was here as a boy in repertory.

BURTON. When exactly were you here, Mr. Gosport? (*Getting out notebook and pencil.*) Could you pin it to a definite date? I ought to ring up the *Argus* about this.

ARTHUR. Well, let me see now. (*He ponders deeply.*) Yes, I can tell you exactly. It was the year Gladys Cooper opened in *The Sign of the Door.*

BURTON. I'm afraid I don't remember that, Mr. Gosport. (*To* JACK.) Do you?

JACK. No. (*To* ARTHUR.) I suppose you couldn't remember anything else that happened that year? A war, or something like that?

ARTHUR. No, I don't think there was a war. Wait a moment—

I do remember something that happened that year. There was some sort of commotion——

JACK. A commotion? An earthquake?

ARTHUR. No, no. Something to do with trains. They didn't run. And newspapers too. There weren't any notices. And then I was made to drive a tram, for some reason——

JACK. 1926. The general strike.

ARTHUR. Thank you. That's right. That's what it was called. The general strike.

BURTON. (*Writing down the date.*) 1926.

ARTHUR. Excuse me . . . I must get a cup of tea before I look at six girls . . .

He goes off.

BURTON. Bit scatter-brained, isn't he?

JACK. I doubt if you can scatter a void.

BURTON. I thought he was supposed to be an intellectual sort of chap.

JACK. He's an actor, Mr. Burton.

BURTON. Now perhaps you wouldn't mind giving me a bit more dope on the Gosports for the *Argus*.

JACK. All right, but very quickly. I've got a hundred things to do.

BURTON. How long have they been married?

JACK. Fifteen years.

BURTON. Any children?

JACK. One—little Basil——

BURTON. Oh. And how old is little Basil?

JACK. Thirteen.

BURTON. Up here?

JACK. No. At school——

BURTON. Going to be an actor too?

JACK. Judging by his behaviour, yes. Besides—he's a Gosport.

BURTON. I see. Now how would you describe these Gosports? Would we offend anyone if we called them the most famous married couple in the theatre?

JACK. You wouldn't offend the Gosports, Mr. Burton, which is the main thing. Besides it's reasonably true.

BURTON. Always act together, don't they?

JACK. Yes.

BURTON. Always as husband and wife?

JACK. No. Usually as lover and mistress. The audience prefers that—it gives them such a cosy feeling to know they're really married after all.

BURTON. Now, about this tour. How long is it?

JACK. Sixteen weeks out, then London——

BURTON. Oh. They *are* going to London, then?

JACK. Only for four weeks. If you play in the West End for longer than that you become commercial.

BURTON. I see. What after that?

JACK. Belgrade, Bucharest, Warsaw, Riga, and Moscow.

BURTON. Oh. What about the Iron Curtain?

JACK. The Gosports could make any curtain rise.

BURTON. What plays are they taking?

ARTHUR, *tea in hand, wanders on and begins fussing mildly in the background, removing a pot of artificial flowers from one place on the stage and putting it in another; then changing his mind and putting it back again.*

JACK. *Romeo, The Winter's Tale, Macbeth,* and a modern play in verse called '*Follow the Leviathan to My Father's Grave*'.

BURTON. What's that about?

JACK. Here's Mr. Gosport, he'll tell you.

BURTON. What's the new play about, Mr. Gosport?

ARTHUR. Death. My wife's got the best part in it. I only play the pencil-sharpener in the last act.

He replaces the pot once more and wanders off.

BURTON. Well, perhaps he'll tell more about it to the *Argus* critic.

JACK. I doubt it.

ARTHUR reappears.

ARTHUR. There's a baby here, in the wings. It looks exactly like someone I know. Who is it?

JACK. I've no idea, I'm afraid.

ARTHUR. It's very careless of people, leaving babies in the wings. There might be a very nasty accident. Somebody might easily trip over it and ruin their exit. See that it's removed before rehearsal.

JACK. Yes, Mr. Gosport.

ARTHUR. And in future, if people bring babies to the theatre, see that they're kept in the proper place.

JACK. Yes, Mr. Gosport. Where's that?

ARTHUR. I don't know.

He goes off again.

JACK. Well, is there any more help I can give you, Mr. Burton?

BURTON. No, thanks. I think that's all. It only remains for me to wish you a very successful opening, which I'm sure you'll have.

JACK. Thank you very much.

They shake hands. MURIEL *and her* SOLDIER *appear suddenly on Juliet's balcony.*

MURIEL. (*Attacked with vertigo.*) Oo—Tom! Look where we've got ourselves to!

JACK. Madam—will you and your friend kindly leave this theatre?

MURIEL. No, I won't. I've told you. I want to see my Dad.

JACK. And I've told you your Dad isn't here.

MURIEL. Oh, yes, he is. He's not at The Palace, like you said. He's here. I've seen his name on the posters.

JACK. Well, you can't see him now, anyway. Anyway, who is your Dad?

MURIEL. Gosport's the name.

JACK. Gosport?

MURIEL. Yes. Arthur Gosport. **He's** an actor.

JACK. Oh. I see.

He signs urgently to the prompt corner. JOHNNY *appears.*

So you're the daughter of Arthur Gosport, are you?

MURIEL. Yes, that's right. And this is my husband.

TOM. How do?

JACK. I'm most delighted to meet you both. I simply can't apologize enough for having been so very rude. (*To* JOHNNY.) Oh, Johnny. This lady is Mr. Gosport's daughter, and this is her husband. Would you be so kind as to—er—look after them both? Just—er—show them around, would you?

He makes a quick, violent gesture of his thumb, unseen by the two on the balcony. JOHNNY *nods.*

JOHNNY. O.K., Mr. Wakefield.

He goes off.

JACK. Now, Miss Gosport——

MURIEL. (*Giggling.*) Mrs. Palmer.

JACK. I do beg your pardon, Mrs. Palmer. Now, if you and
your husband would be so very kind as to step through that
window there and down the steps, you'll find such a nice
gentleman who's going to take such very good care of you
both.

MURIEL. Oh. Thanks—you're a pal. Come on, Tom.

She disappears from view. TOM *waves cheerfully to* JACK *and follows
her.*

BURTON. Lor' love us! What will they think up next?

JACK. Amazing, isn't it?

BURTON. (*Shaking his head, sadly.*) It's a funny world ours,
isn't it?

JACK. Side-splitting.

The IST HALBERDIER *comes on mouthing and muttering anxiously
to himself.*

BURTON *exits.*

JACK *shakes his head wearily. Then looks at his watch.*

JOHNNY *reappears.*

All right?

JOHNNY. I'll lock 'em in one of the downstairs rooms. I'd better
not shove 'em out as the doorman's off and they might get
in again.

JACK. Quite right. Which room will you put them in?

JOHNNY. I'll put them in number three. There are six other
girls there waiting for someone.

JACK. (*Wearily.*) I wonder whose daughters they are. O.K.,
Johnny. Thanks.

He goes off as the HALBERDIER *approaches* JACK.

HALBERDIER. Mr. Wakefield, do you think it ought to be:
Faith, we may put up our PIPES and begone, or FAITH,
we may put UP our pipes and begone?

JACK. What about, Faith, we may put up our pipes and
(*roaring*) BEGONE?

HALBERDIER. That doesn't sound quite right to me.

JACK. It sounds awfully right to me. What's happened to
your Mum?

HALBERDIER. Oh, she's gone.

JACK. (*Grimly.*) That's very lucky for *her*.

A very good-looking, smartly dressed girl (JOYCE LANGLAND) *appears
on the stage and stands, evidently a little awed by her surroundings.
The* HALBERDIER *wanders off, still muttering.*

JOYCE. Jack——

JACK. (*Surprised.*) Joyce! (*He approaches her and kisses her warmly.*)
Why on earth didn't you let me know you were coming up?

JOYCE. I didn't have time.

JACK. What do you mean, you didn't have time?

JOYCE. I've got some news for you which I had to tell you
myself, so I just jumped on the first train.

JACK. Oh, darling! How wonderful!

JOYCE. (*Disappointed.*) You've guessed.

JACK. Your father's changed his mind. Darling, you're a
magician. How did you work it?

JOYCE. You worked it. He was terribly impressed with your
letter.

JACK. So he should be.

JOYCE. Then I told him your war record.

JACK. That was a mistake, wasn't it?

JOYCE. You got the D.F.C.

JACK. Only because the C.O. liked the pantomime I produced
for the chaps. I say, darling, are we rich?

JOYCE. We'll pay super-tax, anyway.

JACK. Oh, darling, how marvellous! I don't have to work any
more?

JOYCE. Not in the theatre, anyway.

JACK. Oh. But I do have to work?

JOYCE. He's going to take you into the firm.

JACK. Oh. I thought there was a catch.

JOYCE. Darling, it's not a catch. Jack—it's not that you don't
want to give up the theatre, is it?

JACK. Good lord, no! I'd give up the theatre tomorrow if I
could.

JOYCE. Well, now you can.

There is a pause, broken by the HALBERDIER *who has wandered on to the stage a few seconds before.*

HALBERDIER. Faith, we may put up OUR pipes and begone.

JACK. Look, old chap—do you mind awfully going and doing that somewhere else? I've got things on my mind.

HALBERDIER. Sorry, Mr. Wakefield. This is my great chance, you know—and I don't want to muck it up. (*Muttering.*) That's it. I know. Faith, we may put up OUR pipes and begone.

He goes off.

JACK. Darling, I think I'd better finish the tour.

JOYCE. (*Horrified.*) The whole tour—forty-six weeks?

JACK. No, no. Only England. After London they'll have to get someone else. But I can't let them down without fair warning.

JOYCE. No. I see that. There's only one thing I'm frightened of though, Jack. Shall I tell you what it is?

JACK. That I haven't the guts to leave them at all?

JOYCE. It's not only the Gosports I'm worrying about. It's the theatre.

JACK. The Gosports are the theatre. There is no theatre apart from the Gosports.

JOYCE. Darling, don't exaggerate.

JACK. I'm not. I mean the Gosports are eternal. They're the theatre at its worst and its best. They're true theatre, because they're entirely self-centred, entirely exhibitionist, and entirely dotty, and because they make no compromise whatever with the outside world.

JOYCE. Then what about this idea of theirs of theatre with a social purpose?

JACK. Theatre with a social purpose, indeed! It's a contradiction in terms. Good citizenship and good theatre don't go together. They never have and they never will. All through the ages, from Burbage downwards, the theatre—the true theatre—has consisted of blind, anti-social, self-sufficient, certifiable Gosports. The point is that if I have the courage to leave the Gosports, I have the courage to leave the theatre.

JOYCE. And have you?

JACK. Yes. I hate the theatre. I shall leave the theatre without the faintest regret, and for a week afterwards I shall barely draw a sober breath in celebration.

JOYCE. (*With a sigh of relief.*) And I'll be at your side in that. Good. Will you go and tell them now, then?

JACK. Now?

JOYCE. Yes. There's a break on, isn't there?

JACK. (*Slowly.*) Yes. Is this a test of my courage?

JOYCE. That's it.

JACK. All right. I might as well get it over with. Besides, I'm giving them plenty of notice, aren't I?

JOYCE. (*Smiling.*) Yes. Plenty.

JACK. (*Annoyed.*) I'm not in the least afraid of them, you know, if that's what you think.

EDNA, *in dressing-gown and chewing a sandwich, wanders on from the wings.*

EDNA. I'm a bit worried about the balcony, Jack. It seems very wobbly to me.

JACK. It's being seen to, Miss Selby. Er—Miss Selby——

EDNA. (*Turning.*) Yes?

JACK. Could I introduce Miss Langland?

EDNA. Oh yes. How do you do? (*She shakes hands.*) You're a serving wench, aren't you?

JACK. Er—no. She's not in the company at all. As a matter of fact, Miss Selby—she's the girl I'm going to marry.

EDNA. Marry! My dear, how wonderful! How simply wonderful! Oh, Jack, darling, I'm so glad. (*She embraces him warmly. To* JOYCE.) And you too, my dear. (*She kisses her.*) So pretty you are, and so young and what an enchanting little frock! Oh, I'm so happy for you both, I feel I want to cry and ruin my make-up. Arthur must be your best man, and I'll be godmother to your first. When's the wedding to be?

JACK. (*Exchanging glances with* JOYCE.) After the provincial tour —when we come to London.

EDNA. Oh, good! (*To* JOYCE.) It would have been far too long a time to wait for him, wouldn't it—forty-six weeks?

JOYCE. (*Surprised.*) Yes. I did feel that, I'm afraid.

EDNA. Don't be afraid, dear. You're quite right to be impatient.

I was, when I married Arthur. (*She strokes* JOYCE's *face.*)
Dear little child. I'm so happy for you. So you'll be coming
to Europe with us, will you?

JOYCE. Er—no, Miss Selby. I won't.

EDNA. No? Well, perhaps you're wise. It's going to be rather
uncomfortable for all of us, I expect. Still, won't you miss
him, being gone all that time?

JACK. Well—the fact is, Miss Selby—you see—I—er—well—
this is the point—I'm not sure that I'm going to Europe
myself.

EDNA. Not going to Europe? (*She looks mildly surprised then
appears to see daylight.*) Oh, I know what you mean. Some
nasty creature must have sneaked to you about what
Arthur was saying the other day about Ronnie Williams
coming to stage-manage for us. But you mustn't worry, my
darling. It was only because Ronnie Williams stage-
managed for us for so long—practically before you were
born, my darling—and Arthur heard he was out of a job,
and you know how tactless he is, the poor old thing—but he
really didn't mean it, I know he didn't——

JACK. (*Desperately.*) Look, Miss Selby—it's got nothing to do
with Ronnie Williams——

EDNA. You're hurt, my precious. I'm so sorry. But I can
promise you most faithfully that there was never, never any
question of our not taking you to Europe. We all love you
and admire you far too much——

JACK. Thank you very much, Miss Selby, but——

EDNA. Now I don't want to hear anything more about it. Just
forget the whole thing and pretend it never happened.
You're coming with us to Europe. I promise you. Goodbye,
you dear things. (*She blows them a fond kiss.*) You look so
pretty, the two of you, standing there together.

She goes off.

JACK. (*To* JOYCE.) Look, darling, perhaps a dress rehearsal
isn't the best moment to break it to them. What about
tomorrow—or after the first night?

JOYCE. Or after Sheffield, or after London, or after the European tour? No, Jack, darling, something tells me that if

you don't do it now, during this break, you never will——

JACK. I could write them a letter——

JOYCE. I thought you said you weren't afraid of them?

> ARTHUR *wanders on and makes straight for the flower pot, removing it, in the background, to another spot.*

JACK. I know. I'll tell *him.* He's really much easier to deal with than she is.

JOYCE. (*Indicating* ARTHUR.) Well, now's your chance, then.

> JACK *starts violently; then braces himself and takes* JOYCE *by the hand up to* ARTHUR.

JACK. Oh, Mr. Gosport.

ARTHUR. Yes.

JACK. Could I introduce Miss Langland?

ARTHUR. Oh. How do you do. Have you read *The Winter's Tale?*

JOYCE. Er—no. I'm afraid I haven't.

ARTHUR. Well, it's not a difficult part. It's about a girl who's abandoned by her father when she's a baby, and then many years later they meet——

JACK. Er—Miss Langland isn't here about *The Winter's Tale,* Mr. Gosport. (*In a firm, measured voice.*) She's my fiancée, we're getting married after the provincial tour, and I'm not coming with you to Europe.

ARTHUR. Yes. I see, my dear fellow. Now what about those girls for *Winter's Tale?* Are they here?

JACK. Yes, I think so. Did you hear what I said, Mr. Gosport?

ARTHUR. Yes, of course. I think I'd better see those girls straight away. Have them in, one by one, would you? (*He puts the pot in another place.*)

JACK. Yes, Mr. Gosport. (*Calling.*) Johnny. Are the girls here for *Winter's Tale?*

JOHNNY. (*Off.*) Yes. Seven of them.

JACK. That's right. Mr. Gosport will see them now, separately.

JOHNNY. (*Off.*) O.K.

ARTHUR. (*Indicating pot.*) How do you like it here, Jack?

JACK. Much better.

ARTHUR. (*To* JOYCE.) What do you think, Miss—er—Hrrhm?

JOYCE. I think it's charming, there.

ARTHUR. No. I don't think I like it there very much. (*He removes it.*)

JACK. Mr. Gosport, I don't think you quite grasped what I said just now.

ARTHUR. (*Annoyed at the implication.*) Of course I did, my dear fellow. You said you thought the pot looked better there, but I don't agree——

JACK. No. Before that. I told you I was getting married——

ARTHUR. Getting married? I'm absolutely delighted, my dear chap. (*He shakes hands.*) Who to?

EDNA *comes on.*

ARTHUR. Edna, I've thought of an entirely new way of dying.

EDNA. Have you darling? How exciting.

ARTHUR. Bring on the tomb, someone.

JACK. Yes, Mr. Gosport. (*Calling.*) Johnny, give me a hand with the tomb.

JOHNNY. (*Coming on.*) Yes, Mr. Wakefield.

He and JACK *bring forward the tomb and* JOHNNY *goes off.*

ARTHUR. (*Going over to* JOYCE.) Now, young lady—perhaps you would be kind enough to take up a position there—thank you. (*To* EDNA.) The beauty of it is in its simplicity. Now I must get you something to lie on.

He takes a mackintosh from JOYCE *and spreads it on the tomb.* EDNA *lies on it.*

Thank you.

JACK. Look, Mr. Gosport, there's something I've got to tell you before you die.

ARTHUR. Well, if she can't do the quick change in time, she'll just have to wear the black velvet all through.

JACK. But Mr. Gos——

ARTHUR. That's all there is to it. I don't want to hear another word about it.

(*Adopting his dying pose.*)

Now. Come, bitter conduct, come, unsavoury guide!
Thou desperate pilot, now at once run on,
The dashing rocks thy sea-sick weary bark!
Here's to my love! (*Drinks.*)—Oh true apothecary!
Thy drugs are quick.—Thus with a kiss I die.

And a very spectacular death it is. JOYCE, *despite her prejudice, is thrilled.*

JOYCE. (*To* JACK.) That was wonderful!

ARTHUR. (*Overhearing.*) Oh, did you·like it, Miss—Hrrhm? I'm so glad. You didn't think it was too much?

JOYCE. Oh no. Not a bit—I thought it was thrilling.

EDNA. (*Sitting up.*) Jack, darling, don't you think your little friend must be feeling awfully cold, standing on this draughty stage in that thin little frock? Wouldn't she be much better off in a nice warm dressing-room?

JACK. (*Resignedly.*) Yes, Miss Selby. (*To* JOYCE.) Darling, run along to my room, would you? It's number fourteen on the second floor. I'll join you when I can.

JOYCE. All right. (*As she goes.*) Now, don't let me down, Jack. Before the break is up.

EDNA. Such a sweet little face.

JACK. Before the break is up. I promise.

JOYCE *goes out.*

EDNA. Arthur, it's a lovely death, but I'm not absolutely sure it doesn't go on perhaps a hair too long. I don't think we'll put it in tonight.

ARTHUR. (*Knowing he has lost.*) All right, darling. I just thought it was worth trying—that was all.

The HALBERDIER *comes on, still muttering.*

HALBERDIER. Oh, Mr. Gosport. Are you ready for me yet?

ARTHUR. No. In a minute. I'm seeing some girls first. Just wait there.

He motions him to a corner of the stage, where the HALBERDIER *sits, mouthing intermittently.*

All right, Jack. Ready for *The Winter's Tale*.

JACK. (*Calling.*) All right, Johnny. Send the first lady on, will you?

JOHNNY. (*Off.*) O.K.

JACK. (*Calling.*) What is the lady's name, please?

Whispers off.

JOHNNY. (*Off.*) Muriel Palmer.

JACK. (*Writing it down.*) Muriel Palmer.

And MURIEL PALMER *comes on, followed at a few yards' interval by her* SOLDIER HUSBAND. JACK, *busy with his notebook, does not immediately look up.*

MURIEL. (*With a joyous cry, pointing at* ARTHUR.) There he is! That's my Dad! Daddy, I'm your daughter, and you're my Dad.

ARTHUR. Er—what text are you using, Miss, er—hrrhm?

JACK. (*Interposing quickly.*) Excuse me, Mr. Gosport, but I know about this young lady. She's been annoying us all the evening. (*To* MURIEL.) How did you get out of that room?

MURIEL. A young man came and unlocked us and told me and six other girls to come on the stage separately as Mr. Gosport was waiting for us——

JACK. Oh God! All right. Well, now, are you going to go quietly or shall I have to ring up for the police?

MURIEL. Ring up the police? Go ahead. I don't mind. I haven't done anything wrong. I just want a few words with my Dad, that's all. That's my Dad, all right. I recognize him from Mum's picture on the piano.

TOM. Even in this country you can't arrest a girl for talking to her Dad, you know.

MURIEL. You can't scare me, young man.

JACK. All right. (*Calling.*) Johnny! Ring up the police station and ask them to send a man round. We're having trouble.

ARTHUR. (*To* JACK.) Do I understand that this lady claims that I'm her father?

MURIEL. Your name is Gosport, isn't it?

ARTHUR. Arthur Gosport. Yes.

MURIEL. (*Chattily.*) Well, I'm your daughter, Muriel. You've never seen me, because I was born after you left Mum. This is my husband, Tom—he's your son-in-law.

TOM. How do?

MURIEL. And I've brought someone else along that I thought you'd like to meet. Tom! (*She signs to him to go to the wings.*)

TOM. O.K., Mu.

ARTHUR. Just a minute. (*To* MURIEL.) You mentioned just now a character called Mum. Could you be more explicit, please? Where does this Mum person live?

MURIEL. Same old place. Number twenty-one Upper Brecon Road.

ARTHUR. Opposite a puce, rectangular building—with a notice board outside, saying Thy Days are Numbered?

MURIEL. That's right. The Baptist Chapel.

ARTHUR. And is Mum's name—Florence?

MURIEL. Flossie. That's right.

ARTHUR. (*Whimpering.*) Flossie! (*With a wail.*) Oh, no, no. It can't be!

MURIEL. Oh yes, it is, Dad.

EDNA. Arthur! You can't mean——

ARTHUR. Yes, yes, oh yes! It's true. I know it now. (*Pointing tragically.*) You've only to look at her face to see it. The living image of her dreadful mother.

MURIEL. Well, really! That's a nice way to talk, I must say——

JACK. (*Taking charge.*) Look, Mr. Gosport—as we've never seen the lady's dreadful mother, perhaps there's some other way we could test her story. (*To* MURIEL.) When were you born?

MURIEL. January 15th, 1927.

JACK. (*To* ARTHUR.) When did you last see Flossie?

ARTHUR. Don't cross-examine me! I don't know. I can only tell you that I am absolutely convinced of the truth of this girl's statement. This is my daughter, Mabel——

MURIEL. Muriel. Mu for short.

ARTHUR. My daughter, Muriel. Mu for short.

He sinks down on to a stool, his head in his hands. EDNA *loyally goes to his side to comfort him.*

(*To* MURIEL.) Why are you here? What do you want?

MURIEL. Want? I don't want anything. Just to say hullo, that's all. It seemed silly being in the same town, and for us not even to meet each other. Mum didn't want me to come, but I thought Dad'll be interested to see what I look like, and to meet his son-in-law. Besides I've got such a nice little surprise for you. (*Calling.*) Come on, Tom. I want to introduce you to your grandson.

TOM *appears, wheeling a pram tenderly towards the group, who are too frozen with horror to move.*

ARTHUR. (*At length.*) My—grandson?

MURIEL. That's right, Dad. Come and look.

Very slowly ARTHUR *rises and, with* EDNA *on one side and* JACK *on the other, gazes down on the pram.* MURIEL *and* TOM *complete the group. There is a long pause.*

ARTHUR. (*Slowly, at length.*) It looks—(*With a sob.*)—like Beerbohm Tree——

EDNA. (*Hopelessly.*) No, darling. The terrible thing is—it looks awfully like you.

ARTHUR. Don't say that, Edna!

MURIEL. Yes, he's the image of his Grandpa, isn't he? The ickle, chicka-widdy-biddy woo. Go on, Grandpa, tickle his little tummy.

ARTHUR. I refuse to tickle his little tummy.

EDNA. (*To* TOM.) How old is it?

TOM. Five months. You're Edna Selby, aren't you?

EDNA. Yes.

TOM. I saw you in Shakespeare once, in Birmingham. You were the Queen, weren't you, when Mr. Gosport was Hamlet?

EDNA. I have played it—yes.

TOM. (*Cheerfully.*) Well then in a sort of way, that makes you our little Ted's great-grand-mama, doesn't it?

EDNA. No, it doesn't. Not in any sort of way, and please, don't say it does. (*Reproachfully.*) Arthur—how could you!

ARTHUR. (*Pointing to the pram.*) I am not responsible for Ted.

EDNA. (*Pointing to* MURIEL.) But you are responsible for Mu.

ARTHUR. (*Tragically.*) I was a mere boy—a wild, hotheaded, irresponsible, passionate boy—a Romeo of seventeen——

EDNA. And your Juliet was Flossie.

ARTHUR. She was my landlady's daughter. I loved her, for a time, with all my heart and mind. She loved me too, in her way—but not enough. She never even came to the theatre to see me act. Of course it had to end, as all such mad, youthful follies must.

EDNA. (*Pointing to the pram.*) It didn't have to end in this.

ARTHUR. And I say unto you, the sins of the fathers shall be visited upon the children even unto the third and fourth generation. You know the line——

EDNA. It seems to have got up to the fourth generation far too quick. (*Pointing to the pram.*) Oh, Arthur, it's not in my nature to reproach you for what is past and done, but I do think you've been terribly, terribly foolhardy. (*To* TOM.) Please remove this.

TOM. O.K. If that's the way you feel——

MURIEL. (*To baby.*) Didn't they appreciate him, then? Come along, then, my icky-wicky-chick-a-boo! (*She begins to wheel the pram out.*) Come along, then! Say ta-ta for now, Grand-daddy——

ARTHUR. (*Sinking again into an attitude of tragic despair.*) Oh, my God! Edna! What am I to do?

Once more EDNA *takes his hand in silent but loyal sympathy.*

The PALMERS *wheel their baby out.*

There is a pause, broken by the HALBERDIER, *who, throughout the preceding scene, has been mouthing intermittently in the background, more or less oblivious of what has been going on.*

HALBERDIER. (*Attempting a new reading.*) Faith, we may put UP our PIPES and begone.

ARTHUR. Jack, what am I to do?

JACK. (*Reassuringly.*) Well, Mr. Gosport, they haven't bothered you at all for twenty years. I don't see any reason why they should in the future.

ARTHUR. Yes—but that child! (*With a shudder.*) That horrifying child!

JACK. No one need know about that. Ask your dau— Mrs. Palmer, to keep the whole thing secret; and if I might venture to suggest it, send an occasional little present to them for the baby.

EDNA. A nice little box of jujubes, flavoured with prussic acid.

ARTHUR. I don't think it's in quite the best of taste to make a joke of that sort, Edna. After all, the creature is my grandson. (*In agony again.*) Oh, God! my grandson!

EDNA. Never mind, my darling. These things can happen to any of us.

ARTHUR. But why, when I'm playing Romeo of all parts? Why couldn't it have turned up when I was playing Lear?

EDNA. That's life, my darling.

ARTHUR. Of course we shall have to cancel the performance now.

JACK. Look, Mr. Gosport—I really don't think you'll find it necessary to do that——

ARTHUR. How can I play a boy of seventeen with a grandson in the wings, mocking me with that repulsive leer of his, every time I go on?

JACK. Because it won't be in the wings. First thing tomorrow morning I shall go and see—er—Mrs. Palmer's mother. I'd better have her address again.

ARTHUR. Twenty-one Upper Brecon Road.

JACK. (Writing it down.) Thank you. And what is her name?

EDNA. Flossie.

JACK. I know. I meant her surname.

ARTHUR. Gosport, I suppose.

JACK. Gosport?

EDNA. What an odd coincidence!

JACK. Mr. Gosport—did you—did you marry Flossie?

ARTHUR. Oh yes. She made rather a point of it, I remember.

EDNA. Arthur! You mean your daughter isn't illegitimate?

ARTHUR. Oh no. She's perfectly legitimate, I think.

EDNA. (Annoyed.) Well, really? Of course that puts an entirely different complexion on the whole thing. It's going to make *me* look very silly—if that gets out.

ARTHUR. It all happened such a long time ago, darling, and I really didn't see why I should bother you with the whole, rather sordid, story.

JACK. (Quietly.) Mr. Gosport—when did you divorce your first wife?

ARTHUR. Let me see, now. I left her to take a part in a revival of *The Passing of the Third Floor Back* at Barnes.

JACK. I said, when did you divorce her? This is rather important. You did divorce her, didn't you?

ARTHUR. Yes, of course I did, my dear fellow. I remember perfectly.

JACK. Did you divorce her or did she divorce you?

ARTHUR. We divorced each other, my dear chap.

JACK. In law that isn't quite possible, Mr. Gosport. Who was awarded the decree nisi—you or your wife?

ARTHUR. Decree nisi? What's that?

JACK. It's the decision awarded by the judge in a divorce action.

ARTHUR. A judge? I don't remember a judge. I'm sure if there'd been a judge, I'd have remembered. There was a solicitor—I know that—and a lot of documents to sign——

JACK. (*His voice becoming gradually edged with horror as the truth becomes clearer.*) Mr. Gosport—one solicitor and a lot of documents don't make a divorce, you know.

ARTHUR. My dear fellow, don't fuss! Everything was perfectly legal and in order, I assure you.

JACK. You don't think it might just have been a deed of separation that you signed, and not a divorce at all?

ARTHUR. Of course it was a divorce. It must have been a divorce. The solicitor's name was Jenkins. He had Commissioner of Oaths on his glass door, I remember.

MURIEL *and her* SOLDIER *wander on.*

MURIEL. Hullo, Dad. Just been having a look round the stage. Don't mind, do you?

JACK. (*Urgently.*) Mrs. Palmer, if I ask you a straight question, will you please give me a straight answer?

MURIEL. All right. Fire away.

JACK. Is your mother divorced?

MURIEL. Divorced? Mum? Of course not.

JACK. (*Quietly.*) Thank you. That was what I had already gathered.

MURIEL. Mind you, she's often thought of divorcing Dad, but somehow never got round to doing it. Not that she's got a good word to say for him, mind you. She says he was the laziest, pottiest, most selfish chap she's ever come across in all her life. 'He'll come to a sticky end,' she used to say to me, when I was a little girl. 'You mark my words, Mu,' she used to say, 'if your Dad doesn't end his days in gaol my name's not Flossie Gosport.'

JACK. Your mother, Mrs. Palmer, is plainly a remarkable prophetess. Would you and your husband mind returning to No. 21 Upper Brecon Road as I have a rather important little matter to discuss with your Dad, who will be getting in touch with you in due course.

MURIEL. O.K. Well, ta-ta for now, Dad.

ARTHUR. Ta-ta and I will arrange for three complimentary seats to be left in your name for the Thursday matinée.

TOM. Thanks a million, Dad.

ARTHUR. I'm not your Dad, you know.

TOM. In law, old cock, in law.

MURIEL *and* TOM *go off.*

There is a pause, after they have gone.

EDNA. (*To* ARTHUR.) Darling, I must say it looks as if you've been very, very careless.

ARTHUR. Darling, there must be some hideous mistake. The whole thing is absolutely ridiculous. Jack, you must fix it.

JACK. Mr. Gosport and Miss Selby—I'm afraid this is something that not even I can fix. You must face, both of you, a very unpleasant fact. You are bigamously married.

There is another pause.

ARTHUR. (*Calling.*) Miss Fishlock!

MISS FISHLOCK. (*Off.*) Yes, Mr. Gosport.

ARTHUR. Come here a moment, would you?

MISS FISHLOCK *comes in, notebook and pencil at the ready.*

Miss Fishlock, it appears that my wife and I have committed bigamy. You'd better ring up the London Office at once and inform Mr. Wilmot.

MISS FISHLOCK. (*Faintly.*) Yes, Mr. Gosport. What—did you say—you and your wife have committed?

ARTHUR. Bigamy.

MISS FISHLOCK *sways slightly and is supported by* JACK. *Then clutching her pencil firmly, she bravely writes down the fatal word— or its shorthand equivalent.*

MISS FISHLOCK. Yes, Mr. Gosport.

EDNA. Silly word, isn't it? It sounds almost as if Arthur and I had committed a serious crime——

JACK. I hate to alarm you, Miss Selby, but that is exactly what Mr. Gosport has committed.

ARTHUR. You mean, I might have to pay a fine—or something like that?

JACK. (*Gently.*) Miss Fishlock, do you happen to know the maximum penalty for bigamy?

MISS FISHLOCK *nods, biting her quivering lower lip.*

ARTHUR. What is it, Miss Fishlock?

MISS FISHLOCK. (*In a whisper.*) Imprisonment—for life.

There is a stunned silence.

EDNA. And—does that apply to me too, Miss Fishlock?

MISS FISHLOCK. No, Miss Selby. You haven't committed any crime—(*Nearly in tears.*)—only Mr. Gosport.

EDNA. (*Aghast.*) They wouldn't *separate* us?

JACK. I'm afraid they would, Miss Selby.

EDNA. Oh, no, they wouldn't. They couldn't. If Arthur has to go to prison, I shall go too.

JACK. I doubt if that is allowed, Miss Selby. Is it, Miss Fishlock?

MISS FISHLOCK. No, Mr. Wakefield. I don't know of any— prison—where—convicts—are allowed to take their wives with them——

The thought is too much for her. She bursts frankly into tears and runs into the wings.

ARTHUR. (*Calling after her.*) Miss Fishlock! Miss Fishlock! What an idiotic woman, to get so hysterical!

EDNA. (*Approaching him and hugging him.*) Oh, my darling, I won't let them take you from me. I won't! I won't!

ARTHUR. Darling, there's nothing at all to get so worked up about. I'll make a public apology, divorce Flossie properly, and marry you again.

EDNA. But that would be such horrible publicity——

ARTHUR. The Arts Council will fix that. (*Suddenly galvanized into life.*) Now don't let's waste any more time. We've got to get to work.

His eye lights on the HALBERDIER who, all this time, has been patiently sitting in the background waiting to be called for rehearsal. You! I'll do your line now. (To EDNA.) Darling, do you mind taking up your position in the potion scene, after you've drunk the potion.

While ARTHUR *is placing* EDNA *where he wants her for the scene,* JACK *goes up to the* HALBERDIER.

JACK. My God! How much did you hear of all that?

HALBERDIER. Oh, that's all right, Mr. Wakefield, I'm not a tattle-tale. Wish me luck, Mr. Wakefield. This is my great chance——

ARTHUR. (*Turning.*) All right, Mr.—— Hrrhm. We're ready for you. Now, I'll give you your cue.

HALBERDIER. Thanks, Mr. Gosport.

ARTHUR. Leave a five-second pause, come on, look down at the bed and see what you take to be a dead body. Now I want to get from your expression that you realize that this girl, at whose wedding you have been hired to play, has taken her own life, presumably because she couldn't face her marriage with Paris, and that she has died for love of another. Your face should express understanding of the undying conflict between spiritual love and this gross, mundane world.

HALBERDIER. Gracious!

ARTHUR. Well, if you can't do it, just look sad. Then turn and say your line to your fellow musicians who we presume to be offstage, there. (*He points.*) Understand?

HALBERDIER. Yes, Mr. Gosport.

ARTHUR. All right. Go off. Jack, music.

The HALBERDIER *runs off.*

JACK. Panatrope.

ARTHUR. The heavens do lower upon us for some ill.

Move them no more by crossing their high will.

After the correct time interval, the HALBERDIER *comes on, acting hard. He gazes down at* EDNA, *and contrives to look very sad, sighing deeply and shaking his head. Then he turns slowly and faces* GEORGE CHUDLEIGH, *who has come on silently behind him.*

HALBERDIER. ⎫
GEORGE ⎬ Faith we may put up our pipes and begone.

ARTHUR. What? Oh Mr. Hrrhm—you've come back.

GEORGE. I just felt I couldn't desert you both in the hour of your great affliction.

ARTHUR. Our great affliction?

JACK. Oh, my God! How did *you* hear?

GEORGE. I was in The Feathers, and a chap in the company came in and told us all how Mr. and Mrs. Gosport were likely to get a life-sentence for bigamy——

JACK. Oh, God! The news must be half over Brackley by now——

He runs off.

EDNA. (*Calling after him.*) Don't worry, Jack. The company, I know, will stand by us. (*To* GEORGE.) Mr. Chudleigh, it was naughty of you to leave us so suddenly, but I think I know what was the matter—we all of us suffer from an occasional *crise de nerfs.*

CHUDLEIGH. *Crise de* what!

EDNA. Nerves, Mr. Chudleigh, nerves. Now come with me and I'll give you a nice strong cup of tea.

They go off together.

ARTHUR, *during this, has been staring, chin in hand, fixedly at the set. The* HALBERDIER *has been staring fixedly, and despairingly, at him.*

HALBERDIER. Mr. Gosport?

ARTHUR. Yes?

HALBERDIER. Do you want me any more?

ARTHUR. What? Oh, no, thank you.

HALBERDIER. You couldn't—let me have another line to say —some time—could you?

ARTHUR. (*Abstractedly.*) I'll keep you in mind.

HALBERDIER. (*Sadly.*) Thanks, Mr. Gosport.

ARTHUR *goes off.*

JACK *comes back.*

JACK. Too late! it's out of The Feathers and into the Green Horse, now. They've all heard it.

JACK *wearily subsides on the stool. The* HALBERDIER *approaches him timidly.*

HALBERDIER. Mr. Wakefield?

JACK. Yes?

HALBERDIER. Do you think I should give up the theatre?

JACK. Why ask me?

HALBERDIER. You know so much about Life.

JACK. What has Life got to do with the theatre?

HALBERDIER. (*He wanders to the wings.*) It's an awful shame about
that line. It came at such an important time, with Miss
Selby and Dame Maud on, and after a pause and with a
chance for face-acting. The London critics might have
noticed me——

JACK. (*Sympathetically.*) I rather doubt that. The potion scene
comes very soon after the interval.

HALBERDIER. Well, cheeribye.

JACK. Cheeribye.

The HALBERDIER *goes out sadly.*

JOHNNY'S VOICE (*Off.*) Mr. Wakefield!

JACK. (*Calling.*) Yes, Johnny?

JOHNNY'S VOICE. (*Off.*) The lady in your dressing-roon says
I'm to tell you time is getting on and you're not to forget
your promise.

JACK. (*Calling.*) All right. Thank you.

Enter DAME MAUD.

DAME MAUD. What is this terrible news?

JACK. Oh, Dame Maud, have you been to The Feathers!

DAME MAUD. I just looked in for a little refreshment and heard
this abominable slander. Jack, have some pity on an old
lady and tell me it isn't true.

JACK. I'm afraid it is true, Dame Maud.

DAME MAUD. I see. Well of course I suppose you know who's at
the bottom of it all, don't you?

JACK. No. Who?

DAME MAUD. The Old Vic.

JACK. Oh, I don't think so, Dame Maud.

DAME MAUD. My dear Jack, are you quite blind? It's as clear
as daylight to me. They stick at nothing, that lot, absolutely
nothing. I'm going to ring them up this moment and tell
them exactly what I think of them.

JACK. No, Dame Maud, you mustn't. You really mustn't.

DAME MAUD. And Sadler's Wells.

DAME MAUD *goes off followed by* JACK.

The stage is empty a moment, and then a uniformed POLICEMAN *walks
on from the wings with firm measured tread. He looks round him.*
JOHNNY, *still busy on the balcony, comes on.*

POLICEMAN. Who's in charge here, please?

JOHNNY. Mr. Wakefield. He'll be back in a minute.

After shaking the balcony once more JOHNNY *goes off.*

> JACK *comes on and stops dead at sight of the* POLICEMAN.

JACK. (*Murmuring.*) Oh God!

POLICEMAN. You Mr. Wakefield?

JACK. That's right, yes. Yes, I'm Mr. Wakefield, officer. Yes, that's quite correct.

POLICEMAN. I understand you want assistance.

JACK. Assistance?

POLICEMAN. One of your chaps rang up to say you were having bother at the theatre.

JACK. (*Infinitely relieved.*) Oh, that! Oh yes. Of course, I'd forgotten. (*He laughs, rather hysterically.*) Well, well, well! Just fancy your taking all that trouble to come round here. I do think that's good of you, officer—but as a matter of fact it was all a mistake—an utter misunderstanding——

POLICEMAN. You're not having any bother?

JACK. Oh, no, no, no! No bother in the world. Not a trace of bother. Everything's quite, quite perfect.

POLICEMAN. Then I don't know what you're doing wasting our time——

JACK. Oh, my dear old chap—I can't tell you how sorry I am about that. It's awful to think of you walking all that way from the police station on a wild-goose chase. Look, sit down, my dear fellow, do. (*He brings up a stool.*) Make yourself comfortable and I'll get you a nice drink. A nice large drink. What would you like? Whisky?

The POLICEMAN *nods.*

> Yes. I thought you would. Now just stay there. Don't move, will you? There are all sorts of dangerous contraptions in a theatre and you might hurt yourself and that'd be dreadful. Just sit there and relax and I'll dash and get you an enormous zonk of whisky——

He goes off, still burbling.

The POLICEMAN, *sitting patiently on the stool, is evidently rather surprised at the extreme affability of his reception. There is a pause, then* DAME MAUD *crosses the stage, another glass of Guinness*

clutched in her hand. She does not at first see the POLICEMAN.
When she does she utters' one single hoarse and strangled scream,
and sinks slowly to the floor in a dead faint. The POLICEMAN *rises,*
startled, as JACK *comes back with a whisky.*

POLICEMAN. Here, quick! There's an old lady having a fit——

JACK. What? Oh, it's Dame Maud. Oh lord! I suppose she
saw you—I mean—she goes off at the slightest thing, you
know. (*Calling.*) Johnny, Johnny! Come here, quick!

JOHNNY *comes on.*

Give me a hand with Dame Maud.

JOHNNY. Took queer, is she?

JACK. Just one of her dizzy spells——

POLICEMAN. I'd better lend a hand—I know my first aid.

JACK. Oh no. Please don't bother. You really mustn't trouble
yourself, officer. It's nothing at all. She's always doing this.
She's over a hundred, you know—poor old thing. Just sit
down and be comfortable, and pay no attention at all.

DAME MAUD. (*As she is carried off.*) Get me a drink, for God's
sake!

JACK *and* JOHNNY *carry her into the wings.*

The POLICEMAN *settles down once more on his stool. There is another*
pause and EDNA *comes on quickly.*

EDNA. Jack—are we doing the farewell——

She sees the POLICEMAN *and stands quite motionless looking at him*
as he rises politely. Then, very slowly, she walks towards him.
(*Sadly, resignedly, and melodiously.*) Ah, well. There is no
purpose to be served, I suppose, in kicking against the
pricks.

POLICEMAN. Beg pardon, ma'am?

EDNA. Constable—I only want to say one thing. In fifteen
years my husband and I have never spent a single night
apart——

POLICEMAN. (*Politely.*) Is that so, ma'am? Just fancy!

EDNA. Not one. If we were separated, I think we would die.

POLICEMAN. Would you indeed, ma'am?

EDNA. I want you to know that nothing can keep us apart.
Nothing; and no one—not even you, constable—can come
between us now. If you take him, you must take me too.

POLICEMAN. (*After a pause, stunned with bewilderment.*) I see, ma'am. I'll bear that in mind.

JACK *comes back and gasps as he sees* EDNA *with the* POLICEMAN.

JACK. Oh, Miss Selby, Dame Maud has been taken a bit faint. She's calling for you urgently.

EDNA. (*Tragically.*) What can that matter now? I've been telling the constable——

JACK. (*Hastily.*) Isn't it nice of the constable to come dashing round just because he heard we were having a little trouble in the theatre—especially when we're not having any trouble at all—are we?

EDNA. (*Understanding slowly.*) Oh. Oh, I see. Constable, dear constable, perhaps you'd better forget what I said just now——

POLICEMAN. I'll try to, ma'am, I'm sure.

EDNA. Just a little secret between the two of us, eh? (*To* JACK.) What a beautiful line of the neck the constable has, hasn't he, Jack?

JACK. Beautiful.

POLICEMAN. Here, I say!

EDNA. Goodbye, constable, and thank you for your great, great kindness to us all. I shall never forget it.

She goes off.

POLICEMAN. That was Edna Selby, wasn't it?

JACK. Yes, officer. You mustn't, you know, pay too much attention to anything she might have said to you. She's suffering from the most terrible first-night nerves.

POLICEMAN. Oh, is that the way it takes them?

JACK. Nearly always. Now, if you've quite finished your drink, I'd better escort you out——

POLICEMAN. Thanks. I can find my own way out——

JACK. Oh. Well, it's rather complicated and I wouldn't like you to be bothered by any of the other actors.

POLICEMAN. Are they all suffering from first-night nerves, then?

JACK. Nearly all of them. Come along, officer. I'll just clear a way for you——

He and the POLICEMAN *move to the wings.* JACK *goes out.*

The POLICEMAN *goes back for his helmet, which, in his confusion, he has left by the stool.* ARTHUR *comes in.*

ARTHUR. (*Explosively.*) Well, really, inspector. This is too much! I do think you might have waited until after the performance.

POLICEMAN. Well—Mr. Gosport, sir, I've got my work to do—you see——

ARTHUR. But, my dear inspector, you mustn't listen to a word my wife says. I can assure you we're divorced. There's no doubt at all about it.

POLICEMAN. Is that so, sir? I'd no idea.

ARTHUR. And anyway, we haven't spoken a single word to each other since the general strike.

POLICEMAN. That's too bad, sir. Your wife gave me to understand quite different——

ARTHUR. Of course she would, my dear fellow. She's out for publicity, I suppose. But I'll tell you something else, my dear chap. (*Confidentially.*) I'm not at all sure that my child is really mine——

POLICEMAN. Good gracious!

JACK *comes back in a hurry.* ARTHUR *goes up to balcony.*

JACK. My God! Mr. Gosport, Miss Selby's ready for the farewell. Officer, come this way, please! Please come this way! (*He drags the* POLICEMAN *away from* ARTHUR. *In a low voice.*) You mustn't pay any attention to him either. Least of all to him.

POLICEMAN. First-night nerves too?

JACK. Far worse than that. He's completely and utterly off his rocker. It's terribly, terribly sad——

POLICEMAN. Lor' love us! But he can still act?

JACK. Yes, he can still act. That's all he can do. Come along, officer, please.

He gets him off the stage.

JOHNNY *has come on to the balcony and is affixing a rope ladder to it.* ARTHUR *and* EDNA *appear on the balcony.*

JOHNNY *goes off, shaking his head.*

ARTHUR. Give me the lighting for the farewell, please.

The light comes down to give a rosy dawn effect.

All right.
Let me be ta'en, let me be put to death;
I am content, so thou wilt have it so.
I'll say yon grey is not the morning's eye,
'Tis but the pale reflex of Cynthia's brow;
Nor that is not the lark, whose notes do beat
The vaulty heaven so high above our heads:
I have more care to stay than will to go:
Come, death, and welcome! Juliet wills it so.
How is 't, my soul? let's talk; it is not day.

EDNA. It is, it is; hie hence, be gone, away!
It is the lark that sings so out of tune
Straining harsh discords and unpleasing sharps.
Some say the lark makes sweet division;
This doth not so, for she divideth us;
Some say the lark and loathed toad change eyes;
O! Now I would they had chang'd voices too,
Since arm from arm that voice doth us affray,
Hunting thee hence with hunts-up to the day.
O! now be gone; more light and light it grows.

ARTHUR. More light and light; more dark and dark our woes.

MISS FISHLOCK *suddenly flies on from the wings, and her counte-
nance, transported with joy, is suffused with the rosy gleams of the
sun now rising on Verona.*

MISS FISHLOCK. (*In great excitement.*) Mr. Gosport—Miss Selby
—I know you'll forgive me for interrupting you. I have
important news.

ARTHUR. Yes, Miss Fishlock?

MISS FISHLOCK. I got through to Mr. Wilmot and gave him your
message. He was most calm, most kind, most helpful, and
most reassuring. He is coming down to Brackley tomorrow
morning by an early train, in person.

EDNA. How very good of him!

MISS FISHLOCK. What is more he gave me a message to pass on
to you both. He says you are on no account to worry yourselves about this matter. He says he happens to know there
can be no danger whatever of—of—what we feared——

ARTHUR. (*Triumphantly.*) I knew it!

MISS FISHLOCK. He says it will probably be necessary for Miss Selby to sign a document saying that at the time she married you, Mr. Gosport, she was aware that you were already married. That, of course, would have the effect of making your second marriage null and void.

ARTHUR. Oh. That's splendid!

MISS FISHLOCK. There can therefore be no question of your having committed an offence in law. Oh, Mr. Gosport, he was so wonderfully brave. He went on to say that there should be little difficulty in your getting a divorce from this —this other person. Then, afterwards, should you and Miss Selby still wish it, you could get married again. Only no publicity, of course. And that, of course, would settle the entire problem once and for all. (*She beams gladly at the balcony, conscious of a duty well performed.*)

EDNA. How brilliant he is, isn't he, Arthur? I really don't know why anybody ever works for another management.

ARTHUR. Thank you, Miss Fishlock. You've done extremely well. I'm very grateful.

MISS FISHLOCK. I knew you'd both be pleased. Oh, Mr. Gosport —I'm so glad—I really am. I do congratulate you. And you too, Miss Selby.

EDNA.
ARTHUR. } (*Murmuring.*) Thank you, Miss Fishlock.

MISS FISHLOCK *goes off, again in tears, but this time, of joy.*

EDNA. Arthur, don't you think you ought to say a few words to the Company? I know they'll all be overjoyed at the news.

ARTHUR. Oh. Very well. (*Calling.*) Jack, assemble the Company, would you?

JACK *appears.*

JACK. They're mostly in front already, Mr. Gosport. (*Looking at front of house.*) Remain in your seats down there—everyone else on, please.

ARTHUR. Oh, right. (*To the House.*) Ladies and Gentlemen. With regard to this subject of bigamy—the danger point is past. I am sure you will be delighted to hear that Mr. Wilmot has discovered a way by which my marriage to Miss Selby can be rendered entirely illegal——

There is a little flutter of handclapping from the wings.

Thank you very much. Nor would it be right to let this occasion pass without extending on your behalf, on Miss Selby's and on mine, our most grateful thanks to Mr. Wilmot, without whose co-operation and—ingenuity—and *savoir-faire*—this very happy result would barely have been possible.

Another outburst of applause, louder than the first. Mr. Wilmot's spies, one feels, are everywhere.

Also to Miss Fishlock, who, as usual, has had to do most of the donkey-work, and has done it, as always, far better than anyone would ever expect.

One solitary clap for MISS FISHLOCK.

And lastly, Ladies and Gentlemen, to yourselves for the great loyalty you have shown in this moment of crisis to my wife, that is to say, Miss Selby, and myself. A thousand thanks. And one other thing. I'm not a difficult man in the theatre, as you know, but I would like to have it perfectly clear that I consider a very great deal of time has been wasted during this break for tea. Please see that it doesn't occur again. And now—back to work.

ARTHUR *goes off.*

EDNA. Just a moment, everyone. I also have an announcement to make. I know you will all be overjoyed to hear that Miss Fishlock with characteristic ingenuity has at last successfully completed the National Insurance forms for the entire company.

Enter ARTHUR.

ARTHUR. Bravo. (*To* EDNA.) Let's just finish the climb down, my dear.

EDNA. Yes.

ARTHUR *climbs on to ladder.*

Since arm from arm that voice doth us affray,
Hunting thee hence with hunts-up to the day.
O! now be gone; more light and light it grows

ARTHUR. More light and light; more dark and dark our woes.

EDNA. Then, window, let day in, and let life out.

ARTHUR. Farewell, farewell! one kiss, and I'll descend.

He begins to climb down.

EDNA. Art thou gone so? Oh Arthur—I've just thought of something quite, quite dreadful.

ARTHUR. What?

EDNA. Little Basil.

ARTHUR. Little Basil? (*Calling.*) Miss Fishlock!

MISS FISHLOCK *flies on again.*

MISS FISHLOCK. Yes, Mr. Gosport?

ARTHUR. Ring up Mr. Wilmot immediately and inform him that he appears to have made little Basil into a little bastard——

MISS FISHLOCK. Yes, Mr. Gosport.

She goes off.

ARTHUR. What's more there's far too much light on this scene —don't you agree, dear?

EDNA. Yes, dear, I do. Especially on the balcony.

ARTHUR. (*Calling.*) Jack!

JACK *comes on.*

There's too much from here and too much from there. (*Waving his arms to left and right.*) Now is everyone ready?

JACK. You can't get the lights much lower than this, Mr. Gosport, or they'll go out altogether——

ARTHUR. Nonsense, my dear fellow.

The tabs draw revealing the Verona scene with the TWO HALBERDIERS GEORGE CHUDLEIGH, *and* INGRAM *grouped.*

Now—are we all here? I just want to do the duel.

DAME MAUD *comes on to the balcony.*

DAME MAUD. As you've stopped, dear, I thought you wouldn't mind if I gave you another teeny little hint——

EDNA. Not just now, Auntie Maud. Do you mind? Perhaps tomorrow——

DAME MAUD. Tomorrow will be far too late.

EDNA. (*Paying no attention.*) There's still too much on the balcony, Jack.

JACK. (*Shouting.*) Bring it down more, Will! It'll never stand it, Miss Selby.

EDNA. I'm sure it will—the lights never let us down.

ARTHUR. (*In Verona.*) Now, Tybalt, take the villain back again

That late thou gav'st me; for Mercutio's soul
Is but a little way above our heads,
Staying for thine to keep him company;
Either thou, or I, or both, must go with him.

INGRAM. Thou wretched boy, that didst consort him here.
Shalt with him hence.

ARTHUR. This shall determine that.

INGRAM. What! Art thou drawn among these heartless hinds?
Turn thee—look upon thy death!

JOYCE. (*Shouting above the din.*) Jack! Jack! Time's up.

JACK. What? Oh, clear the stage, will you, darling? We're
extremely busy.

JOYCE. No. I won't. Have you told them yet?

JACK. Told them what? Oh that. No, I haven't. Look, darling,
I'm afraid you'll have to wait for me, that's all. I can't
leave these two now. I realize that. How can I let them go
behind the iron curtain without one sane man to look after
them?

JOYCE. Sane? You're not sane! You're as mad as they are.
This madhouse has infected you too.

JACK. Madhouse? This isn't a madhouse. It's just an ordinary
dress rehearsal, that's all—now clear the stage, darling.

EDNA. Jack, dear, there's still too much light on this balcony.

JACK. If you take the lights down more than this, Miss Selby,
they'll fuse.

EDNA. Let them fuse.

ARTHUR. (*Still in Verona.*) Again, please. That's too quick.

JOYCE. It's no good, Jack, I'm leaving you. You'll never get
out of this, it's bedlam, and you're in it for life. Goodbye,
Jack, goodbye.

She runs off the stage.

JACK. Joyce!

DAME MAUD. (*Looking down from the balcony.*) Now that girl has
talent. Who is she? Arthur—who was that girl?

ARTHUR. (*Still arranging the fight in Verona.*) I don't know,
Auntie Maud. Get her name, will you, Jack?

JACK. I've got her name, Mr. Gosport. It's Joyce Langland.
She was my fiancée.

ARTHUR. Good. We'll try her for *Winter's Tale* tomorrow. Now this duel is getting very sloppy. Let's go back.

EDNA. There's still too much light, Jack.

JACK. Yes, Miss Selby. Take it down more, Will. And try those thunder and lightning cues 2, 3, and 4.

The lights suddenly go out.

My God! They've fused.

Summer lightning is now playing fitfully on the scene.

ARTHUR. (*Calling.*) House lights. House lights.

The house lights go up. MR. BURTON *rushes on.*

BURTON. (*In a frantic voice.*) Take those lights out! It's seven-thirty. There's an audience in front. Look!

He points. A row of startled faces gaze at the now visible audience, and then they scatter in panic to the wings.

The house lights go out. There is a moment's black-out, disturbed by summer lightning and a roll of thunder. Then the stage lights come on again, revealing an empty stage. ARTHUR *comes on slowly carrying his pot.*

JACK. (*Off, whispering frantically.*) Mr. Gosport! Mr. Gosport! The audience is in front.

He beckons him to the wings. Other faces and other beckoning figures appear, but ARTHUR *is oblivious. He walks slowly round the pot, then, dissatisfied with its appearance, picks it up once more and walks slowly out, to the strains of the overture.*

THE CURTAIN FALLS